"Some Christians avoid the book of Revelation, thinking it is only for the brilliant or the paranoid. In this clear and engaging book, Nancy Guthrie walks us through the meaning of this crucial book of the Bible, showing us how it is about blessing. This book wouldn't fit in a conspiracy theorist's underground bunker, but it is needed for people who wonder how the fears and worries and regrets of our lives can be transformed by what Jesus showed John on the island of Patmos two thousand years ago. After reading *Blessed*, you will never again skip past Revelation in your Bible reading but will turn there with wonder and confidence, expecting to see Jesus. It will leave you informed, pondering, and, yes, blessed."

Russell Moore, Public Theologian, *Christianity Today*; Director, *Christianity Today's* Public Theology Project

"The book of Revelation is daunting and even discouraging for some believers, and we have a tendency to ignore it. Nancy Guthrie has written a wonderfully clear, accessible, and faithful interpretation of the book. The theological vision of the book is captured in her exposition, but the book doesn't stop there. Guthrie explains in a remarkable way how the book of Revelation applies to us today. Laypeople, students, and anyone who wants to understand the book of Revelation will profit from reading and studying this book."

Thomas R. Schreiner, James Buchanan Harrison Professor of New Testament Interpretation, The Southern Baptist Theological Seminary

"The only thing more frightening than the book of Revelation is Christian books about the book of Revelation—the deluge of cross-references, the eye-wateringly complex predictions about the future, the various millennialisms. Not so with this book. Nancy believes that, like all of Scripture, Revelation is intended to make sense to ordinary Christians. Its meaning is well within reach to anyone who is willing to read—prayerfully and carefully in context—the words on the page. Nancy makes it seem so simple, vivid, heart-warming, and practical—surely that's what God intended when he gave the prophecy to his servant John as a blessing for all who read it and take to heart what's written in it."

Andrew Sach, Pastor, Grace Greenwich Church, United Kingdom; coauthor, *Pierced for Our Transgressions* and *Dig Deeper*

T0035887

"This guide through the book of Revelation is exactly what is needed for individuals and groups who want to study Revelation without being intimidated. It is solidly researched and sound but written with a wide audience of readers in mind. It is engaging and winsome, with attention to personal applications. Guthrie commendably stands with readers in admitting when there are challenges and difficulties. But she encourages people not to stop when confronting challenges, but to continue to learn from what is clear in the message of Revelation. As the title indicates, the book shows us the blessings to be found in Christ."

Vern S. Poythress, Distinguished Professor of New Testament, Biblical Interpretation, and Systematic Theology, Westminster Theological Seminary

"I was helped tremendously by this book. Nancy carries us through Revelation with anticipation and wonder. While some readers will not agree with all of Nancy's conclusions, we will all stand with her in awe of a great God. We will leave with a renewed sense of endurance to flee evil and to cling to Christ until we reach the end."

Colleen McFadden, Director of Women's Workshops, Charles Simeon Trust

"What I often mean by the word *blessed* is not even close to what Christ secured for us. If you want to know how much better, read this book."

Michael Horton, J. Gresham Machen Professor of Systematic Theology and Apologetics, Westminster Seminary California

"Nancy Guthrie reminds us that Saint John wrote about dragons, eagles, and beasts—not to fuel twenty-first-century speculation about their precise physical referent, but to motivate the church toward godliness in the midst of a pagan culture. Revelation invites the church to gather around the throne of the holy God, Lamb, and Spirit and worship in every aspect of life. We need more books such as this on the capstone of the Bible's storyline, and I'm eager to see how God will use this volume for his glory!"

Benjamin L. Gladd, Associate Professor of New Testament, Reformed Theological Seminary

Blessed

Blessed

Experiencing the Promise of
the Book of Revelation

Nancy Guthrie

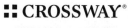
WHEATON, ILLINOIS

Library of Congress Cataloging-in-Publication Data

Names: Guthrie, Nancy, author.

Title: Blessed: experiencing the promise of the book of Revelation / Nancy Guthrie.

Description: Wheaton, Illinois : Crossway, 2022. | Includes bibliographical references and index.

Identifiers: LCCN 2021038563 (print) | LCCN 2021038564 (ebook) | ISBN 9781433580208 (trade paperback) | ISBN 9781433580215 (pdf) | ISBN 9781433580222 (mobipocket) | ISBN 9781433580239 (epub)

Subjects: LCSH: Bible. Revelation—Commentaries.

Classification: LCC BS2825.53 .G88 2022 (print) | LCC BS2825.53 (ebook) | DDC 228/.07—dc23

LC record available at https://lccn.loc.gov/2021038563

LC ebook record available at https://lccn.loc.gov/2021038564

---

*In profound humility, and with deep admiration, I dedicate this
book to my brothers and sisters around the world who live under
constant threat and have experienced significant loss because of their
bold allegiance to Jesus and their refusal to compromise. You are
among those of whom the world is not worthy (Heb. 11:38).*

*I will not likely meet you in this lifetime. But one day I will gather
with you around the throne of God and the Lamb. We will sing together
about the worthiness of the Lamb and praise the Lord God Almighty
for the way he has executed his justice. One day we will be face to face
with our Savior, and I anticipate he will look you in the eyes and say,
"You conquered by the blood of the Lamb and by the word of your
testimony, for you loved not your life even unto death" (Rev. 12:11).*

*Until then, I'm praying for you. I'm asking God to fill you
with grace and peace. I'm asking him to strengthen you for
patient endurance as we wait for our King to come.*

Contents

Introduction

I SHOULD PROBABLY begin with a confession.

A number of years ago, when I was first asked to help teach a study of Revelation at my church, I began looking for a way out of it, a good excuse to say no. I was completely intimidated. I thought of Revelation as an impossible-to-understand collection of strange creatures and events that I would not be able to make sense of myself, let alone teach to anyone else.

But then I thought, *I should probably read through it before I say no.*

So I started reading. And just three verses in I read this: "Blessed is the one who reads aloud the words of this prophecy, and blessed are those who hear, and who keep what is written in it, for the time is near" (Rev. 1:3). When I read that, I thought to myself, *Would I ever want to say that there is a blessing from God that I'm not really interested in receiving?* I kept reading, all the way to the end, and there it was again: "Blessed is the one who keeps the words of the prophecy of this book" (Rev. 22:7) and "Do not seal up the words of the prophecy of this book" (22:10), which Eugene Peterson paraphrases, "Don't put it away on the shelf" (Rev. 22:10 MSG). When I read that, I thought to myself, *That's essentially what I've done. I've put this book on the shelf assuming I won't be able to understand it, and don't really need to.* I realized I needed to take Revelation off the shelf and invest myself in reading, hearing, understanding, submitting to, and rejoicing in this book.

Perhaps you sense in yourself the same need. If so, I'm really excited to open up this book with you in the pages ahead.

Before we begin, however, I want to do three things. First, I want to explore some reasons we have for ignoring or neglecting the book of Revelation. Second, I want to make a case for why investing in understanding this book is worthwhile. Third, I want to present a few basics for grasping the message of this book that will help us as we work our way through it.

Reasons We Avoid Revelation

1. We're afraid we won't be able to understand it.

Revelation is filled with strange creatures, other-worldly imagery, and scenes that we find difficult to imagine and decipher. It demands that we use our imaginations, and we're not really used to doing that when reading the Bible. Revelation is written in a genre of literature we're not used to reading and therefore don't instinctively know how to read and understand. This means that if we're going to rightly understand it, we've got to develop our skills for reading the literary genre of apocalyptic prophecy. As we do, we find this book opening up to us.

Revelation was not written for scholars, so you don't have to be a scholar to understand it. It is a letter written to ordinary believers in the first century with the expectation that they would understand its message. It was written to unveil or reveal hidden realities, not to make them harder to see and understand.

Revelation was not written to create confusion, conflict, or fear in those who read it. Rather, it was written so that ordinary believers who hear it and embrace what is written in it will not only be able to understand it; they'll be blessed by it—blessed in a countercultural way that the world simply cannot understand and does not value.

2. We know there is lots of disagreement about Revelation.

The fact that there is lots of disagreement about Revelation is true. There are a variety of approaches to how to read and understand Revelation, some more valid than others. And there are lots of people who have very strong opinions about how to read and understand

Revelation. Sadly, the varying approaches of interpretation can tend to create a barrier that makes this a closed book to many. And I think that's tragic.

Let me just tell you upfront: if you start into this book hoping to find either an ally or sparring partner for your thoroughly convinced interpretive or eschatological views, you may be disappointed. While my views on some disputed things may be evident in places, it is not my goal to make an argument against opposing views. I simply don't have the space or inclination for that. In most instances I'm not going to present a variety of views and make a case for my own view. I'm just going to state what I think the Scriptures present to us. I'm not interested in critique or controversy or speculation; I'm interested in presenting what is clear and cannot be ignored.

3. We think Revelation is mostly or completely about the future with nothing practical for us today.

Most people assume that Revelation is primarily or even exclusively about the future. But think for a minute. Would it really make sense that John would address a letter to seven churches in the first century that was mostly about things only the generation alive at the return of Christ would need to know and recognize? Doesn't it make far more sense that John wrote to believers in his day as well as to believers in every era between his day and the day of Christ's return about what they need to know, how they are to live, and how they can cope with the harsh realities of life in this world?

Revelation presents a past, present, ongoing, and future reality that servants of Jesus living in between his ascension and return need to see. It sheds light on history as it has unfolded in the past and is unfolding right now. It serves as a corrective to any assumptions we might have that the status quo will continue, and that resistance to the world's system is futile.

Clearly there are things described in this book that are yet to happen. There is a future culmination of the ongoing conflict that has been a reality in our world ever since God put enmity between the serpent and the woman in Eden. There will be a final battle. Jesus will return. And Revelation is going to help us to see these things more clearly. But that doesn't mean it is entirely or even primarily future focused.

Revelation is actually less about *when* Jesus will return and more about *what* we are to do, *who* we are to be, and *what* we can expect to endure as we wait for Jesus to return to establish his kingdom.

We tend toward being very pragmatic. We want to walk out of Bible study with a to-do list and may assume that the cosmic struggle represented in Revelation doesn't lend itself to practical application. But that simply isn't so. Revelation presents a repeated call that is urgent for every one of us to respond to right now, today. Revelation has everything to do with how we invest the capital of our lives, what is worth getting excited about, or being afraid of. Revelation speaks to our big and little compromises with the world around us, how we view political and governmental systems, and what we expect our money can provide for us.

If we are concerned with what's practical, the day will come when we will look back and it will be clear to us that there was nothing more practical than prayer, nothing more practical than perseverance, and nothing more practical than praising the triune God even when evil was pressing in on us. We'll discover that worship was the "ultimate subversive activity" in a world of idolatry and materialism.[1] Enduring in our allegiance to King Jesus even when it costs us, and living as if we do not expect this world to applaud us, approve of us, or satisfy us, is subversive. It's shocking. And at the same time, it is the ordinary Christian life. It is what is expected of a citizen of the kingdom of heaven living in the kingdom of the world.

*4. We know that there is a lot about persecution of believers
in Revelation, and that makes us uncomfortable.*

Maybe it isn't so much the strangeness or the controversy of Revelation that keeps us from this book. Perhaps, for many of us, it is our love

---

1 Iain Duguid, "Doxological Evangelism in Practice: Preaching Apocalyptic Literature," Westminster Conference on Preaching and Preachers, Westminster Theological Seminary, October 21, 2020.

of comfort and our lack of ability to relate to being under assault as a believer. The threat of being exiled to an island prison for declaring allegiance to King Jesus is so very far away from the comfortable lives many of us live. We simply find it hard to relate to the tension, the threat, the life-or-death consequences in this book. It is hard to relate to crying out "How long?" when we have the security of a nice house and a good job, a football game to watch on a big-screen TV, and food being delivered to our front door. If we're honest, perhaps our comfortable lives and all we're looking forward to acquiring and accomplishing and experiencing in this life make us perfectly content for Jesus to wait a while before he comes back to intervene in the affairs of this world.

Perhaps it is not until we dare to allow ourselves to be moved by the reports of believers in other parts of the world being tortured or killed for their faith, or when we sit with a woman who has been raped or saw her husband killed in front of her eyes by Islamic extremists, or when we consider real people whose churches have been burned and their pastors executed that we finally feel the ache expressed in Revelation by the believers asking how long it will be until Christ comes to set things right. Revelation invites us to share the ache of the persecution endured by our brothers and sisters around the world and throughout history. And it speaks into this ache, telling us that the days of evil having its way in this world are numbered.

Reasons We Should Study Revelation

1. We might not be able to understand everything in Revelation, but we can understand its central message.

If our goal in studying Revelation is to nail down what every image portrays, what every symbol stands for, what every detail means, we're likely going to be frustrated. Our goal, instead, should be to listen for and take to heart what is really clear.

To help you grasp the central message of Revelation, I've prepared a personal Bible study to go along with this book that you can find at nancyguthrie.com/revelation. You will get much more out of this book if you have spent some time answering a few questions on the biblical text before you read each chapter. At my website you'll also find a complete leader's guide that includes discussion questions to help you if you are leading a group through Revelation using this book.

We're living in such a divided time. We all have our opinions, as well as opinions about whose opinions are worth considering. And that is certainly the case regarding the book of Revelation. Some of us may be more comfortable focusing on interpretive issues or nailing down the details than opening up our lives to the self-examination this book demands of us. You and I can understand the central message of this book. The more significant question is whether or not we're willing to embrace and live in light of it.

2. We need to see this world, and our lives in this world, through the perspective of heaven.

We sometimes foolishly assume we have all of the data we need to evaluate what is happening in our world. But we don't. Our perspectives are limited by our humanity and our earthly vantage point. In the book of Revelation, we find that a curtain was pulled back for John so that he could see beyond the time and space of this earthly life into the heart of ultimate reality. He was enabled to see what is happening in this world, not from the perspective of this earth, but from the perspective of heaven. As we take in what he saw, we find that we are better able to see the true nature of things. Rather than view this world's offerings as attractive, from heaven's perspective we can see how ugly and unsatisfying they are. Rather than seeing the persecution of a faithful believer as a tragic defeat, we're able to see it as a glorious victory.

3. We want the blessing that is promised to those who "hear and keep" this book.

Many of us have a rather lightweight perception of what it means to be *blessed*. Revelation is going to correct some of our assumptions about what the blessed life looks like for ordinary believers like you and me. And since the blessing promised in Revelation is reserved for those who "hear and keep" what is written in this book, we're going to be challenged to think through what it will mean and require for us to hear and keep it. Revelation is going to add some meat to the bones of our understanding of what the blessed life really is.

4. We need to live out of the story Revelation tells.

Every one of us lives out of the story that we believe is true. Some of us live out of the story called "the American dream." Some of us live out of a story that must end with "happily ever after." Some of us have come to think that we can craft our own life story toward the end that most appeals to us. There is a story that you and I should be living out of, a story that should shape how we live today and every day to come. According to Jesus, the kingdom of God is the story. And the book of Revelation helps us to see where that story is headed so that we can live out of it in joyful anticipation.

What We Need to Get the Most Out of Studying Revelation

1. We need to be ready to use our visual imaginations.

In many places in Scripture the biblical writers tell us what they *heard* the Lord say to them. But Revelation is different. John writes about what he *saw* in four different visions—a vision of Christ, a vision in heaven, a vision in the wilderness, and a vision on the great high mountain. John draws magnificent pictures with his words, pictures that are intended to make an impression and communicate a reality.

You and I live in a world that is vivid to us. We are inundated with images throughout the course of a typical day. And these images threaten to define reality for us. But they are not a full picture of reality. Revelation is presenting to us a fuller picture of reality that we cannot see with our physical eyes. It is providing for us an opportunity to see beyond the time and space of this world, and to see all of it from heaven's perspective.

The pictures Revelation sets before us can be strange or, in some cases, nonsensical. But these startling, compelling, even shocking images are intended to jolt us out of our complacency regarding the evils of this age and the unimaginable blessedness of the age to come. As we process Revelation's vivid pictures we're meant to feel the hot breath of the beast and smell the sulfur from the pit and see the rainbow around the throne. These images are intended to shake us out of our sleepiness and apathy and the détente we may have made with the world's ways. Our prayer should be that as we see these things, they will make a deep impression on us, changing how we feel and what we fear and what we want. That's their intended purpose.

2. We need to develop our skills in interpreting symbols.

Revelation uses a lot of symbolism. John's visions include descriptions of physical objects or phenomena that actually represent something else. Of course Revelation is not the first place symbolism is used in the Bible. For example, in Exodus 19:4, when God says to Israel, "I bore you on eagles' wings," he is not saying that he used eagles to fly his people out of Egypt. The symbol of an eagle communicates something about the speed and strength of his rescue. Jesus used many symbols to represent aspects of his own person and work, saying that he was a good shepherd, the bread of life, and the vine. Similarly, but perhaps more pervasively, John uses symbols to communicate sometimes complex realities. Babylon as a symbol of worldly idolatry and immorality. The sea is a symbol for the chaos and threat of evil. Colors and numbers have symbolic meaning.

Sometimes the meaning of Revelation's symbols is plain or is even stated explicitly. For example, we're told that lampstands represent the churches (1:20), white linen represents the righteous acts of the saints (19:8), and the ancient serpent is the devil (20:2). And sometimes it's more challenging to grasp with confidence what is being communicated.

Some interpreters insist that if we don't read every image in Revelation literally, we're not taking the Bible seriously. But an important aspect of taking the Bible seriously is recognizing and interpreting each part of it in the literary genre used by the human author as inspired by the divine author. To interpret symbols symbolically is not spiritualizing the text; it is rightly interpreting the text. For example, when we read about the Lamb standing as though it had been slain, we instinctively know that John is using symbolism to communicate something about the crucified Christ. When he speaks of God and the Lamb being seated on a throne, we know that he is using symbolism to communicate something about the sovereignty of God over the universe and over history. When he speaks of the beast, he is communicating something about the nature and intentions of Rome in his day and in every government that has set itself against God and his people since then. When he describes a dragon with seven heads and ten horns, he is communicating something about the terrifying power of Satan. In using symbols this way, John reveals the true nature of things.

Our first and best step to rightly interpreting various symbols will be to explore if and where a symbol appears in earlier books of the Bible and allow that to significantly inform our understanding. Then we must consider what the symbol would have meant to the first-century audience of this book. Many of the symbols in Revelation find resonance in the specific social, political, cultural, and religious world of the first century. They are not a system of codes waiting to be matched for meaning with people and events in our current day. Rather, they have theological and spiritual meaning pertinent to the first readers of Revelation, and that meaning must inform how we interpret their meaning for us today.

3. We need to have our eyes and ears open for Old Testament imagery and allusions.

In the book of Revelation, John was clearly writing down what he saw and heard. But his book is filled with allusions to the Old Testament, and there are at least two reasons for that. The first reason is that John saw into and wrote about the same heavenly reality that Isaiah, Daniel, Ezekiel, and Zephaniah saw into and wrote about. No wonder the throne John saw is a lot like the throne Isaiah saw. No wonder the kingdom crushing other kingdoms is a lot like the kingdom Daniel saw. No wonder the new Jerusalem John saw is a lot like the city Ezekiel saw. They were seeing the same things!

The second reason Revelation has so many images from the Old Testament is that John was thoroughly saturated in the Hebrew scriptures. These images were implanted into his consciousness and imagination. It makes sense that he would draw upon words and images he was familiar with to write down descriptions of what he saw. Unlike other parts of the New Testament that set off quotes of the Old Testament, Revelation doesn't call attention to its Old Testament quotes and allusions. It's more subtle. It assumes that those reading and hearing it will recognize its Old Testament allusions and make the connection. So rather than constantly quoting the Old Testament, John simply sees everything and describes everything through the lens of the Old Testament.

4. We need to have a sense of how the book is organized.

There are a number of ways to understand how the book of Revelation is organized.[2] Kevin DeYoung presents several possible approaches, including seeing Revelation as divided into two main sections: chapters 1 to 11 introducing the story of God's triumph, and chapters 12 to 22 explaining the story in greater detail; or divided into four main sections, each beginning with John writing "what must soon take place" or "what must take place after this" (Rev. 1:1, 19; 4:1; 22:6). Another way DeYoung suggests it can be divided into four parts would be to organize it into the times John says he was caught up in the Spirit and was given a vision (1:10; 4:2; 17:3; 21:10).[3]

We're going to see that numbers are very significant in the book of Revelation. They express the sovereignty of God over history. The number four speaks of completeness in a universal, global, or worldwide sense. The number six refers to humanity. The number seven speaks of

---

2 Vern Poythress presents numerous ways to outline Revelation in "Outlines of Revelation," Westminster Theological Seminary, accessed October 6, 2021, http://campus.wts.edu/~vpoythress/nt311/nt311.html.

3 Kevin DeYoung, "Revelation, Coronavirus, and the Mark of the Beast: How Should Christians Read the Bible's Most Fascinating Book? (Part 1)," Kevin DeYoung blog, The Gospel Coalition, May 26, 2020, https://www.thegospelcoalition.org/.

completeness, perfection, and salvation. It represents God's sovereign plan in its perfection and completeness. The number ten speaks of completeness in the human experience or dimension. And the number twelve speaks of completeness in terms of the community of God's people, a unity in diversity.

The number seven is especially important in Revelation (used 53 times), so we shouldn't be surprised that another way the book could be organized is in seven sets of seven:

Prologue (1:1–3)
1. Seven churches (1:4–3:22)
2. Seven seals (4:1–8:5)
3. Seven trumpets (8:6–11:19)
4. Seven great signs (12:1–15:4)
5. Seven bowls of wrath (15:1–16:21)
6. Seven messages of final judgment (17:1–18:24)
7. Seven last things (19:1–22:5)
Epilogue (22:6–20)

The most important thing we need to understand about the organization of Revelation is that it retraces the same events from different angles, each with a different emphasis or focus. As modern thinkers and readers, we tend to expect events depicted in a piece of writing to be in chronological order. In fact, many interpreters attempt to force the events depicted in the book of Revelation into chronological order. But if we try to do that, we find that Jesus is depicted as coming again numerous times and there are numerous "final" judgments. If we were to attempt to impose a chronological reading on it, we would see a back and forth between people persecuting the people of God and being judged for it and then persecuting them again. And we know that doesn't make sense.

Instead of reading through Revelation as a chronological depiction of events, it helps us to recognize that John repeatedly rehearses events taking place between the first and second coming of Christ. In this way he brings us to the end of history repeatedly in the book and then starts over again, showing the same period of time from a different angle. Earlier in the book he focuses more on the time leading up to the second coming of Christ in final judgment and salvation. And later in the book, the focus is more on those final events. In "each series of seven (seven seals, seven trumpets, and seven bowls), and also within the interlude of Revelation 12 to 14, the reader is brought to 'the end.'"[4] So as each of these sections begins, it is as if John picks up his camera and moves it to another location or angle and shoots the same scene again, each time adjusting his lens to focus in on different aspect of the scene and with a greater intensity. This means that Revelation is made up of seven sections that are parallel to each other—seven sections that depict the same period of time—the time in between Jesus's first and second coming—from a variety of angles.[5]

5. We need to replace an unhealthy fascination about the future with a determination to follow Christ in the present.

While some people want to avoid Revelation, others are enormously interested in it. But sometimes that interest isn't particularly healthy. Some are fascinated by the possibility of matching up what they hear about on the news with strange details or images in the book. If that's what you're hoping for in this book, I might as well tell you that you are going to be disappointed, perhaps even annoyed. But, more impor-

---

4   Joseph R. Nally Jr., "Recapitulation: Interpreting the Book of Revelation?," Third Millennium Ministries, accessed September 7, 2021, https://thirdmill.org.

5   For more about Revelation's recapitulation of sections that are parallel to each other, see William Hendrickson, *More than Conquerors: An Interpretation of the Book of Revelation* (Grand Rapids, MI: Baker, 2015), 25–26, who writes, "Different sections ascribe the same duration to the period described. According to the third cycle (chapters 8–11) the main period here described is forty-two months (11:2), or twelve hundred and sixty days (11:3). Now, it is a remarkable fact that we find that same period of time in the next section (chapters 12–14), namely, twelve hundred and sixty days (12:6), or a time and times and half a time (3 and 1/2 years) (12:14). A careful study of chapter 20 will reveal that this chapter describes a period that is synchronous with that of chapter 12. Therefore by this method of reasoning, parallelism is vindicated. Each section gives us a description of the entire gospel age from the first to the second coming of Christ." See also, Anthony Hoekema, *The Bible and the Future* (Grand Rapids, MI: Eerdmans, 1994), 223–26, and G. K. Beale with David H. Campbell, *Revelation: A Shorter Commentary* (Grand Rapids, MI: Eerdmans, 2015), 22–25.

tantly, if that is what you want most to get out of studying the book of Revelation, you're going to be too preoccupied with the future to grasp its implications for you in the very real present.

Revelation wasn't written to entertain, or to set out a timeline for the future, or to satisfy our curiosity about when Christ will return. Revelation was written to fortify Christians to live in the world, enduring its harsh treatment and alienation, with a firm confidence that this world is not all there is, and that, in fact, what may seem like defeat is going to give way to victory.

If, when we finish this study, we can explain every symbol, identify every Old Testament allusion, and trace every connection but are still intimidated by the world's opinion of us, still enamored with the world's wealth, still attracted by the world's comfort and pleasure, then we will not have truly heard and kept its message. We will not have truly understood and embraced the book of Revelation.

My goal is to open up this text to you, taking away the intimidation or fear factor. I want to focus your attention on the Lamb standing as though it had been slain, to help you listen to the voice of him who is Faithful and True, to encourage you to open the door to him who knocks, to challenge you to welcome the authority of the King of kings, to invite you to pull up a chair at the marriage supper of the Lamb, to direct you to find your home in the new Jerusalem.

It is my goal to cut through the confusion and help you to see the beauty, the hope and help, that is uniquely presented in this book. I want to focus your gaze on the glorious Son of Man and to instill in you a determination to overcome the world. I want you to be drawn into the worship around the throne. I want you to feel the relief that someone was found worthy to open the scroll. I want you to sense the reality of the judgment to come to all who refuse to become joined to Christ as well as the relief, the rest, and the reward to come to those who belong to him. I want to help you to see this world for the Babylon that it is so you'll be motivated to flee from it to the new Jerusalem where God himself will make his home with you. I want you to get goose bumps because you can almost taste the food that will be served at the marriage supper, and can almost feel your tears being wiped away, and can almost see the eyes of your Savior looking into yours as you finally see him face to face.

I've realized something as I've been studying Revelation. We begin our study of this book thinking that our biggest challenge is going to be understanding it. And it isn't. The biggest challenge is opening ourselves up to the adjustments in our lives that this book calls for. Yet this biggest challenge is also what promises the greatest blessing. So let's work our way through the book of Revelation, stopping at every step along the way to consider what it means for us to hear and keep what is written in it so that we can anticipate experiencing its promised blessing.

Seven "Blessed" Statements in the Book of Revelation

Blessed is the one who reads aloud the words of this prophecy, and blessed are those who hear, and who keep what is written in it, for the time is near.
—Revelation 1:3

And I heard a voice from heaven saying, "Write this: Blessed are the dead who die in the Lord from now on." "Blessed indeed," says the Spirit, "that they may rest from their labors, for their deeds follow them!"
—Revelation 14:13

(Behold, I am coming like a thief! Blessed is the one who stays awake, keeping his garments on, that he may not go about naked and be seen exposed!)
—Revelation 16:15

And the angel said to me, "Write this: Blessed are those who are invited to the marriage supper of the Lamb." And he said to me, "These are the true words of God."
—Revelation 19:9

Blessed and holy is the one who shares in the first resurrection! Over such the second death has no power, but they will be priests of God and of Christ, and they will reign with him for a thousand years.
—Revelation 20:6

"And behold, I am coming soon. Blessed is the one who keeps the words of the prophecy of this book."
—Revelation 22:7

Blessed are those who wash their robes, so that they may have the right to the tree of life and that they may enter the city by the gates.
—Revelation 22:14

1

Blessed by Hearing the Revelation of Jesus

Revelation 1:1–8

THE BIG REVEAL. That's what home makeover shows are all about. It all starts with a property that has . . . potential. Of course, it also has problems. The renovators make a plan. Unexpected challenges like rotted subfloors and sinking foundations pop up along the way. The clock is ticking. The budget is stretched. An unnumbered crew of electricians, woodworkers, and decorators have been at work behind the scenes. And then we finally get to what we've all been waiting for—the big reveal. On *Fixer Upper*, Chip and Joanna Gaines position themselves at the far ends of two panels that feature a life-sized photo of the property before they began work on it. And then the panels are pulled back. What has been hidden is finally revealed.

That image of pulling back the curtain so that we can see what renovation experts and their crew have been working to re-create helps us to understand what the book we are beginning to study is all about. God has been and is now at work in a realm that we can't see into with human eyes. But so that we could know what he has done, is doing, and will do to renovate the home he intends to share with us, God pulled back the curtain and invited John to look. John wrote down what he saw for us. Revelation is John's written record of what he saw behind the veil that separates heaven and earth. This is the biggest of all big reveals, especially when we consider who is revealing it to us. The book begins:

The revelation of Jesus Christ. (Rev. 1:1)

If we were reading this book in Greek, it would tell us that this is the *apokalypsis* of Jesus Christ. To apocalypse is to unveil or uncover something previously hidden. It's helpful to begin our journey through this book here because so many of us have come to think of Revelation as a mysterious book, a closed book, a book that is hard to make sense of—even a book that people seem to like to argue about more than understand or apply. But evidently this book was not written to confuse us or frighten us or divide us into opinionated camps. Rather, it was written to give servants of Jesus Christ in the first century, and servants of Jesus Christ living in every century since then, confidence in what God is doing to bring about his intended purposes for his world.

Of course, unveiling or uncovering what is hidden isn't what most people think of when they hear the word *apocalypse*. Most people think of apocalypse as a cataclysmic event that will usher in the end of life on earth as we know it. And, yes, the book of Revelation does reveal some things about the way in which life on earth as we know it will come to an end as it gives way to a new heaven and a new earth. But this book is not merely or perhaps even primarily about the future. It has some significant things to reveal to us about the present.

To help us understand what John meant when he spoke of this book as an apocalypse, it can be helpful to recognize that this isn't actually the first time this word has been used in the New Testament. Jesus used the word two times when he declared, "I thank you, Father, Lord of heaven and earth, that you have hidden these things from the wise and understanding and revealed [apocalypsed] them to little children. . . . And no one knows the Father except the Son and anyone to whom the Son chooses to reveal [apocalypse] him" (Matt. 11:25–27). Later in the Gospel of Matthew we read that after Peter affirmed that Jesus is "the Christ, the Son of the living God," Jesus said that flesh and blood hadn't revealed [apocalypsed] this to Peter but rather, "my Father who is in heaven" (Matt. 16:16–17).

When the apostle Paul sought to describe how he came to understand the gospel, he wrote, "I did not receive it from any man, nor was I taught it, but I received it through a revelation [apocalypse] of Jesus Christ" and that God "was pleased to reveal [apocalypse] his Son to me" (Gal. 1:12, 16). Even though Paul had spent his whole life studying the scrolls of the Old Testament, he couldn't see who Jesus really was until God supernaturally revealed, or "apocalypsed," it to him on the road to Damascus.[1]

John was given an apocalypse of Jesus Christ and wrote down what he saw in the pages of Revelation. Here, what has been hidden will be revealed—the hidden resurrected and glorified Christ, the hidden angelic and demonic hosts, the hidden hypocrisy of false believers, the hidden beauty of the bride of Christ, the hidden ugliness of the world's system, the hidden plan for the renewal of all things. As we study this book, we're going to discover that an apocalypse can reveal to us that some of the things that we thought were important, beautiful, or secure are actually fleeting, ugly, and destined for destruction. Some of what we're investing our lives in, counting on, hoping for, and depending on is not as significant or certain as we thought it was. As we work our way through the book of Revelation, the true nature of these things will be uncovered so that we can see them through the lens of reality, from the vantage point of heaven itself.

Hearing Revelation as Apocalyptic Prophecy

So the word *apocalypse* simply means "uncovered" or "revealed." But after John wrote the book of Revelation, the word *apocalyptic* also came to describe the unique genre of literature that is reflected in Revelation

---

1 Tim Mackie presents these previous New Testament uses of the Greek word *apokalypsis* in "Apocalyptic Please—Apocalyptic E1," *The Bible Project* (podcast), April 27, 2020, https://bibleproject.com/.

as well as some other prophetical books in the Bible such as Daniel and Ezekiel, and in the Olivet Discourse in Matthew and Mark. Biblical apocalyptic, as a subset of prophecy, emphasizes the lifting of the veil between heaven and earth in order to allow the prophet to see a fuller picture of the way in which God is working out his plans for his world.

In apocalyptic literature we often read accounts of dreams, visionary experiences, or journeys to heaven in which the writers use vivid symbolism to describe what they saw and the message that was mediated to them by a heavenly or angelic being. Apocalyptic is generally otherworldly so that when we read it, we feel like we are "lost in a fog of imagery."[2]

Perhaps the most succinct way to describe apocalyptic literature is to say that it describes earthly events from a heavenly perspective. Common features and characteristics in apocalyptic prophecy in the Bible include:

- heavenly visions
- angels and demons
- bizarre creatures
- symbolic imagery and numbers
- abundant use of metaphor
- cataclysmic events
- scenes of judgment and destruction[3]

It's safe to say that most of these things are outside of our everyday life. Sometimes you and I need something out of the ordinary to really shake up our thinking and adjust our perspective. It has to be bold, dramatic. And that's exactly what we're given in the book of Revelation and other apocalyptic prophecy. Revelation shakes us out of our complacency and out of what may have become a deeply entrenched way of looking at the world and our lives.

2   Tim Mackie, "The Jewish Apocalyptic Imagination—Apocalyptic E4," *The Bible Project* (podcast), May 18, 2020, https://bibleproject.com/.

3   This list is adapted from a similar list by David R. Helm in "An Approach to Apocalyptic Literature: A Primer for Preachers," Charles Simeon Trust, 2009, https://simeontrust.org/.

In biblical apocalyptic prophecy the secret things of God that are inaccessible to normal human knowledge about the outworking of his plans for history are revealed. The curtain is drawn back so that we can see that the powers of this world will be overthrown and replaced by the kingdom of God. We could think of it as a news report on what is happening on earth as reported from heaven. Angels and demons that are active on the earth are in full view. We see past, current, and future events in cosmic technicolor, communicated to us in the form of images and impressions, metaphors and symbols.

For some of us, the otherworldly nature of this type of literature is off-putting. As soon as we start reading about dragons and beasts with many eyes or locusts with human faces, some of us think, "Forget it. Let's study something more straightforward. Let's be comforted by the Psalms or challenged by Jesus's teaching in the Gospels. Let's trace Paul's argument in Romans." But we have much to gain by stretching ourselves to rightly interpret what the divine and human authors chose to write to us in the form of apocalyptic. Revelation has its own unique way of pressing us into Christ, illumining the person and work of Christ, nourishing our love for Christ. It simply won't allow us to rest on the laurels of seasons in the past when we lived by faith and were bold in our testimony to Jesus Christ. It demands fresh obedience and boldness from us today. It won't allow us to settle for a go-to-church-on-Sunday-and-live-like-everyone-else-all-week kind of faith. It intends to shake us out of apathy and compromise. It intends to infuse our worship with wonder.

While the creatures and events in what John has written about may seem fantastical, perhaps even the product of a vivid imagination, John wants to be clear that he isn't making this up. He is testifying to what he saw. In fact, in the very first verse, he tells us where his visions originated and how they came to him:

> The revelation of Jesus Christ, which God gave him to show to his servants the things that must soon take place. He made it known by sending his angel to his servant John. (Rev. 1:1)

God the Father gave this revelation to Jesus, who made it known to John by sending his angel to John. And by writing down what he saw and heard, John passed it along to the servants of Jesus. From God the Father → to Jesus → to Jesus's angel → to John → to the servants of Jesus. And what was contained in what was given through this chain of provenance? "The things that must soon take place."

What does that mean? Actually, to speak this way of the age in between the ascension of Jesus and his bodily return is consistent with what is written throughout the New Testament. Paul ended his letter to the Romans saying that "the God of peace will *soon* crush Satan under your feet" (Rom. 16:20). James exhorted his readers to be patient and establish their hearts because the Lord "is *at hand*" (James 5:8) and the Judge is "standing at the door" (5:9). Peter warned his readers to be sober and watchful in prayer since "the end of all things is *at hand*" (1 Pet. 4:7).

When we read that this book is about "things that must soon take place" and that "the time is near," we're meant to see that what is written in this book about the coming of the kingdom of God was set in motion by the death, resurrection, and ascension of Jesus. As John wrote, the kingdom of God was spreading throughout the world as the gospel went out, and those who once belonged to the kingdom of darkness were being transferred to the kingdom of Jesus (Col. 1:13). The opposition to the kingdom of God portrayed in Revelation wasn't merely something off in the future. It was a present reality for those who first heard this book read to them, and it is a present reality for us now.

[John] bore witness to the word of God and to the testimony of Jesus Christ, even to all that he saw. (Rev. 1:2)

John saw into heavenly realities and then, similar to prophets in the Old Testament, he was charged to write down all that he saw.[4] He was

---

4 In the Old Testament book of Daniel, we read that God sent the angel Gabriel to lift the veil so Daniel could see how the angel Gabriel was delayed because he was doing battle with a demonic force. In Ezekiel, we read that a voice from heaven told Ezekiel to write down his visions of the

invited into the heavenly throne room to see who is there and what they are doing, out to an earthly wilderness to see the world's system, and onto a high mountain from which he could see the new Jerusalem. Revelation is a written record of all that John saw in these visions.

Can you imagine seeing into heavenly realities and then trying to put it into words that people who hadn't seen it themselves would be able to understand? How would you have the vocabulary for it? You'd have to compare what you saw to things your readers were familiar with. You'd be trying to paint pictures with words, which is exactly what John does in this book.

Hearing Revelation as a Promise

These pictures painted by words in this book are intended to affect us deeply. In fact, there's a promise in this book for those who will open themselves to be changed by what they see:

> Blessed is the one who reads aloud the words of this prophecy, and blessed are those who hear, and who keep what is written in it, for the time is near. (Rev. 1:3)

Blessing, according to this verse, is first for those who would read this book aloud. Revelation was originally intended to be read out loud to the seven churches it was addressed to. It was written in such a way that when those in the churches of John's day heard it read to them, they would be able to get its message. That means it was written to convey a message and stir the imagination rather than to trace an argument. It was written to evoke worship, confidence, anticipation, and hope in those who heard it read to them. It was written for listeners to get a sense of the big picture rather than obsess over the details. And the same goes for us. For some of us, the idea that we would not try to nail down with certainty the meaning of every word of the text we're studying goes against our instincts in what we would define as "serious Bible study."

---

glory of God on the move. In Zechariah, the prophet records eight visions that include horses, horns, lampstands, and a flying scroll.

We want to come away from our study with a clear understanding of every detail in our text. But studying Revelation requires a different set of skills. "It is more like studying an Impressionist painting; if we look too closely, we might lose sight of the big picture."[5] If we insist on owning every detail of its fantastical images, we'll be in danger of missing the message.

Imagine that you are part of one of those seven churches in Asia who first received this letter. A reader has stood up in the midst of your gathering to read a letter that John the apostle has addressed to your church. You're on the edge of your seat. And then he begins to read. Very quickly you realize you have some adjustments to make in the way that you listen and process what he's written because this is not like any of the other letters from Paul or Peter or James or John that have been circulated and read aloud to your church before. The reading of this letter is more like a dramatic performance. Everyone in the room is having a similar experience. Their perception of what is really happening in your church and in the world is being altered by the experience of entering into John's dramatic visions.

As you walk back home past all of the Roman architecture and evidence of Roman rule, you would find that you're now seeing it through the lens of the vivid counterimages contained in John's letter. You've seen an alternative reality that is true reality, and it has changed how you see everything else. John's "blessed are those who read aloud the words of this prophecy" has proved true. God has blessed the reading aloud of his word, evidenced by the way in which all who heard it read at your church are thinking and feeling, singing and suffering, worshiping and waiting. You have been blessed by it. But not merely by hearing it. You've been blessed because what you heard is changing how you think, how you feel, what you say, what you believe.

There is no magical blessing in simply hearing what is revealed in Revelation. There's no blessing for those who hear it but choose to

5   Iain Duguid, "Doxological Evangelism in Practice: Preaching Apocalyptic Literature," Westminster Conference on Preaching and Preachers, Westminster Theological Seminary, October 21, 2020.

ignore it, reject it, rebel against it, or simply treat it as fodder for their curiosity. The blessing is for those whose lives are impacted and shaped by what is in it. It changes their priorities. It builds up their courage. It impacts how they spend their money. It leads them to worship in spirit and in truth. It sends them to their knees in prayer. It emboldens their witness. It takes away their fear of death. It fills their imagination and fuels their anticipation of where history is headed, and it shapes their understanding of how their suffering will resolve in the new heaven and the new earth.

The first servants of Jesus who heard what is written in Revelation were believers around Asia in the first century. It was exactly what they needed to hear in their day. But it wasn't just what *they* needed to hear. John wrote it down for every believer in every century since then. It has always been exactly the truth believers need to hear, the reality believers need to see. It shows us:

    ~ the opposition we can expect to escalate

      ~ the endurance we need to cultivate

        ~ the judgment we will celebrate

          ~ the victory in which we will participate

            ~ the enemy Jesus will annihilate

              ~ the sorrow he will alleviate

                ~ the creation he will regenerate

                  ~ the marriage he will consummate

                    ~ and the home we can anticipate sharing with him forever.

That's what I call blessed.

Hearing Revelation as a Letter

So Revelation is an apocalyptic prophecy, which is its own unique literary genre. It includes the promise of blessing for those who hear and keep it. It is also a letter or epistle. After John explains the provenance and promise of the book, he addresses a specific group of recipients:

John to the seven churches that are in Asia. (Rev. 1:4a)

Revelation doesn't simply *contain* letters to the seven churches; it *is* a letter that John intends to be circulated to seven churches in Asia. It was written to meet the very real needs of believers in his day. Some of them were compromised and needed to be jolted out of it. Some of them were enduring costly persecution and needed to be strengthened for it. All of them needed to understand the cosmic battle against evil being waged in heaven and earth that will resolve in the establishment of God's kingdom at the coming of the King.

So why these seven churches? There were certainly other churches in Asia. We're going to discover that the number seven has tremendous significance in Revelation. Something is being communicated whenever we come upon seven of anything in the book. Seven is one of the numbers of completeness. So, by addressing seven churches, John is saying that his letter is written to the church as whole, to Christians throughout the centuries. Each of the seven churches addressed represents struggles and victories that are present in the church in every generation. The comforts in it aren't reserved only for believers living in Asia at the end of the first century, and neither are its commands.

After stating who the letter is being written to, we get a sense of what is being imparted to them by means of this letter:

> Grace to you and peace from him who is and who was and who is to come, and from the seven spirits who are before his throne, and from Jesus Christ the faithful witness, the firstborn of the dead, and the ruler of kings on earth. (Rev. 1:4b–5a)

We've read other letters in the New Testament that begin with a greeting of grace and peace. So perhaps it is easy to read right through this greeting as standard politeness. But I don't think we should. John knows that if the believers who will hear this letter read to them are going to be able to keep or obey what is written in it, they will need supernatural help. They are going to need grace to persevere instead of compromise. They'll need peace if they are to endure constant conflict with the world's system. This kind of grace and peace has only one source. And that is exactly who John says will provide it. Each member of the Godhead is getting in on it.

John works his way through Father, Spirit, and Son as the source of this grace and peace. Here he refers to the Father as "him who is and who was and who is to come." We're about to read about some very difficult realities. In facing those, we can be sure of the support of the God "who was"—the God who has always been a helper to his people—and the God "who is" even now caring for his people. We're about to read about some stark realities in the future. We can be sure of the sovereign oversight of the God "who is to come" over those realities. Then he speaks of the Holy Spirit as "seven spirits who are before his throne." We can be sure that the Holy Spirit will deliver this grace and develop this peace in the servants of Jesus. Then he gives us three names or titles for the Son, and each one speaks grace to us and brings us peace:

~ Jesus is the faithful witness. We can trust that Jesus will tell us the truth about ourselves, about the world we're living in, about the future, about everything.

~ Jesus is the firstborn of the dead. He was the first human to rise from the dead and never die again. But he won't be the last! He is our hope for life beyond this life when our lives are threatened.

~ Jesus is the ruler of the kings of the earth. Sometimes it seems to us like governments and organizations and philosophies and the dominant culture have all of the power in this world. But they don't. Someone is ruling over them. Their days are numbered.

These three titles for Jesus seem to move John to praise. We can almost picture him looking up from what he's writing, lifting his hands toward heaven, and saying:

To him who loves us and has freed us from our sins by his blood and made us a kingdom, priests to his God and Father, to him be glory and dominion forever and ever. Amen. (Rev. 1:5b–6)

John is moved to worship this triune God who is revealing so much about who he is, what he is doing, and what he is about to do in "the things that must soon take place." It's not some remote robotic being revealing these things. He's receiving this revelation from someone "who loves us." It is always easier to hear hard things when they come from someone who loves us, isn't it? And how do we know he loves us? John stated it clearly in one of his earlier letters, which we know as 1 John. "In this is love, not that we have loved God but that he loved us and sent his Son to be the propitiation for our sins" (1 John 4:10). The love of Jesus toward us is not merely sentimental; it's sacrificial. He actively demonstrated his love for us by offering himself as a substitute in such a way that sin doesn't have the power over us that it once had. We've been "freed from our sins by his blood"— freed from its penalty and its power.

In the next verse, John combines familiar images about the Messiah from Daniel 7:13 and Zechariah 12:10 to turn our gaze toward anticipation of the day when Jesus will come again to this earth in power and glory:

> Behold, he is coming with the clouds, and every eye will see him, even those who pierced him, and all tribes of the earth will wail on account of him. Even so. Amen. (Rev. 1:7)

The whole world will see him when he comes. His coming will not be a secret. But his coming will not be a day of celebration for all who see him. For those who have rejected him, ignored him, and refused his offer of grace and mercy, his coming will be a day of great wailing and mourning. All those who crucified him, rejected him, mocked him, and refused to believe in him will finally see his glory. And it will bring them to their knees, weighted down by sorrow and regret.

Finally, John enables us to hear God himself speak. What God says about himself assures us that he is a reliable source for all we're about to read in this book:

> "I am the Alpha and the Omega," says the Lord God, "who is and who was and who is to come, the Almighty." (Rev. 1:8)

Think for a minute about all that someone who is and who was and who is to come has seen. Think about all that he knows, all that he understands from his perspective. And then imagine that he wants to pull back the veil between heaven and earth so that you will be able to see, know, and understand these things. Imagine that he wants you to have his perspective on what is going on in the world, his perspective on what is going on in your life. That is the great purpose of the book of Revelation. God has chosen to apocalypse, or reveal, his perspective to us so that we can meet the uncertainty, the unfairness, and the undoing of life in this world with faith and hope.

Two times in just these opening eight verses God has identified himself as the one "who is and who was and who is to come." We're going to hear him say it again in 4:8. And then we're going to hear him say it again later in the book, except it will be slightly different. Later, we'll hear him identify himself as the one "who is and who was" (11:17; 16:5). He'll leave off the "and who is to come." Why? Because he will have come!

Finally, God identifies himself as "the Almighty" (1:8). God reveals himself to a people who may have wondered if he was aware of their suffering, if they should really put their lives on the line for the gospel, if they were risking everything for something that wasn't real or true, and he reminds them of his name—a name that reflects the reality that he has the power and position to control everything. Oppressive governments are under his control. False teachers are under his control. Evil is under his control. The suffering of his saints is under his control. The destruction of the devil is under his control. Time is under his control. The earth and stars are under his control. Everything is under his control because he is not just mighty; he is the Almighty.

Imagine what it would mean for us if none of what we've been shown in these first eight verses were true. What if God did not choose to reveal or uncover these things for us? What if he did not act to reveal to us where history is headed? The sorrow and persecution that so many endure for him would seem meaningless and truly unbearable. Imagine if we had no resource for grace or peace. Without Jesus as the faithful witness, how would we know what is true in a world of so many lies? Without Jesus as the firstborn from the dead, how would we have any hope of life beyond our number of years on this earth? Without Jesus as the ruler of kings on earth, what would keep us from despair over the corruption, oppression, and misery that is so pervasive in our world? If Jesus did not love us by freeing us from our sins, we would still be ruled by them in the here and now, and we would be destined for destruction because of them in the hereafter. If he had not made us a kingdom and priests to his God and Father, our lives would have no dignity or purpose.

But instead, he who is the Alpha and the Omega has revealed to us what we can expect in this in-between time—in between his ascension to heaven and his return to this earth. He who is and who was and who is to come is present with us now by his Spirit and will be fully and intimately present with us when he comes. Because he is the Almighty, we can rest knowing that he has the power to provide the blessing promised in this book, to accomplish the elimination of evil and suffering portrayed in this book, and to prepare us as a bride to present to the Son as pictured in this book.

Hearing and Keeping Revelation 1:1–8

Earlier we read that those who hear and keep what is written in the book of Revelation are blessed. So beginning in this first chapter, and in every chapter that follows, we want to ask a very practical and hopefully penetrating question: What will it mean for us to "hear and keep" it? What will it look like for us to live in light of what has been revealed? We need to know, because this is where the blessing is. And we want every blessing God has for us.

To hear and keep Revelation 1:1–8 means that we hear it as something God wants us to know. More significantly, we hear it as something we simply *must* know if we're going to be able to live as servants of Jesus, waiting for him to come again. So perhaps it leads us to pray as we begin our study of Revelation, "Lord, I want to see everything you want to show to me. My eyes, my heart, and my mind are all open."

It means that we open ourselves up to being moved and challenged and perhaps shocked out of our complacency by what John saw. We refuse to take a casual or merely intellectual approach to what is being shown to us. Instead, we are desperate enough for the blessing this book promises that we are open to being wrong, open to coming under conviction and responding in repentance, open to having our deeply entrenched ways of interacting with the world challenged and changed. Are you that desperate?

To hear and keep these verses is to rest in God's sovereign control over the past, the present, and the future in such a way that we aren't constantly feeding on regret over the past, frustrations in the present, and fears about the future. Instead, we want to live in the light of the grace that has covered our past and is empowering us to live in the present as those who have really been freed from our sins by his blood. We have peace now because we really do believe that we have been and are now loved in the way we most need to be loved. And we have peace about the future, because we know that the Alpha and Omega, the Almighty, has it firmly in his grip. He will bring everything John saw to pass.

Perhaps hearing and keeping these first eight verses of Revelation means that we get on our knees and pray, "Lord, I need this revelation of who you are to do more than simply inform me. I need this revelation to move me. I need this revelation of your eternity and your sovereignty to fill me with the courage to live in light of it. I need this grace and peace to permeate—even define—my life. I need for you to radically adjust my perspective about what is real, what is worthwhile, and who is worthy of my worship."

These first eight verses are a bit like the buildup to the big reveal on a home improvement show. We've been introduced to the person who has been at work behind the scenes. We've heard his promise of blessing, the assurance of his love, and the extent of his power. God himself is pulling back the curtain, and he has invited us to see into the reality we most need to see. And so we find ourselves on tiptoes, anticipating all that he has to show us—to apocalypse to us—about the coming of his kingdom.

2

Blessed by Seeing the Glorified Jesus

Revelation 1:9–20

HAVE YOU EVER had a first impression of someone and then later you saw another side of him or her that caused you to realize that you had missed something—that there was far more to that person than you recognized at first—far more than meets the eye?

That's what happened to me when I first saw David Guthrie around the halls of the office at Word, Incorporated, where I worked. When he moved from Portland, Oregon, to Waco, Texas, in August 1985, he had a head of dark hair and a full, dark beard. I remember noticing that he wore, well, comfortable shoes, and my impression of him from seeing him in the hallway at the office was that he was very serious.

But then he came to choir practice at my church. Our choir was going to be premiering a new Word musical at a workshop for ministers of music, and as Word's marketing person, he came to talk to the choir about the event. He was so comfortable in front of a group of people. His voice. His wit. His confidence. And then as I was walking to my car in the parking lot after rehearsal, I saw him crawl into his car—a red Mazda RX7 two-seater sports car. And I thought to myself, "I think I may have seriously underestimated this guy." He suddenly seemed far more interesting and, might I say, far more attractive than I'd given him credit for.

Sometimes our estimation of people stays stuck on our first impression or stuck on what they were like when we knew them as kids, or in college, or some other time in our past. In fact, that may be the case for some of us with Jesus. Perhaps somewhere along the way we came to an understanding of who Jesus is, why he came, what he's all about. And it stuck. We have never taken the time to evaluate if the Jesus we see in our mind's eye lines up with the real Jesus. Revelation shows us that there is far more to Jesus than meets the eye, perhaps far more than we have seen before.

Most of the pictures of Jesus we have in our mind that shape our understanding, our response, and maybe even our obedience to Jesus have been taken through the lens of the Gospels. And those pictures are good. They are true. They show us what he was like when Jesus took on flesh and lived on this earth for thirty-three years. They don't necessarily show us what Jesus is like now in his glorified humanity, ruling and reigning in heaven. But in Revelation 1, John writes down what he saw when the curtain between heaven and earth was pulled back for him so that he could see Jesus as he truly is—today, right now.

Suffering on Account of Jesus

Let's look first at who this vision of Jesus was given to:

> I, John, your brother and partner in the tribulation and the kingdom and the patient endurance that are in Jesus . . . (Rev. 1:9a)

It was given to John who identifies himself as a "brother and partner" of those he was writing to. What makes them brothers and partners is that they are all "in Christ." He is writing to those who, like him, have become joined to Christ by faith.

Notice the three things John shares with those to whom he is writing—tribulation, the kingdom, and patient endurance. He shares with them the kind of tribulation that Jesus described when he said, "They will deliver you up to tribulation and put you to death, and you will be hated by all nations for my name's sake" (Matt. 24:9). John shares with his readers about being part of the kingdom. And what is required of all kingdom subjects living in this time in between Jesus's ascension and his second coming? Patient endurance, patiently enduring the suffering that is inherent in identifying with Jesus.

We should probably circle those two words in our Bibles: patient endurance. We're going to hear them again and again as we work our way through Revelation (2:2, 3, 19; 3:10; 13:10; 14:12). In fact, if someone were to ask you what the book of Revelation is about, a good answer would be, "Revelation is a call to patient endurance of tribulation as we await the coming of Christ's kingdom in all of its fullness." The idea that the Christian life is or should be defined by patient endurance shouldn't actually sound new to us. Jesus promised that "the one who endures to the end will be saved" (Matt. 24:13). And Paul wrote that "if we endure, we will also reign with him" (2 Tim. 2:12).

John goes on to tell us the setting in which, in the midst of tribulation, he was given a vision of the King of this kingdom:

> I, John . . . was on the island called Patmos on account of the word
> of God and the testimony of Jesus. (Rev. 1:9b)

John had been banished by the Romans to a rocky island prison. This wasn't unique in the first century. The Romans often exiled political prisoners to islands in the Aegean Sea. So why was John exiled to Patmos? John writes that he was there "on account of the word of God and the testimony of Jesus." John's testimony about Jesus and his kingdom was viewed as a political crime. He was living in a world ruled by Rome where the emperor Domitian demanded to be worshiped as a god. But all who were partners in the kingdom—the kingdom of Jesus—could not say, "Caesar is Lord." Instead, they boldly declared that Jesus is Lord. And it cost them.

John's boldness about King Jesus had been costing him since shortly after Pentecost when he and Peter were arrested by the temple authorities for healing a man in the name of Jesus who had been lame since birth, and then calling those who witnessed the miracle to faith in Christ. But after arresting them, the priests didn't know what to do with them, so they simply warned them not to speak or teach at all in the name of Jesus and released them. In response, Peter and John said, "We cannot but speak of what we have seen and heard" (Acts 4:20).

It was just a short time later that John and the other apostles were back at Solomon's Portico at the temple. People were bringing the sick and those afflicted with unclean spirits, and they were all healed. This time the high priest arrested the apostles and put them in prison. But during the night an angel opened the prison doors and led them out. So the next day they went right back to the temple to continue declaring the good news of Christ. The religious leaders were infuriated and wanted to kill them but were afraid of how the people would respond. So the apostles were beaten and ordered, once again, not to speak in the name of Jesus, and then released. Acts 5:40–41 records that John and the other apostles "left the presence of the council, rejoicing that they were counted worthy to suffer dishonor for the name."

King Jesus was so real and so precious to John that he would rather be exiled to a barren island prison than not talk about him. And as I think about this, it causes me to ask myself some questions. First, am I willing to be excluded, indicted, even imprisoned, because Jesus has become so precious to me and so compelling to me that I just can't keep from talking about him openly to anyone who will listen? I don't have to fear being exiled to a rocky island prison for speaking about Jesus as Lord. But if I did, would there be enough evidence to convict me? Do I love his word that much? Have I testified of Jesus that clearly?

As a prisoner on Patmos, John likely spent his days doing manual labor. History tells us that in the marble mines on the Isle of Patmos, "men worked chained to their slave barrows."[1] Probably no one else on Patmos even kept track of what day it was. But John did. It was

---

1   Herbert Lockyer, *All the Apostles of the Bible* (Grand Rapids, MI: Zondervan, 1972), 97.

the Lord's day, the first day of the week. And on this particular Lord's Day, the veil between heaven and earth was pulled back for him:

> I was in the Spirit on the Lord's day, and I heard behind me a loud voice like a trumpet saying, "Write what you see in a book and send it to the seven churches, to Ephesus and to Smyrna and to Pergamum and to Thyatira and to Sardis and to Philadelphia and to Laodicea." (Rev. 1:10–11)

When John writes that he was "in the Spirit," we are to understand that he was having the same kind of experience Old Testament prophets had. John "was taken up into a trancelike, visionary state"[2] by the Spirit of God to receive revelation from God. And like Old Testament prophets such as Moses, Isaiah, and Jeremiah, John was commanded to write down what he saw in a book.

But there was a challenge for John in describing what he saw. He simply didn't have the words to describe the heavenly things he saw and heard, so we hear him doing his best to make it understandable to the people in the seven churches, writing repeatedly, "It's like . . . It's like . . . It's like . . . It's like . . ." This is the language of metaphor and analogy. Because he didn't have words to describe the heavenly things he saw, he drew upon the best things he could to describe it using imagery his readers and those who would hear it read to them would be familiar with. As John described what he saw in this vision and in the three additional visions he will write about in Revelation, rather than understanding him as describing things in literal terms, we need to understand him describing them analogically saying, "It's *like* this." When we say what he's describing is not literal, we're not saying that it wasn't real. John is looking into the heart of ultimate reality. We're simply saying that he is using metaphorical language to describe what is real. "This does not show us what Jesus *looks* like

2   Richard D. Phillips, *Revelation*, Reformed Expository Commentary (Phillipsburg, NJ: P&R, 2000), 61.

but rather what Jesus *is* like, symbolically depicting his person and work."[3]

Turning toward the Vision of Jesus

The voice John heard was loud, like a trumpet. Unavoidable. Unignorable. Inescapable.

> Then I turned to see the voice that was speaking to me, and on turning I saw seven golden lampstands, and in the midst of the lampstands one like a son of man, clothed with a long robe and with a golden sash around his chest. (Rev. 1:12–13)

"I saw," he says, "one like a son of man." In other words, he saw someone who looked human. John looked at his glorious Lord, and the first thing that struck him was the humanness of Jesus. It reminds us that Jesus didn't just take on flesh for the years he walked on this earth. He's still a human being as he sits on the throne of heaven. But he is not an ordinary human being. John recorded in his Gospel that Jesus prayed on the night before his crucifixion, "And now, Father, glorify me in your presence with the glory that I had with you before the world existed" (John 17:5). In Revelation 1 we see that God answered that prayer. His glory is no longer veiled. He's still flesh, but his earthly, perishable flesh has been transformed into imperishable, heavenly flesh. Right now, Jesus Christ is the first and only glorified human being. But he won't be the last.

When John writes that he saw someone "like a son of man," he's expressing more, however, than simply that he's seeing a glorified human being. He's connecting the person he saw with the person Daniel saw and wrote about when the curtain between heaven and earth was pulled back for him seven hundred years before John. Daniel wrote:

> I saw in the night visions,
> and behold, with the clouds of heaven

3 Phillips, *Revelation*, 64.

    there came one like a son of man,
and he came to the Ancient of Days
    and was presented before him.
And to him was given dominion
    and glory and a kingdom,
that all peoples, nations, and languages
    should serve him;
his dominion is an everlasting dominion,
    which shall not pass away,
and his kingdom one
    that shall not be destroyed. (Dan. 7:13–14)

The "son of man" Daniel wrote about is a commanding, redeeming, glorious figure, and Daniel's prophecy about him shaped the Jewish people's expectations for what the Messiah would be like. It's no wonder that the people in Jesus's day had such a hard time believing Jesus when he referred to himself as the "Son of Man," clearly connecting himself to the person Daniel saw. From their vantage point, Jesus was an ordinary person from the humble town of Nazareth. He had a rag-tag group of followers. How could this simple man be the "son of man," given dominion and glory and kingdom, as Daniel had prophesied?

Even those closest to him, the disciples, struggled to accept that the Jesus they saw eating with prostitutes, sleeping on the boat, and walking the streets with dusty feet was really the "son of man" they had been waiting for. Surely even after Jesus ascended into heaven, it didn't come naturally to them to imagine him as the glorified Son of Man seated at the right hand of God.

Jesus gave John this revelation and told him to write it down, because he wanted them and wants us to see him as he is. He doesn't want us to have our mental picture of him stuck on how he looked for the thirty-three years he walked this earth. John's vision shows us Jesus as he is and as he wants to be known. It also shows us where he prefers to be:

> And in the midst of the lampstands one like a son of man, clothed
> with a long robe and with a golden sash around his chest. (Rev. 1:13)

His Preferred Place

John saw Jesus "in the midst of the lampstands." There is a lot of imagery used in Revelation that is challenging to understand, but we don't have to wonder what these lampstands represent. We are told later in this first chapter that the lampstands represent the churches (1:20). When John turned to see the voice that was speaking to him, the first thing that caught John's attention was Jesus standing in the midst of his people.

Were these early Christians wondering if the church would be snuffed out as persecution increased? When they gathered to hear this letter read to them, it must have provided deep encouragement to see that Jesus was not standing off at a distance while his followers suffered for him. He was right there with them, walking in the midst of them, keeping their fire for the gospel burning, correcting them, watching over them, strengthening them.

Some people in this world today are so suspect of the church. They've seen too much of what they've labeled as hypocrisy, and even though they might be interested in Jesus, the last place they want to be found is in the church. But Jesus is not ashamed to be found in the midst of his imperfect church. It is his preferred place to be. He chooses to be in and among his imperfect people who follow and serve him in imperfect ways. What a relief.

His Priestly Work

As Jesus is standing in the midst of his suffering church, he is wearing "a long robe," which is a description of the high priest of the Old Testament. If you've studied Hebrews, then you'll remember that it emphasizes that Jesus is the perfect, ultimate high priest and that "we do not have a high priest who is unable to sympathize with our weaknesses, but one who in every respect has been tempted as we are, yet without sin" (Heb. 4:15). So standing in the midst of his suffering church is our high priest—our mediator—representing us before the Father, interceding for us, protecting us from any accusation that might damn us through the once-and-for-all sacrifice of himself.

John writes that Jesus had "a golden sash around his chest," which is the description not only of a high priest but of a king. The people of John's day needed to see the authority of Jesus as king. They were suffering under a government that criminalized their faith in Jesus. This vision of Jesus as a king must have filled them with confidence to know that he—not the Roman government or any other power—is in charge of what is happening in this world.

His Perfect Wisdom

John's gaze went from what Jesus was wearing to the hair on his head:

> The hairs of his head were white, like white wool, like snow. (Rev. 1:14a)

We think of white hair as indicating advancing age. But this stunning white hair of Jesus reveals his eternal wisdom, which is demonstrated in his righteous judgments. Having already connected his vision to Daniel 7, John's first hearers and readers would have connected this description of the risen Jesus to Daniel's description of the Ancient of Days who sits on the throne, having "clothing . . . white as snow, and the hair of his head like pure wool" (Dan. 7:9). Our instinct might be to wonder if John is confusing the son of man with the Ancient of Days, but what he's really doing is *connecting* the son of man to the Ancient of Days. "John attributes to the Son of Man white hair, even though in Daniel 7 the white hair belongs to the Ancient of Days. The white hair, of course, isn't literal but indicates the wisdom and omniscience of the Son of Man; thus there is no doubt the Son of Man is divine."[4]

This means that not only does Jesus know exactly what to do; what he does is absolutely pure and right. Jesus is absolutely pure in what he

---

4 Thomas Schreiner, *Hebrews–Revelation*, ESV Expository Commentary (Wheaton, IL: Crossway, 2018), 564.

thinks and what he says and what he does. He never has mixed motives. He is wisdom incarnate. He is holy, holy, holy.

His Penetrating Gaze

His eyes were like a flame of fire. (Rev. 1:14b)

Imagine what it must have been like for John to look into eyes that were like a flame of fire. John must have felt this fiery gaze penetrate into his very soul, exposing any shallowness and sinfulness that was there.

Jesus doesn't just look at us; he looks into us. And if we are willing to hold his gaze, he will burn away what is meaningless and frivolous and contaminating. We're going to see in the next chapter that Jesus will speak to the church of Thyatira about her toleration of sexual immorality and idolatry as one who "has eyes like a flame of fire" (2:18). He's seeking her purity and pointing out what is contaminating her.

Of course, when we picture someone whose eyes are like blazing fire, we imagine that person must be very, very angry. There are numerous places in the Old Testament where we read about God's anger burning against his enemies. God is angry against sin. His righteous anger burns against evil and injustice and unrighteousness, and as much as we might like to point in someone else's direction, this reality should make every one of us want to run and hide.

But when we see the fire in his eyes, rather than prompting us to run away from him, it should make us want to run to him, welcoming him to burn away what is displeasing to him. Jesus invites us to come to him so that we can be confident that when the day comes that we look into his fiery eyes, we will experience his full salvation, not his fiery judgment.

His Permanent Foundation

His feet were like burnished bronze, refined in a furnace. (Rev. 1:15a)

Bronze is a combination of tin and copper. Both tin and copper are relatively soft on their own, but when they are melted and mixed together, they become bronze, which is strong and hard and resistant to corrosion. So to say that his feet were like burnished bronze that has been refined in a furnace is to say that the foundation of Jesus's power has been tested by fire and will endure.

This is the firm foundation our lives are built on when they are built on Jesus Christ. Our lives become as secure, as enduring, as his. He is our source for patient endurance as his strength flows into us.

His Powerful Voice

Before we are told what the Son of Man says, we are told what his voice sounds like. Remember that John had heard the voice of Jesus before. But what John heard on this day was different:

> His voice was like the roar of many waters. (Rev. 1:15b)

This voice John heard speaking to him thundered with the power of a waterfall drowning out all other sounds of voices. Think Niagara Falls or the loudest rainstorm you've ever heard. The voice of the glorified and enthroned Jesus is commanding, unavoidable, overwhelming. When he speaks, he cannot be ignored.

There are some voices in our lives for which we sometimes wish we had a volume-adjustment knob so we could turn down the level of intensity. But this is a voice we don't want to adjust downward. To hear the powerful voice of Jesus is to hear the voice that imparts life and wisdom. We don't need to deflect or defend ourselves from what he says to us. We don't want to argue with him. We want to welcome whatever it is he has to say to us. What a blessing to hear the powerful, penetrating, and perfectly reliable voice of Jesus speaking into our lives.

His Prized Possession

> In his right hand he held seven stars. (Rev. 1:16a)

In his right hand—the hand where a person holds what is precious to him, what he intends to use, what he wants to keep close—Jesus holds seven stars. And once again, we don't have to try to guess what these seven stars in John's vision represent. We're told in verse 20 that "the seven stars are the angels of the seven churches." According to G. K. Beale, this may suggest that while the lampstands represent the church on earth, the stars represent the church in heaven.[5] And Jesus is holding them close.

His Penetrating Word

From his mouth came a sharp two-edged sword. (Rev. 1:16b)

This striking image of a sharp sword proceeding from his mouth is used three other times in Revelation (2:16; 19:15, 21). Each time, the sword is a metaphor for words of judgment spoken by Jesus. As John heard Jesus speak, he felt the penetrating power of his words. But notice this sword is double-edged. It has two sides. It cuts two ways. The words of Jesus proclaim salvation for the believer and destruction for the unbeliever. His word provides conviction and comfort, commands and promises, punishment and reward. He speaks grace to his people, and destruction for his enemies.

What Jesus has to say is not always a comforting word. Sometimes he comes to rebuke and chastise. And can we be honest and admit that we don't always want to hear what he says to us? We resist what he has to say to us to our own peril. Tim Keller says, "If your God never disagrees with you, you might just be worshiping an idealized version of yourself."[6] A sharp sword cuts. The words of Jesus cut through our stubborn resistance. They expose the shallowness of our comfortable Christianity. They pierce through our carefully cultivated reputation for always being right. And we are better for it.

His Personal Radiance

The last aspect of Jesus that John describes is his face:

His face was like the sun shining in full strength. (Rev. 1:16c)

---

5   G. K. Beale with David H. Campbell, *Revelation: A Shorter Commentary* (Grand Rapids, MI: Eerdmans, 2015), 48.

6   Tim Keller (@timkellernyc), Twitter, September 12, 2014.

This is the same radiance that Moses was exposed to so that his own face began to shine so brightly that people couldn't look at him. This is the radiance that was promised by Aaron when he was instructed to bless the people, saying, "The LORD make his face to shine upon you and be gracious to you" (Num. 6:25). This, my friends, is the face we long to see, the radiance we long to bask in for all eternity.

Sometimes it feels so good to go outside in the sunshine and look up with our eyes closed and soak in the radiant goodness of the sun. I suppose that when we do that, we could think of it as a little taste of heaven. Except that we won't be damaged by this exposure. We'll be blessed by it. The Lord will make his face shine and shine and keep shining on us. We're going to spend eternity basking in the rays of his grace toward us.

When John saw the face of Jesus shining like the sun, it wasn't actually the first time he had seen it. Shortly before his crucifixion, Jesus took Peter, James, and John up on a mountain. What happened there is described in Matthew 17:

> He was transfigured before them, and his face shone like the sun, and his clothes became white as light. . . . The disciples . . . fell on their faces and were terrified. But Jesus came and touched them, saying, "Rise, and have no fear." (Matt. 17:2–7)

Interestingly, exactly the same thing happened when John saw the glorified Jesus in his vision on Patmos:

> When I saw him, I fell at his feet as though dead. (Rev. 1:17a)

Isn't this how those who have seen Christ in all of his heavenly glory have always responded? When Isaiah "saw the Lord sitting upon a throne," he said, "Woe is me!" (Isa. 6:1–5). When Daniel saw and heard the son of man that John saw, he wrote, "I fell on my face in deep sleep with my face to the ground" (Dan. 10:9).

Why would this be the response of every prophet who sees the glory of God in the person of Jesus? Perhaps it is because most of the time we see ourselves in light of other humans around us and determine that, by comparison, we look pretty good. But, evidently, coming into the presence of the glorified Jesus makes the disparity between his perfection and holiness and our sinfulness unbearable so that all a person can do is fall down as though dead.

Falling at the Feet of Jesus

John fell down before Jesus in worship and wonder and submission and stillness—which is the only appropriate response to seeing Jesus as he truly is.

Have you ever been so captivated by Jesus that you've been willing to fall before him—yes, in your heart, but how about physically—in humility and repentance and surrender? There is something that impacts the heart in the physical act of lifting up our hands, getting on our knees, and prostrating ourselves before Jesus, isn't there? So what keeps us from it? Perhaps we're too proud, too in control, to fall at the feet of Jesus.

To fall at the feet of Jesus is to finally come to the place that our reputation doesn't matter anymore, our pride doesn't matter anymore. It is to come to the place that *Jesus is all that matters.*

John had seen the penetrating gaze of blazing fire in the eyes of this glorious heavenly King looking in his direction, exposing his hidden thoughts. He had seen his own filthiness in light of the pure white robes of Jesus and his own foolishness in contrast to the white-haired wisdom of Jesus. He'd been pierced to the core by the two-edged sword of Jesus. John was undone. Perhaps he thought he was going to die right then and there. And then something happened:

But he laid his right hand on me. (Rev. 1:17b)

Jesus reached out to John and touched him.

Responding to the Touch of Jesus

How beautiful is it that this magnificent, powerful figure John saw would also be so loving that he would reach out and touch John in his state of being utterly undone?

This is, in fact, what Jesus always does when a person comes to the place of seeing his or her own desperate sinfulness in light of his perfect holiness and bows before him in humility and need. Jesus touches us and gives us new life. Until he does, we are spiritually dead, unable to reach out to him. And then, in grace and mercy, he makes the first move toward us.

~ He reaches out to touch spiritually dead little boys and girls and awakens them to his kindness and love.

~ He reaches out and touches spiritually dead young men and women, instilling in them passion to live for him.

~ He touches spiritually dead older men and women, who may have spent a lifetime in church without ever really coming alive to him, making them flush with joy over Jesus.

When Jesus touches us, he heals us and cleanses us and remakes us. When Jesus reached out to touch John, he said:

Fear not, I am the first and the last, and the living one. I died, and behold I am alive forevermore, and I have the keys of Death and Hades. (Rev. 1:17c–18)

So much of what is in Revelation can seem scary. So it helps us to know that Jesus doesn't want us to be afraid. What he wants John to write down is not meant to scare us. It is meant to instill confidence and hope so we will not have to face the future gripped by fear.

When Jesus says to John and to you and me, "I am the first and the last," he is saying that everything started with him and everything will end with him. He's saying, "Your life begins when I reach out and touch you, and you come alive spiritually. And when your physical life comes to an end, I will be there to care for you for all eternity." My friend, all of your anxiety about the future finds relief in Jesus himself.

What does it mean that Jesus holds the keys of death and Hades? The person who holds the keys controls access. The person with the keys opens and closes.

Imagine what this meant to John as he wasted away on Patmos, perhaps wondering if he would die there. Imagine what it meant to the believers in these early churches who would read John's record of this encounter with Jesus. Some of them had seen their loved ones taken from them and thrown to the lions and perhaps then lived each day and night wondering if they would be next. Imagine the comfort and confidence it must have given them to hear Jesus say, "I'm in charge of death and the place you go when you die." It meant that they didn't have to be afraid that someone or something might prematurely take their lives or the lives of those they loved.

And neither do we.[7]

Because Jesus is in charge of life and death, Jesus says to you and me today, "I've got the keys in my hand to the place of the dead. No one goes there unless and until I open that door. I hold the keys because I died. I went into the place of the dead myself and emerged with the keys in my hand. I can open the gates of eternal death for those who don't want me, and I can shut the gates of eternal death and open up the gates of heaven to those who want to live forever with me."

Have you needed to hear Jesus say, "Don't be afraid. I hold the keys to death"? I have.

In 1998 my husband and I had a daughter we named Hope. That name seemed to fly in the face of everything about her life because, from the world's way of looking at things, Hope's life was hopeless. Hope was born with a rare metabolic disorder called Zellweger Syndrome. It meant that she was missing a tiny subcellular particle that rids the cells of toxins. On her second day of life, a geneticist told us that there was no treatment, no cure, and that most children with the syndrome live less than six months.

So when we took Hope home from the hospital, we weren't taking her home to live with us; we were taking her home to die.

I remember when that reality began to really hit me after we'd been home a couple of weeks. We know everyone will die someday, but this

---

7   A form of the previous two paragraphs first appeared in my book, *Hearing Jesus Speak into Your Sorrow* (Carol Stream, IL: Tyndale, 2009), 143–44.

was different. I realized that the day was quickly approaching when Hope would either die in my arms or I would go to her crib and find her dead. And fear began to settle in on me. I feared what her death would be like—for her and for me—and how difficult her life might become as we waited for that day to come.

Hope was with us 199 days. The day I dreaded came when David got up in the middle of the night to check on her, and she was cold to the touch.

Jesus, the one who holds the keys to death, opened the door for her.

You may have also faced a day like that, a death like that. Or maybe you have a deep-seated fear about the death of someone you love. Or maybe it's your own death that fills you with fear. This is why we really need to gaze intently at the glorified, resurrected Jesus that John presents for us in the words of this book. Through the words of this book, Jesus reaches out to us, assuring us that we don't have to be afraid, because he holds the keys to death.

Because Jesus emerged from death with the keys of death in his hand, and because he is alive forevermore, the day is coming when Jesus is going to give Hope, and you and me, a glorious resurrection body that looks like his! One day, Paul tells us in Philippians, Jesus is going to "transform our lowly body to be like his glorious body, by the power that enables him even to subject all things to himself" (Phil. 3:21). One day, he who holds the keys to death is going to lock the door to death for good and throw away the keys. As we'll read later in Revelation, "death shall be no more" (21:4).

Aren't we blessed to have this kind of hope and assurance?

Hearing and Keeping Revelation 1:9–20

Hearing and keeping John's message in this passage may mean that we must begin to see ourselves as partners in the tribulation that is in Jesus. We may need to readjust our expectations of the Christian life away from a life in which Jesus protects us from every earthly harm and the Father answers all of our prayers in the affirmative, on our timetable.

Hearing and keeping this part of Revelation is going to look like patiently persevering through being misunderstood, criticized, sidelined, disregarded, mistreated, and perhaps even worse, because of our affiliation with and affection for Jesus. Keeping this word is going to mean that instead of resenting the tribulation that is part of being a citizen of his kingdom, we expect it, even rejoice in it, because John has given us a glimpse of the King. We find that seeing the glorified and ascended Jesus in his eternal, authoritative, powerful, triumphant, compassionate reality is what we need to patiently endure the tribulation inherent in being in Jesus until his kingdom comes.

As we take in this vision of Jesus as he is now in all of his resurrected glory, it causes us to sense the penetrating gaze of his eyes like a flame of fire. It makes us want to build our lives on his solid foundation. We want his voice in our lives to be unavoidable and unignorable.

As we hear the powerful, penetrating voice of Jesus saying to us, "Don't be afraid . . . I hold the keys to Death," it begins to change everything about the way we think about life and death. We're not so afraid anymore. We can surrender our need to always be in control, confident that Jesus not only holds the keys in his hands; he holds us in his hands as well.

We live in a world where everything is reduced so we can take it in quickly and easily. Blog posts usually have about eight hundred words, and tweets are limited to 280 characters. How different is Jesus as he is revealed in Revelation 1. Instead of reducing Jesus to simplified, understandable, manageable terms, the vision that John was given and wrote down for us expands our vision and engages our imagination. It causes us to open ourselves up to someone bigger and grander and more captivating and commanding than we've ever seen before. And we find ourselves blessed—blessed by seeing the glorified Jesus.

3

Blessed by Being Known by Jesus

Revelation 2:1–3:22

REMEMBER GETTING THAT sealed envelope from your teacher in grade school that contained the all-important report card, which we were to give to our parents to read, sign, and return? Carrying it home to my parents, I usually didn't have much to worry about when it came to my grades, but I do remember more than one teacher writing a comment about my behavior. My second-grade teacher wrote: "Nancy talks too much." (And to Miss Swartz I would like to say, as I fill up this book with words, "Look! I'm still talking too much!")

In a sense, Revelation 2–3 is like a report card for each of the seven churches in Asia sent to all of the churches to read. Their evaluation has been conducted not by a second-grade teacher but by the one who is, who was, and who is to come, the glorious king John described in detail in chapter 1. Yes, he sees behavior, but he sees much deeper than that. His knowledge extends into the interior of the heart, to the level of motive and belief.

Imagine what it must have been like for the people in these seven churches when this letter arrived and included a report card on their spiritual condition. They gathered together, perhaps in someone's home, and then the messenger who arrived with the letter stood up to read it to the group. As he began reading, they heard who the letter was from.

It was from Jesus himself. And they heard who it was written to. This letter was addressed to them.

What did Jesus want to say to them? What did he want to reveal to them?

Then the messenger continued reading. As they heard, "To the angel of the church in Ephesus write . . . ," you can almost see the members of the church in Ephesus startle and come to attention. They were about to hear what the ascended Jesus had to say to them in particular. Of course, it wasn't just the Ephesians who would hear what Jesus had to say. As the messenger made the rounds of these seven churches, reading this letter out loud, each of the churches heard what Jesus had to say, not just to them but to the other churches as well. Imagine what it must have been like, after hearing the frankness of the first few letters, to wait for Jesus to address your church. He's not letting anything slide. His words are "full of grace and truth" (John 1:14).

What Jesus had to say was powerful. It was personal. They had heard what John had already written about Jesus standing amongst the lampstands, and when they heard it, it must have given them a sense of comfort. But now they're getting a fuller picture of what his presence among them means. It means he sees everything. He knows everything—the good and the bad, the commendable and the contemptible. He knows what needs to be encouraged and affirmed and what needs to be confronted and condemned.

The big questions for those who first heard this letter read were these: *Do we have ears to hear what Jesus has to say to us? Are we open to seeing ourselves as he sees us? Or will we deflect, defend, or dismiss what he has to say? Will we sit in the room with our fellow believers inwardly pointing a finger at others who really need to hear what Jesus has to say while assuming that we are doing just fine? Or will we do what he calls us to do even though it will be costly, humbling, and hard?*

Of course, these are questions we must ask ourselves as well. Jesus loves his people too much to only tell us what we want to hear. Before we turn up the volume to hear what Jesus has to say to his church—his church in the first century and in every century since then—we need to make a decision to be open to it—open to being exposed, convicted, and challenged to change. Only people with a great deal of spiritual pride or with a very hard heart could immerse themselves in the truth-telling of Jesus in these two chapters and maintain any sort of comfortable distance or spiritual aloofness.

Are you willing to put yourself, right now, into a posture of humility and reception of what Jesus wants to show you about yourself? Will you respond to his call to correction, repentance, and perseverance? Are you open to the self-examination these two chapters require? If you aren't, you may be in real spiritual danger. And if you are, you can be sure that you are headed for real spiritual renewal and joy.

The Jesus Who Knows

In these two chapters, as Jesus speaks directly to each of the seven churches in Asia, his messages follow the same basic pattern. First, Jesus describes himself using images and terms that are very similar to how John describes Jesus in Revelation 1. But the images he selects to describe himself to each church are not random. Each descriptor reflects an aspect of who he is, an aspect of his character, his power, and his purpose that is needed or applicable to the issues in that particular church. In the way that each of these letters begins and ends, we see that Jesus, in his person and in his promises, is what we need most. Jesus is the source for what we need to patiently endure as we live our lives in this world with all of its temptations and trials.

After introducing himself, each message begins with Jesus saying, "I know . . ." To most he says, "I know your works." He's saying, "I know how your faith is being lived out. I know the fruit that is being produced in your life." He knows the good and the bad, the big and the small, the public and private outworkings of being in relationship with him. In two cases, Jesus points to knowing something slightly different. For Smyrna, he says that he knows the tribulation they've experienced, their poverty, and the way they've been slandered by Jews. For Pergamum he says, "I know where you dwell" (2:13). He knows the environment they're living in and the ways in which that environment puts unique pressures on them.

Over and over again to these churches Jesus says, "I know." And we can be sure that he would say the same thing to us. Jesus knows. He knows us better than we know ourselves. We have incredible powers of self-deception and denial. Jesus sees and knows the truth about us that we most need to know. And because he loves us and is bent on blessing us, he is willing to tell us the truth, even though it might be uncomfortable for us to hear.

Jesus Knows What and Who You Really Love

If we look at a map of the churches in Asia, we see that Ephesus was the city closest to Patmos. It makes sense that this letter would start its circular journey there. The church in Ephesus is where Paul spent three years teaching the word of God (Acts 20:31). Apollos and Timothy and John himself taught there. Ephesus was an extremely well-taught church from the time the church was first planted.

> To the angel of the church in Ephesus write: "The words of him who holds the seven stars in his right hand, who walks among the seven golden lampstands. I know your works, your toil and your patient endurance, and how you cannot bear with those who are evil, but have tested those who call themselves apostles and are not, and found them to be false. I know you are enduring patiently and bearing up for my name's sake, and you have not grown weary." (Rev. 2:1–3)

One of the things that Jesus knows, something that made his heart glad, was that the church in Ephesus had real doctrinal discernment. They knew how to spot a fake peddler of God's word, and they had persevered in working to make the true gospel known.

> "But I have this against you . . ." (Rev. 2:4a)

I wonder if their hearts sank when they heard these words. *Jesus has something against us? What could it be?*

> You have abandoned the love you had at first. (Rev. 2:4b)

They had started out loving Jesus, loving his word, loving each other, and loving being a part of the change his gospel makes in the lives of all who embrace it by faith. But somewhere along the way, something changed. Perhaps it was cynicism that was the enemy of love. Or perhaps differing opinions and competing agendas crowded out their love for each other. Or maybe they began to love being right more than they loved being a conduit of grace and mercy. Perhaps they became so focused on the truth of the gospel that their love and wonder at it diminished.

Jesus, who knew the true affections of their hearts, then told them exactly what they needed to do to repair this breach of affection:

> Remember therefore from where you have fallen; repent, and do the works you did at first. If not, I will come to you and remove your lampstand from its place, unless you repent. Yet this you have: you hate the works of the Nicolaitans, which I also hate. He who has an ear, let him hear what the Spirit says to the churches. (Rev. 2:5–7a)

They needed to turn around and go in another direction. Remembering what they did when their love for Jesus was new would serve to rekindle the passion of their love for him.

What did you do when you first came to love Jesus? I remember as a teenager spending time in my bedroom reading my green-padded *Living Bible*. Nobody was making me. I wasn't doing it out of some dry sense of duty or even discipline. I just wanted to. I couldn't get enough of it. I loved Jesus, and I loved his word, and I just wanted as much of it as I could get. But it can be hard to maintain that kind of passion, don't you think? Is there anything that could help us to keep pursuing that kind of passion? Yes. A promise:

> To the one who conquers I will grant to eat of the tree of life, which is in the paradise of God. (Rev. 2:7b)

Jesus closed his message to the believers in Ephesus by saying that those who overcome the way that the world seeks to drain commitment to Jesus of personal passion can anticipate eating from the tree of life in the paradise of God. Meditating on this promise has the power to stoke the fires of passion in the hearts of all who want to love Jesus more today and tomorrow than they did yesterday.

Jesus Knows What You're Willing to Suffer For

It was the words of "the first and the last, who died and came to life" (Rev. 1:17–18; 2:8) that John was told to write down for the church in Smyrna. And when we discover what Jesus had to say to them, we understand why he identified himself this way:

> I know your tribulation and your poverty (but you are rich) and the slander of those who say that they are Jews and are not, but are a synagogue of Satan. (Rev. 2:9)

The church in Smyrna was suffering. They were spiritually rich because they were joined to Christ, but they were financially poor. Why? Because their allegiance to Christ prevented them from fully participating in the professional guilds and business community in Smyrna. Many had been disinherited by family for following the Way. The slander that was spread by Jews about them—that they were seeking to usher in a new kingdom at the expense of the Romans—had cost them their livelihoods. Roman citizens in Smyrna didn't want to buy bread from bakers who were part of this church and didn't want to hire them to work in their homes.

I have to imagine that as the Smyrnian believers heard how this message to them from Jesus began, perhaps they would have hoped to hear Jesus say that he was going to do something about this unjust treatment, that he was going to do something to protect them from the suffering they were experiencing. But that's not what they heard Jesus say. Instead, he said:

> Do not fear what you are about to suffer. Behold, the devil is about to throw some of you into prison, that you may be tested, and for ten days you will have tribulation. (Rev. 2:10a)

That would be sobering to hear. Their suffering wasn't going to end or decrease; it was going to increase. It wasn't going away quickly; it was going to last a while. The number ten is used symbolically here to indicate that it was going to last the exact length of time that God intended.

This news, however, came with a corresponding promise:

> Be faithful unto death, and I will give you the crown of life. He who has an ear, let him hear what the Spirit says to the churches. The one who conquers will not be hurt by the second death. (Rev. 2:10b–11)

Jesus's sobering message to the church in Smyrna was that they could expect to be put to death for their allegiance to him. But speaking as the one who died and came to life, Jesus assured them that being put to death would not be the end of their story. When the day comes that every person who has died is called to life to stand before him in the final judgment, the day when all humanity will be divided into those who will go away into eternal punishment and those into eternal life (Matt. 25:46), they could be assured of entering into eternal life.

For many who are reading this book, myself included, the prospect of being put to death because of allegiance to Jesus can seem very remote and unlikely because of the time and place in which we live. Yet we know it is a reality in our world today.

It was only a few years ago when Necati Aydin and Ugur Yuksel, two Turks who had converted from Islam to Christianity, and Tillman Geske, a German citizen, were put to death in the city of Izmir, which is what the ancient city of Smyrna is now called. The three men were at work translating a study Bible into Turkish. Several Turkish youths came to their office, supposedly to explore the claims of Christianity. They tied the three men up and then beat and stabbed them repeatedly.

Semse Aydin, Necati's wife, told *Christianity Today* that she has no regrets about their ministry in Izmir, having seen fifteen people come to faith in three years. "I see my family as victorious," she says.[1]

---

1 Denise McGill, "A Victorious Family," *Christianity Today*, January 4, 2008, https://www.christianity today.com/.

Her words are significant in so many ways. What her family experienced would in no way appear to be victorious in the eyes of the world. The world only sees tragedy in such a story. But when I read her words, I can't help but think that Semse has not only read this message to the church in Smyrna, but she has taken to heart the repeated refrain in each of these seven letters, and in the entire book of Revelation regarding its call to conquer, to overcome, and to be victorious, and its promises to those who do. "The one who conquers will not be hurt by the second death," Jesus said to those in the church in Smyrna so many centuries before. Clearly Semse really believes what Jesus said to the church there so long ago! She has taken Jesus at his word and allowed this heavenly perspective about what is happening in the world to dominate her thinking and feeling rather than embracing a merely earthly perspective about life and death.

Perhaps few would dare to say that she is living the blessed life, but I think she is, don't you? It can't be an easy life. I imagine at times it has been a profoundly lonely life, certainly a perilous life, and yet profoundly blessed in the truest sense of the word.

Jesus Knows What You Really Believe

Writing as he who "has the sharp two-edged sword" (Rev. 1:16; 2:12), which usually refers to words of judgment that come out of his mouth, Jesus began his letter to the church in Pergamum saying:

> I know where you dwell, where Satan's throne is. (Rev. 2:13a)

What is the significance of where they dwell, and why would Jesus describe it as the place of Satan's throne? Pergamum was a place of governmental power, similar to a state capital. It had a magnificent library. It was also a center of Greco-Roman religion. There were temples to several Greco-Roman gods, including a temple to Asclepius, the Greco-Roman god of healing, which featured the symbol of a serpent-entwined staff. Outside the city was a magnificent altar to the god Zeus that overarched the city like a great throne.

So when Jesus said, "I know where you dwell," perhaps he was saying, "I am well aware of the environment in which you are seeking to be faithful to me, the challenges and forces at work in the realm of your every day." He continued:

> Yet you hold fast my name, and you did not deny my faith even in the days of Antipas my faithful witness, who was killed among you, where Satan dwells. (Rev. 2:13b)

In this pagan environment, the people of the church of Pergamum had stood firm in their faith even when one of them, a man named Antipas, boldly told the truth about the kingdom of Jesus and faced death for it. It makes you wonder what Antipas said or did and in what aspect of life in Pergamum he spoke out. Maybe he refused to offer the proper sacrifice to Asclepius when he went to see the doctor. Maybe he argued against the ideas of the most talked-about book at the library. Maybe he refused to get with the program of giving Zeus his due at the gate of the city. Whatever it was, Antipas did not deny his faith, and the rest of the believers there in Pergamum stood with him and with Jesus under pressure.

Jesus continued his word to the church, words that reflected the other side of the two-edged sword:

> But I have a few things against you: you have some there who hold the teaching of Balaam, who taught Balak to put a stumbling block before the sons of Israel, so that they might eat food sacrificed to idols and practice sexual immorality. So also you have some who hold the teaching of the Nicolaitans. (Rev. 2:14–15)

There were some—not all—who held to "the teaching of Balaam." Jesus referenced an event recorded in Numbers 22 in which Balaam, an enemy of God's people, tried to persecute the people of God by putting a curse on them but found greater success by sending young women from Moab into the Israelite camp to lure the men into sexual sin and idolatry. In Pergamum, where so many people practiced the worship of pagan gods, evidently some in the church were being lured into the sexual immorality and idolatry of the culture they lived in, thinking they could combine it with worship of the one true God.

Jesus also said that some of them held to the teaching of the Nicolaitans, who "encouraged cultural accommodation and secular living."[2] We might imagine these Nicolaitans saying to their fellow church members in Pergamum, "There's nothing wrong with saying the words and participating in the ritual feasts that are a part of living in this great city. You'll be able to build relationships this way so that eventually you can share the gospel."

Remember how Ephesus was affirmed for their love for sound doctrine and challenged in losing their first love? In Pergamum the danger was caring little for doctrinal truth and doing nothing to oppose false teaching. The answer to the problem for them both, however, was the same: repentance—turning around to go in a different direction. Jesus said to them:

> Therefore repent. If not, I will come to you soon and war against them with the sword of my mouth. He who has an ear, let him hear what the Spirit says to the churches. (Rev. 2:16–17a)

Those who refused to repent could expect Jesus to come against them. But those who were willing to repent could expect something very different from Jesus:

> To the one who conquers I will give some of the hidden manna, and I will give him a white stone, with a new name written on the stone that no one knows except the one who receives it. (Rev. 2:17b)

This promise is a bit mysterious—hidden manna and a white stone with a new name written on it. Of course, this hidden manna must

2   Phillips, *Revelation*, 114.

have some connection to the manna God rained down on his people during their forty years in the wilderness. Perhaps God was promising these people, who might have been afraid that they would lose their livelihoods, that their refusal to compromise now would result in receiving his heavenly provision in the age to come.

In his commentary on Revelation, Richard Phillips explains that in the ancient world, a white ceremonial stone called a "tessera" had a number of different meanings, and each could be applied to those who overcome.[3] Champions in athletic games in John's day were given a white stone. So perhaps this promise communicates that as they overcame the temptation to compromise, they could anticipate receiving recognition of their victory from Jesus. White stones were given as a token of admission to pagan feasts and festivals. So while they might not be welcomed into the pagan feasts of Pergamum, they could be assured of a place at the table at the marriage supper of the Lamb. Additionally, white stones were used in courts of law, as jurors would vote for acquittal by setting forth a white stone in contrast to a black stone for conviction. So while, like Antipas, they might be convicted in the courts of Pergamum, they could be assured that in the courts of heaven they would be declared not guilty.

Jesus Knows What You're Willing to Tolerate

Jesus's way of introducing himself in his message to the church in Thyatira is, once again, significant:

> And to the angel of the church in Thyatira write: "The words of the Son of God, who has eyes like a flame of fire, and whose feet are like burnished bronze." (Rev. 2:18)

The fire in the eyes and the fire that burnished the bronze make us think about the fiery holiness of God, so we sense that Jesus is going to point out any unholiness that his eyes cannot look upon. But first, he speaks

3 Phillips, *Revelation*, 116.

a word of commendation that must have been deeply meaningful to the believers in Thyatira:

> I know your works, your love and faith and service and patient endurance, and that your latter works exceed the first. (Rev. 2:19)

Jesus was in their midst and he knew the fruit of faith that was evidenced in their lives. He could see how they loved him and each other, how they were serving and staying faithful under pressure. This fruit was not simply evident in their lives; it was growing and increasing rather than simply maintaining or diminishing.

We're coming to expect that there may be a *but* coming, and there is:

> But I have this against you, that you tolerate that woman Jezebel, who calls herself a prophetess and is teaching and seducing my servants to practice sexual immorality and to eat food sacrificed to idols. I gave her time to repent, but she refuses to repent of her sexual immorality. Behold, I will throw her onto a sickbed, and those who commit adultery with her I will throw into great tribulation, unless they repent of her works, and I will strike her children dead. And all the churches will know that I am he who searches mind and heart, and I will give to each of you according to your works. (Rev. 2:20–23)

In spite of their love and faith and service and patient endurance, there was a problem in the church, a problem in regard to holiness: a toleration of sexual immorality and idolatry.

Thyatira was a market city and was "dominated by trade guilds that oversaw its various industries: wool, linen, dyes, clothing manufacturers, leather works, pottery, bakers, and bronze works."[4] Each guild paid homage to pagan gods. Christians who worked in these trades would have been pressured to participate in sacred festivals to these pagan

---

4   Phillips, *Revelation*, 123. Phillips cites Sir William Ramsey, as cited by Leon Morris, *The Revelation of St. John: An Introduction and Commentary*, Tyndale New Testament Commentary 20 (Grand Rapids, MI: Eerdmans, 1969), 69.

gods, which would have included eating meals in their temples and participating in sexual liaisons with temple prostitutes.

Evidently there was an influence in the church, perhaps a woman in the church claiming to be a prophetess, who was encouraging the believers in the church to go ahead and participate in the feasts and the sexual ceremonies. Calling her "Jezebel" was a way of connecting the nature of her influence in the church to the Jezebel we read about in 1 Kings who urged the Israelites to worship Baal and Ashteroth alongside the Lord, which also involved sexual liaisons at the pagan shrines. Essentially, the message of this person to those in the church was that they could do everything their fellow citizens of Thyatira did.

I have to wonder: when encouraging them to go ahead and participate, did she perhaps add, "Jesus knows your heart," suggesting that Jesus would judge their hearts to be in the right place even when their bodies were invested in sexual immorality? If so, in a way she was right. Jesus did know their hearts. His eyes like a flame of fire saw into their souls to see exactly what their hearts were like. And what he saw was not innocence and good intentions but spiritual adultery worthy of eternal punishment. Sexual sin is spiritual adultery. Idolatry is spiritual adultery. No one can persist in sexual sin and idolatry, excusing it either as unchosen orientation or basic human need, assuming that "God knows my heart and he will forgive me," and expect that he or she will not be burned by the fire of God's anger.

In his eyes like a fire we see not just anger against sin but the jealousy of a lover who has been forsaken and betrayed. If "Jezebel" refers to a particular woman, she was probably sitting there as the letter was read (that would be awkward). She had seduced some people in the church at Thyatira to believe that they could give themselves to these pagan gods and still be true to Jesus. But, of course, they couldn't. These were deeds of darkness that would lead not to life but to death, unless there was real repentance.

Evidently not everyone in the church in Thyatira, however, had been seduced by this teaching:

> But to the rest of you in Thyatira, who do not hold this teaching,
> who have not learned what some call the deep things of Satan, to you

I say, I do not lay on you any other burden. Only hold fast what you have until I come. The one who conquers and who keeps my works until the end, to him I will give authority over the nations, and he will rule them with a rod of iron, as when earthen pots are broken in pieces, even as I myself have received authority from my Father. And I will give him the morning star. He who has an ear, let him hear what the Spirit says to the churches. (Rev. 2:24–29)

To those who held fast to Jesus while awaiting his return, refusing to become like the world, Jesus would use them to have an impact on the world. They would exercise "authority over the nations" as they proclaimed the gospel of grace for sinners to the people they worked with and the neighborhoods they lived in so that more Thyatirans would come under the gracious rule of king Jesus, even as they lived in a world ruled by Caesar.

Jesus Knows the Reality of Your Spiritual Condition

We started by talking about getting a report card that served as an evaluation of how we performed in our classes at school. Most of us don't get those anymore. But we do get reports on another kind of examination. Most of us know what it is like to wait in a doctor's office or by the phone at home to get the results of a medical examination. Sometimes we go to get checked out because we experience some pain or a problem. And then other times we go to the doctor thinking we are in good health and are surprised to find out there's a problem. I wonder if that's how it was for those gathered in Sardis when they heard Jesus speak directly to them.

And to the angel of the church in Sardis write: "The words of him who has the seven spirits of God and the seven stars. I know your works. You have the reputation of being alive, but you are dead." (Rev. 3:1)

Wait. What? Dead?
They thought they were alive. And evidently other churches did too.

Why would they have been thought of as "alive"? Perhaps it was because of activity. There was so much going on at the church. So many programs.

So many meetings. So much teaching. Maybe they liked to say, "God told me this," or "God told me that," as if they had some sort of special ability to hear from him that others didn't have, which made them seem so alive.

Let's be honest: it is a good thing to have a good reputation—as a church and as individuals. But evidently we can be fooled by our own good reputation. It is possible to have a reputation that doesn't line up with the reality of who we are. It is possible to have a reputation for being spiritually alive, when the reality of the condition of our souls is quite different. The reality facing the church in Sardis was that there was a spiritual deadness in the church. They were eaten up by a spiritual cancer that was killing them, and they didn't know it. What were the symptoms they and those around them had missed? Evidently it was spiritual sloth. We can deduce that from the treatment Jesus prescribed:

> Wake up, and strengthen what remains and is about to die, for I have not found your works complete in the sight of my God. Remember, then, what you received and heard. Keep it, and repent. If you will not wake up, I will come like a thief, and you will not know at what hour I will come against you. (Rev. 3:2–3)

They were spiritually sleepy. Apathetic. When they heard the word preached, their minds were elsewhere, and it didn't penetrate. They were spiritually weak. Whenever they felt any urge to vigorously pursue life in Christ by meditating on or memorizing Scripture, getting up early to pray, sharing Christ with their pagan neighbor, or by fighting that sin they had given in to over and over again, they decided to lie down until the urge passed. They had a loss of appetite—no hunger for God's word, no desire to learn anything new or to rigorously apply what they already understood quite clearly.

Jesus, the spiritual doctor, gave Sardis both the diagnosis and the treatment the church needed. His prescription was strength training for greater endurance, rigorous remembering and rehearsing the foundational truths of the gospel that had once invigorated them, and turning away from spiritual sloth and toward a more vigorous and engaged life of repentance and faith.

Evidently not everyone in the church had fallen into this spiritual slumber and deadness:

> Yet you have still a few names in Sardis, people who have not soiled their garments, and they will walk with me in white, for they are worthy. The one who conquers will be clothed thus in white garments, and I will never blot his name out of the book of life. I will confess his name before my Father and before his angels. He who has an ear, let him hear what the Spirit says to the churches. (Rev. 3:4–6)

There were a few who had remained faithful, awake, alive. Jesus had a promise for them and for all who were willing to repent and thereby overcome their drift into spiritual sloth. They could be sure that the spiritual life that had been breathed into them when they were joined to Christ would have its full effect. The righteousness of Christ, pictured as white garments, would become an increasing reality in their lives and would be fully realized one day in his presence. When the day comes that the book of life is opened (we'll read more about that day when we get to Revelation 20), and when the list of names in the book is read, they could be sure that they would hear their names.

Jesus Knows Whose Kingdom You Are Committed To

The people in each of these seven churches lived under the rule of the world power in their day—Rome. Of course, those who gathered in these seven churches were citizens of another kingdom, a kingdom at odds with the kingdom of the world, a kingdom that might look weak to the world but is, in fact, growing and spreading and will one day extend to every corner of the earth. Jesus introduced his message to the church at Philadelphia as being the words of the one who holds the keys to that kingdom:

> To the angel of the church in Philadelphia write: "The words of the holy one, the true one, who has the key of David, who opens and no one will shut, who shuts and no one opens." (Rev. 3:7)

What is the key of David, and what is this door that it opens, this open door that no one is able to shut?

All of Revelation, in fact the whole of the Bible, is about the kingdom of God. As the Son of David, Jesus holds the keys to this kingdom. He has thrown open the door for the nations to come in, and nothing can stop it:

> I know your works. Behold, I have set before you an open door, which no one is able to shut. I know that you have but little power, and yet you have kept my word and have not denied my name. (Rev. 3:8)

In his death and resurrection, in his ascension and sending of his Spirit, Jesus has opened the door for the gospel to go forward. Jesus is pointing the church in Philadelphia toward the open door and promising to use them to extend his kingdom to every corner of the earth.[5]

Jesus didn't include in his message to Philadelphia any criticism, as he did in his messages to most of the other churches. He did point out, however, that this young church had "little power." Evidently they weren't a large church with a reputation for doing great things. Maybe this church wasn't populated with impressive people, people with influence or material resources. Maybe they were few in number. But clearly they had done what really mattered to Jesus. They had kept his word and had not denied his rule and authority in their lives. And clearly what he intended to do in and through them was not limited by how much strength they had in themselves. In 2 Corinthians we read that Jesus said to Paul, "My power is made perfect in weakness" (12:9). Evidently Philadelphia was going to be "example A" among the churches of this reality:

> Behold, I will make those of the synagogue of Satan who say that they are Jews and are not, but lie—behold, I will make them come

---

5   While allowing for this view, Thomas Schreiner presents an alternative view, writing, "It may be that the open door refers to an opportunity for mission and evangelism, since elsewhere the NT speaks of an open door with this meaning (Acts 14:27; 1 Cor. 16:9; 2 Cor. 2:12; Col. 4:3). It seems more likely, however, that the reference here is to entry into God's Presence (Rev. 4:1). They have the open door to God's presence and access to the heavenly city." Thomas Schreiner, *Hebrews–Revelation*, ESV Expository Commentary (Wheaton, IL: Crossway, 2018), 590.

and bow down before your feet, and they will learn that I have loved you. Because you have kept my word about patient endurance, I will keep you from the hour of trial that is coming on the whole world, to try those who dwell on the earth. I am coming soon. Hold fast what you have, so that no one may seize your crown. The one who conquers, I will make him a pillar in the temple of my God. Never shall he go out of it, and I will write on him the name of my God, and the name of the city of my God, the new Jerusalem, which comes down from my God out of heaven, and my own new name. He who has an ear, let him hear what the Spirit says to the churches. (Rev. 3:9–13)

Jesus's promise to those who overcome the kingdom of the world by living in it on mission to spread the kingdom of God is that they will be made a pillar in the temple of God and have the name of God and his city written on them. In other words, they will have a permanent place in the temple of God, which is the people of God who will endure into eternity (Eph. 2:22). They may have "little power" now, but the strength of Christ will turn them into pillars of strength. His name will be written on them, an affirmation of their belonging in his city where they will enjoy his presence and protection forever.

Jesus Knows Whom You Are Depending On

If we as twenty-first-century Christians—especially those of us who live in the West—haven't yet been made uncomfortable by these letters to the churches, this last letter may be the one that finally nails us.

And to the angel of the church in Laodicea write: "The words of the Amen, the faithful and true witness, the beginning of God's creation." (Rev. 3:14)

This was Jesus the faithful and true witness speaking. He tells the truth, and sometimes the truth hurts. But if we have ears to hear it, the truth he speaks will ultimately heal.

I know your works: you are neither cold nor hot. Would that you were either cold or hot! So, because you are lukewarm, and neither hot nor cold, I will spit you out of my mouth. (Rev. 3:15–16)

Jesus started almost every letter before this one with a commendation, and as those in Laodicea listened to those previous letters, they must have been imagining all of the things Jesus might commend when he came to them. They saw themselves as a standout church that really didn't need anything—certainly not a rebuke. Imagine their faces as Jesus skipped any kind of commendation and moved directly to rebuke, basically telling them that the way they were living out their Christian lives made him want to vomit. It wasn't false teaching or immorality or idolatry or their lack of courage in the face of persecution that earned his rebuke. He was disgusted by the fact that they seemed to have no sense of their desperate need for him. They saw Jesus as merely a nice addition to all of the things in their life that brought them comfort and security and enjoyment.

For you say, I am rich, I have prospered, and I need nothing,
        not realizing that you are wretched, pitiable, poor, blind,
        and naked. (Rev. 3:17)

Jesus put these words in their mouths in order to clearly articulate the problem. It came down to three words that simply have no place in the life of a Christian: "I need nothing."

~ Jesus had come to them offering the riches of his grace, the riches of his inheritance in the holy land, and by their actions and attitudes, they had said to him in reply, "No thanks. We've got growing savings accounts and reliable insurance policies, so we don't really need treasure stored up for us in heaven."

~ Jesus had come to them offering sight to see what is good and true and eternal, and they'd said, "No thanks, we're good. We've had good educations, and we've got some well-developed ideas and opinions. Really you could probably learn a few things from us, Jesus, about how to best run this world."

~ Jesus had come to them offering to clothe them in the robes of his perfect righteousness, and they'd said, "No need here. We've spent a lifetime making donations to the right ministries and serving on important committees and leveraging our social-media profiles to promote the right positions, and we think that if you look more closely, you'll see that we're doing quite well in regard to personal righteousness on our own, Jesus."

And, of course, many of us, by our actions and attitudes, have said the very same things in response to Jesus's offer of himself to us.

Fortunately, because he is the faithful and true witness, Jesus is not content to allow us to remain self-sufficient and self-deceived. So he says:

> I counsel you to buy from me gold refined by fire, so that you may be rich, and white garments so that you may clothe yourself and the shame of your nakedness may not be seen, and salve to anoint your eyes, so that you may see. Those whom I love, I reprove and discipline, so be zealous and repent. (Rev. 3:18–19)

Jesus's counsel is to come to him with nothing but our need and experience his provision. Though we've been dismissive of his gifts and unreceptive to his provision, instead of turning away from us, he offers himself to us. He wants to penetrate past our self-sufficient deflection into the closed-off areas of our lives. He wants to share life with us in intimate, ongoing fellowship. He wants to move in close to address our need:

> Behold, I stand at the door and knock. If anyone hears my voice and opens the door, I will come in to him and eat with him, and he with me. The one who conquers, I will grant him to sit with me on my throne, as I also conquered and sat down with my Father on his throne. He who has an ear, let him hear what the Spirit says to the churches. (Rev. 3:20–22)

Do you have ears to hear what the Spirit is saying to you and me in this moment? He's saying, "Even though you have discounted the value and necessity of living under my rule and my care in my kingdom, if you will now receive my reproof and respond to my discipline, if you will be zealous to turn away from your self-sufficiency and embrace your desperate need for me, your future will be bright with all the benefits of my kingdom."

Oh, my friend, do you have an ear to hear what the Spirit is saying to you? And are you willing to think through what it will mean to keep it?

Hearing and Keeping Revelation 2–3

We are reminded that Jesus promised that those who are willing to hear and keep the words of this letter—even when, perhaps especially when, what he has to say is a hard and challenging word—will be blessed. So we must ask ourselves, what will it look like for us to hear and keep what we've heard the Spirit saying to us through these letters to the seven churches? Perhaps one way to work through it is to boil down each letter to the questions that the letter poses to each one of us:

~ The letter to the church of Ephesus invites us to ask ourselves: *Has there been a time in my life when my love for Christ and his gospel and his people was greater than it is now? And if so, am I willing to do the things I did when that love was new, not out of duty or legalism but out of desire to rekindle my love for Jesus?*

~ The letter to the church of Smyrna invites us to ask ourselves: *What am I willing to suffer for, because that reveals the true object of my affections? Do I need to readjust my expectations of the Christian life away from expecting Jesus to protect me from suffering, toward expecting him to preserve me through the suffering that is inevitable for a Christian?*

~ The letter to the church of Pergamum invites us to ask ourselves: *What might Jesus point to in my life as an area in which compromise threatens my witness for him and my relationship to him—is it in the entertainment I consume, the ethical standards I hold to, the sexual humor I laugh at, the time and attention I give to sports or politics or my profession?*

~ The letter to the church at Thyatira invites us to ask ourselves: *Have I been seduced by voices inside the church that twist Scripture to justify or minimize sexual sin or idolatry? What teaching am I tolerating, in the church or in the media I consume, that is destructive to Christ's bride and will not prepare her—and me in particular—for patient endurance?*

~ The letter to the church at Sardis invites us to ask ourselves: *Do people around me assume that I am more devoted to Jesus than I really am? What needs to change in order for the reality of my relationship to Jesus to line up with my reputation? What needs to change so that I can be fully awake, fully strengthened, for patient endurance?*

~ The letter to the church at Philadelphia invites us to ask ourselves: *Am I walking through the doors that Jesus has opened for me to share the gospel?*

~ The letter to the church at Laodicea invites us to ask ourselves: *Has material prosperity and comfort kept me from coming to terms with my true spiritual condition?*

Revelation 2 and 3 contain letters written not only to those seven churches in Asia in the first century; the entire passage is a letter to you and me today. Jesus says to you and me: "I know you. I know the good and the bad. I know what needs to happen in your life. I know what I'm preparing for you, and if you will treasure my promises, you will not regret it."

And since he knows it all anyway, we can be honest with him and with others about our failures. We can be honest about recalcitrant sinful habits and patterns that seem to have a hold on us. We can be honest about our lack of love for him and loving other things too much. We can be honest about our sexual past and present. We can be honest about reluctance to be bold in our witness and the ease with which we are willing to compromise. We can be honest because he already knows! He's not surprised by our apathy, our idolatry, our sexual immorality, or our tolerance for those who don't tell the truth about him. And he is present with us to be our provision, our power.

Jesus is holding out a promise of blessing beyond what we could ever think to ask for. He's offering himself to us, providing everything we need for patient endurance as we wait for his return.

4

Blessed by Worshiping the Worthiness of Jesus

Revelation 4–5

I'VE ONLY BEEN TO one college football game. (And I know that as you read that, some of you feel a great deal of pity for me or wonder what planet I've been living on.) A number of years ago the University of Oregon Ducks played against the University of Tennessee Volunteers in Knoxville. David's sister and her husband, both of whom are big Duck fans, came to Tennessee and we drove over to Knoxville, where our son was a student at the time, for the game. It was quite an experience.

Squeezed into my place among the fans in the bleachers, what struck me most was the sense that I was at a worship service. People streamed into the stadium from all over the country, not because anyone made them come but because they couldn't imagine being anywhere else on game day. There was preparation and anticipation and identification with the object of worship in attire, temporary tattoos, and face paint. People got there early because they didn't want to miss anything. Being there was expensive; it required sacrifice. But it was a sacrifice gladly given. There was a liturgy to the event that included a song that everyone knew the lyrics to and sang with gusto.

And when the team took the field, no one had to be told to stand and cheer. I'm not sure I have ever witnessed so much unhindered passion and devotion.

It seemed that nothing could dampen the sheer joy and exuberance about being a part of what was happening in that stadium. It was worth the cost, worth the inconvenience, worth fighting the crowds, worth enduring the thunderstorm that drenched us. Being gathered in a great circle around the team on the field was worth everything it took to be there.

Of course, it isn't just at a college football game that we can witness this kind of glad participation and identification. We see it at political rallies, at product sales conventions, at concerts, and in other arenas of life. The worth of the candidate, the product, and the music make everything it took to be there worth whatever it cost.

So far, Revelation has been a call to be willing to suffer for Jesus, to face loss and hardship, to eschew casual commitment and to embrace rigorous examination. So if we're thinking deeply about this at all, it would make sense that we would ask ourselves: *Is Jesus worth all of the effort and pain and sacrifice it will take to overcome the pull of the world around me to seek first his kingdom and his righteousness?* In reality, this question is answered day by day, week by week, and year by year as our lives demonstrate whether or not we think Jesus is worthy of our worship, worthy of whatever it may cost us to identify with him.

The Scene

As we begin to work our way through Revelation 4 and 5, the first phrase, "After this I looked, and behold . . . ," tells us that we're entering into a second vision experience, which will run from Revelation 4 through 16. John's first vision included seeing and hearing the risen, glorified Jesus and writing down the letters to the churches given to him by Jesus. In reading through and trying to imagine the scene of the first vision, we got the sense that Jesus condescended to enter into John's suffering in Patmos. Jesus reached out to touch him, assure him, and commission him. This second vision seems different. By the means of a visionary state, John seems to ascend to the heavenly throne room:

> After this I looked, and behold, a door standing open in heaven! And the first voice, which I had heard speaking to me like a trumpet, said, "Come up here, and I will show you what must take place after this." (Rev. 4:1)

John was invited to "come up" into heaven and to "come in" the open door to see something.

What is the "heaven" into which John was invited? The Bible uses the word *heaven* to describe several different places. The first heaven is the space that immediately surrounds the earth and extends about twenty miles above the earth where birds fly in our atmosphere, which we read about in places such as Psalm 147:8, which says that God "covers the heavens with clouds." The second heaven is the outer galaxies where the planets revolve around our sun, what we sometimes call "outer space." For example, Genesis 1:17 speaks of God setting the sun, moon, and stars in "the expanse of the heavens."

But John, in this passage, is taken to the same place Paul was also invited into, an experience Paul described in 2 Corinthians 12:2 where he says he was "caught up to the third heaven," which is the place where God dwells. Five times in Ephesians Paul refers to the "heavenly realms." For example, he writes in 1:3, "Blessed be the God and Father of our Lord Jesus Christ, who has blessed us in Christ with every spiritual blessing in the heavenly places."

What Paul saw and recorded in 2 Corinthians 12 and described in Ephesians and the place John was invited to "come up" into was the place of ultimate spiritual reality.

Through John's written account of his vision, you and I get to see into the heart of ultimate reality in the timeless presence of God and his heavenly court. We get to see into heaven as it has been and is since the resurrection and ascension of Jesus to the Father's right hand. In these two chapters we're invited to see the celebration that is taking place right now in heaven. We get to see what is at the center of heaven around which everything revolves. We see the scroll in heaven on which all of God's plans for history are written, and we hear the song being sung in heaven, a song we want to know the words to, a song we want to sing now and into eternity.

As John peered into the heart of ultimate reality, what did he see?

At once I was in the Spirit, and behold, a throne stood in heaven, with one seated on the throne. (Rev. 4:2)

Amidst everything else that John saw, what stood out most, at the center of everything, was a throne. And not just a throne, but an occupied throne.

In the heart of ultimate reality, we see, along with John, what is most important, what really matters. We see what the suffering Christians of John's day needed to see. We see what struggling believers of every age have needed to see—God on the throne of the universe.

As John wrote from Patmos, the Emperor Domitian sat on the Roman throne, demanding to be addressed as "lord and god," which meant that those who called Jesus "Lord" and "God" were being severely persecuted and even put to death. The Roman throne was a source of fear and anxiety for John's readers and a source of unparalleled suffering.

But John was invited to see who is truly on the throne of the universe. John saw someone on the throne whose reign brings terror upon all who reject his offer of grace, and extends mercy to all who will receive it. The one seated on this throne gives abundant and undeserved grace. To all who are willing to come under his authority, his is not a throne to hide from but a throne to draw near to. In this scene, the one seated on this throne is not worshiped reluctantly. He is worshiped enthusiastically and authentically because he is worthy. He is worthy in his beauty, brilliance, and majesty, which John described using the imagery of rare jewels:

He who sat there had the appearance of jasper and carnelian. (Rev. 4:3a)

God sits on the throne of the universe radiating from his being the splendor of his holiness, the beauty of his character, the magnificence of his mercy, the brilliance of his plans and purposes, and the majesty of his sovereign reign.

And around the throne was a rainbow that had the appearance of an emerald. (Rev. 4:3b)

What might John be trying to communicate with this imagery of a rainbow? Remember that God used a rainbow as the sign of his covenant promise spoken to Noah that he would never again destroy the earth by water (Gen. 9:15–17). To see a rainbow is to be reminded of God's mercy in judgment and his covenantal faithfulness.

Most of the rainbows I've seen in my life have been kind of a partial arc or even a patch of color. Only a few times can I remember seeing a rainbow that went in a complete half-circle from one part of the horizon to the other. The most memorable was when David and I went on a trip to Maui to celebrate our tenth anniversary. If you've been to Maui, you may have taken that bone-rattling, terrifying drive to Hanna. If you have, you haven't forgotten it because you thought you wouldn't live to tell about it. But it was worth it because it took you to a place they call the "Seven Sacred Pools," where waterfalls spill down into pools and eventually down into the ocean.

I will never forget climbing our way up the rocks toward the waterfalls, looking back across the ocean and seeing a rainbow out over the ocean that began in one part of the ocean and extended all of the way down into another part of the ocean. The rainbow that John saw in heaven was even better than that. This rainbow encircled the throne. It was a full circle. In other words, John saw the reality of God's faithfulness in its unending completeness.

In the heart of the universe, in the place of ultimate reality, God is on the throne reminding us by flashes of lightning and rumblings and peals of the thunder of his power to judge his enemies. He also reminds us of his love and commitment to those who belong to him, showing us in living, brilliant color that he will be faithful to us.

The Circles

John moves from his focus on the centerpiece of heaven to the circles surrounding the throne of God. God is in the center of everything. Everything revolves around him:

> Around the throne were twenty-four thrones, and seated on the thrones were twenty-four elders, clothed in white garments, with golden crowns on their heads. (Rev. 4:4)

Who are these twenty-four elders? It may be that we're meant to think of the twelve patriarchs plus the twelve apostles so that they would represent the totality of redeemed humanity from both the old- and new-covenant communities of faith.[1] What unites them is the source of their garments and crowns. They are all dressed in the righteousness of Christ given to them when they responded to the gospel in repentance and faith (Gal. 3:8; Eph. 4:24) and are wearing the crown that Jesus promised to all who are faithful unto death (Rev. 2:10). They dared not—in fact, they could not—enter the presence of God with the filthy rags of their own righteousness. They've been cleansed by the blood of Jesus and given a robe of righteousness by Jesus. Dressed for Jesus by Jesus.

The elders are wearing crowns of gold and are seated on thrones themselves. To be joined to Christ by faith is to be invited to reign

---

1 While most commentators I consulted agree that the twenty-four elders represent redeemed humanity from both covenant eras, Tom Schreiner writes that it is "more likely that the twenty-four elders are angels" since when we hear them speak, "they don't include themselves among the redeemed (5:9). Instead the elders exclaim, 'You have made *them* a kingdom and priests to our God, and *they* shall reign on the earth.'" In addition, he writes that "the twenty-four elders are always mentioned alongside the four living creatures and other angels elsewhere in Revelation, which may suggest that they too are angels." Thomas Schreiner, *Hebrews–Revelation*, ESV Expository Commentary (Wheaton, IL: Crossway, 2018), 600.

with him as a kingdom of priests. The highest positions of honor and authority in the universe are positions of service to God. In the unreality of this world, serving Jesus is not a career-advancing, reputation-enhancing, bank-account-building position. But in the ultimate reality of heaven, to serve the Lord is the highest honor and privilege in the universe.

> From the throne came flashes of lightning, and rumblings and peals of thunder, and before the throne were burning seven torches of fire, which are the seven spirits of God, and before the throne there was as it were a sea of glass, like crystal. (Rev. 4:5–6a)

Thunder and lightning are sounds associated with judgment (Ex. 9:23–28; Isa. 29:6). Radiating from the throne of this beautiful, glorious, majestic king is the sound of his perfect justice. Before the throne are the agents who carry out his decrees. And around the throne is a calm restfulness that reflects and reverberates the perfections of the one seated on the throne throughout the expanse of heaven.

This picture of heaven shows us that heaven is not exactly like many of us may have pictured it. It certainly isn't like the way so many people who claim to have died, visited heaven, and come back have described it, as their descriptions are usually strongly human-centered and shortsighted. It is, however, just like other prophets who were invited to see it described it—people like Isaiah and Ezekiel and Daniel. For each of these writers, heaven was not described like a vast vacation destination. And I say this gently to those of you, who, like me, look forward longingly to seeing those you love one day in heaven—the most compelling part of heaven for these witnesses was not seeing those who had died and entered into the presence of God before them. That will be good, but it won't be the best. The centerpiece of heaven, the focal point of this universe, is God on the throne ruling and reigning, surrounded by a sea of glass that perfectly mirrors his glory back to him.

You and I tend to think of this earth as the center of the universe. Most significantly, we think our own private worlds are the center of the universe. We sometimes operate as if everything revolves around us, our needs, our wants, our problems, our pain. But in Revelation 4 and 5, we discover what is truly at the center of the universe, what everything and everyone revolve around.

God is at the center of the universe. His perfection and power shine bright and beautiful. He demonstrates his love for us, not by making us the center of his universe but by inviting us to see him as the center of the universe and the source of our joy forever.

The Celebration

When John saw the one seated on the throne at the center of heaven surrounded by twenty-four elders, it was not a silent scene. They weren't quiet. Surrounding the throne of God is a perpetual party, an unending celebration of the holiness of God. The atmosphere of heaven is continuous celebration of worship:

> Around the throne, on each side of the throne, are four living creatures, full of eyes in front and behind: the first living creature like a lion, the second living creature like an ox, the third living creature with the face of a man, and the fourth living creature like an eagle in flight. And the four living creatures, each of them with six wings, are full of eyes all around and within, and day and night they never cease to say,
>
> "Holy, holy, holy, is the Lord God Almighty,
>   who was and is and is to come!" (Rev. 4:6b–8)

Surrounding the throne are four living creatures. It would be difficult to identify these beings if they were not present in the vision of Ezekiel. There, the "four living creatures" (Ezek. 1:5) have the same appearance as they do here in Revelation 4 with only slight modifications. In Ezekiel 10 they are identified as cherubim, the mighty angelic attendants of God's throne. These are the same creatures that guarded the way to the tree of life when Adam and Eve were expelled from it, the same creatures symbolized in gold atop the ark of the covenant. With the faces of a lion, an ox, a man, and an eagle, they represent all the classes of living beings on earth—man, wild animal, domesticated animal, highest bird. Covered in eyes, they "vigilantly watch over the world as God's agents."[2]

What the four living creatures see before them on the throne they just can't stop talking about. We read that they "never cease to" talk about the holiness and sovereignty of God. They never stop talking about the goodness of what he has done and what he is going to do.

Think of all the ways people talk about God in our world. God's name is uttered in profanity and blasphemy and obscenity and hypocrisy and insincerity. But in heaven his holy name is hallowed, honored, praised, exalted, and glorified without interruption and without end.

Notice John writes that they "never cease to say." What do you "never cease to say"? I spent much of my son's growing-up years afraid that if someone were to someday ask him what he remembers his mother talking about when he was growing up, his answer would likely be, "I remember her always saying, 'Be quiet. I'm on the phone,' or maybe, 'Is your room picked up?'"

So how about you? If people close to you were to finish the sentence about you, "Day and night, she never stops saying . . . ," how would that sentence end?

Would they say, "She never stops saying, 'I'm so busy!'" "She never stops saying, 'Why doesn't anybody help me around here!'" "She never stops saying, 'If only we had more money'; 'If only we had another child'; 'If only we didn't have these kids'; "If only . . .'" We want to be people whose words are marked by worship, not whining, not gossip, not criticism. Worship. Unending, uncompromising worship of the living God on the throne of the universe.

2 Schreiner, *Hebrews–Revelation*, 601.

Next we get to hear what the gathering of redeemed humanity in heaven has to say:

> Whenever the living creatures give glory and honor and thanks to him who is seated on the throne, who lives forever and ever, the twenty-four elders fall down before him who is seated on the throne and worship him who lives forever and ever. They cast their crowns before the throne, saying,
>
> > Worthy are you, our Lord and God,
> >   to receive glory and honor and power,
> > for you created all things,
> >   and by your will they existed and were created. (Rev. 4:9–11)

Worthy. In the heart of ultimate reality there are people like you and me who have gone before us. They're no longer distracted by anything in the created world, no longer concerned primarily with themselves. (What a relief!) And they no longer wonder if following Jesus will be worth what it might cost them. They can see it clearly. He is worthy— worthy to receive all of the glory and honor and power as the center and source of everything good and beautiful.

To worship is to let the worth and wonder of God sink in so that you respond in a wholehearted reorientation of your life. What used to be valuable becomes worthless. What used to seem insignificant or optional becomes of ultimate significance and utmost importance. Seeing what God is worth and giving him the glory and honor he is worthy of is worship.

The Scroll

As John gazed on the one seated on the throne, his attention zoomed in on something in his hand:

> Then I saw in the right hand of him who was seated on the throne a scroll written within and on the back, sealed with seven seals. (Rev. 5:1)

What is this scroll, and why does it matter? The scroll represents the decrees of God concerning the unfolding of God's plans for judgment and salvation that were established before the foundations of the world, set in motion by Christ's death and resurrection. G. K. Beale writes that the scroll contains "all sacred history, especially from the cross to the new creation."[3] The scroll has writing on both sides, indicating that the decrees of God are comprehensive and extensive. What is written on the scroll is precise, and it is sealed to let us know that it is complete and cannot be altered.

The future of this world is not determined by fate or chance. History is the unfolding of God's predetermined plan for all things. And when the scroll in the hands of God is unsealed, the unfolding of the end of history, the final triumph and consummation of God's kingdom begins. We're going to see this in chapter 6 of Revelation as one seal after the other is opened and more and more is revealed of the judgments coming on the earth.

When you see this picture John presents of God on the throne of the universe holding in his hands this sealed scroll on which he's written out his plan for history, you can trust that his plans for this world and for your life are precise and complete. You don't have to live with a sense of regret about your past failures and mistakes, wondering what great plan of God you may have missed out on. You don't have to fear that the evils of some fatal disease or natural disaster or worldwide terrorism are going to derail God's plans for this world or for your life. You can rest in knowing that a sovereign God is seated on the throne, holding in his right hand the sealed scroll, and that nothing happens in this world or in your life that is outside of his control. If you are in Christ, you can be confident that his plans for you are good even when they don't seem that way. He is in absolute control and has loving plans for your future firmly in his grasp.

The Search

Evidently, for the plans that are written in the scroll to be fulfilled, the seals on it must be broken and the scroll opened. And in the drama of Revelation 5, that presents a crisis:

3   G. K. Beale with David H. Campbell, *Revelation: A Shorter Commentary* (Grand Rapids, MI: Eerdmans, 2015), 112.

I saw a mighty angel proclaiming with a loud voice, "Who is worthy to open the scroll and break its seals?" (Rev. 5:2)

Before we deal with the question asked by the angel, perhaps we should deal with more foundational questions. Why does someone need to be found who is worthy to open the scroll? Why can't God on the throne just do it himself? Why doesn't God simply remove the seals and reveal its contents and bring about the consummation of his kingdom?

First we must understand that the scroll reveals God's plan for history and humanity, which includes abundant, undeserved grace for repentant sinners, and unbearable, righteously inflicted, justly deserved judgment on unrepentant sinners.

For God the Father to open on his own the scroll that pours out pardon for sin would be like sweeping sin under the rug of the universe. If God were to open on his own, with no mediator or protector, the scroll that pours out wrath, no one would escape the punishment that will be poured out. Someone must come onto this dramatic heavenly scene to demonstrate the justice of God against evil as well as the sacrifice of God to accomplish salvation.

So in this heavenly drama the search is on for someone who is worthy to open the scroll—someone who is pure and powerful and perfect, someone who can be a mediator between a holy God and sinful people. It is as if a lone voice—the voice of a mighty angel—is calling out into the cosmos, "Who is worthy?"

And the response is—silence.

And no one in heaven or on earth or under the earth was able to open the scroll or to look into it. (Rev. 5:3)

John records his own response to this desperate, unsuccessful search, writing:

I began to weep loudly because no one was found worthy to open the scroll or to look into it. (Rev. 5:4)

John wept with shame for "the failure of the entire human race to be so much less than what God had originally intended for it to be."[4] Perhaps he wept in personal shame, seeing in himself his own failure to live up to what God intended him to be. His weeping, however, was about far more. He wept because if no one was found worthy to open the scroll, then there would be no end to the suffering of this world. There would be no confidence in good triumphing over evil. There would be no assurance that justice will finally be done. There would be no ultimate victory for God's people. No experience of promised blessings. No new heaven. No new earth. No end to sin and death. No hope.

And that would be worth weeping about, wouldn't it? I want to weep at the thought of it.

Then John heard words of hope that must have quickly put an end to his tears:

> One of the elders said to me, "Weep no more; behold, the Lion of the tribe of Judah, the Root of David, has conquered, so that he can open the scroll and its seven seals." (Rev. 5:5)

Finally, someone was found who is worthy! This moment in the drama of Revelation 5 is like the point in a movie when all seems lost, but the hero appears at the very last second to save the day. *Yes, the Lion, the King, the overcomer! That's the answer! He will save us with his power! He will tear those seals to shreds!*

John must have looked up expecting to see a conquering lion. Instead, what he saw was a conquered Lamb:

> And between the throne and the four living creatures and among the elders I saw a Lamb standing, as though it had been slain, with seven horns and with seven eyes, which are the seven spirits of God sent out into all the earth. (Rev. 5:6)

4 Anne Graham Lotz, *The Vision of His Glory: Finding Hope through the Revelation of Jesus Christ* (Dallas: Word, 1996), 127.

John looked up and saw a Lamb. But this was no ordinary lamb. Interestingly this Lamb was alive and standing, yet looked "as though" it had been slain. What made the Lamb look "as though" it had been slain? John was looking at the crucified and resurrected Lord Jesus, in glorified human flesh. It is as if he could still see scars on his brow where the thorns had been pressed in and scars on his hands and feet where the nails had been pounded into them.

In the heart of ultimate reality, John saw a Savior who still bears the marks of his suffering—a Lamb who was slain, yet conquered death.

The Lamb is not slumped in defeat. He has seven horns. Horns are a symbol of strength and power throughout the Bible, including in the book of Revelation. This is a powerful lamb, an incredibly wise lamb—the only creature in the whole of the universe worthy to unfurl the scroll that contains God's sovereign plans for judgment and salvation. When the scroll is opened, the victory he achieved in his death and resurrection will have its full effect in establishing God's rule over the world.

> And he went and took the scroll from the right hand of him who was seated on the throne. And when he had taken the scroll, the four living creatures and the twenty-four elders fell down before the Lamb, each holding a harp, and golden bowls full of incense, which are the prayers of the saints. (Rev. 5:7–8)

The Lamb simply walks over and takes the scroll, asserting his right to rule the world. The prayers of the saints—prayers for God to judge those who continue in rebellion against him, prayers for deliverance from the evil of this world, prayers for his kingdom to come—are being answered.

The Singing

It is at this point in the unfolding drama that the singing begins—a spontaneous outburst of worship from all those who encircle the throne. A mighty chorus of redeemed people begins to sing a song they have never sung before, a song about what has been accomplished in the death and resurrection of Jesus to bring about what God has intended for his people ever since they were forced to leave Eden.

And they sang a new song, saying,

> "Worthy are you to take the scroll
>   and to open its seals,
> for you were slain, and by your blood you ransomed people
>   for God
>   from every tribe and language and people and nation,
> and you have made them a kingdom and priests to our God,
>   and they shall reign on the earth." (Rev. 5:9–10)

This song celebrates the threefold unique worthiness of Christ:

~ "You were slain." Jesus's willing, sacrificial death is the zenith and purest expression of his costly and unconditional love for sinners.

~ "You ransomed people for God." Think of a slave market where people are bought and sold. At the cross, Jesus paid the purchase price of his own blood to buy back or redeem men and women. He bought us back from the slave market of sin.

~ "You have made them a kingdom and priests to our God, and they shall reign on the earth." Through Jesus, our lives have meaning and purpose for eternity.

What makes Jesus worthy? What makes him worthy of your worship, worthy of the whole of your life? Jesus is worthy because he is fully God, fully able to bring about the plans and purposes of the triune God. Jesus is worthy because of the magnitude of his love for sinners demonstrated in sacrifice. He is worthy because he is able to make ordinary people like you and me worthy to be a part of his heavenly kingdom, worthy to serve him in the holiness of heaven, worthy to sit on thrones to rule and reign with him on a new earth.

This song of the worthiness of Jesus is an amazing and important song, isn't it? It's the kind of song I want to sing, don't you?

Do you ever get a song stuck in your brain that you really don't want to be humming but you just can't help it and can't get rid of it? Or have you noticed how an old song can come on the radio that you haven't heard for ten or twenty years and you remember every word? When that happens to me I wonder, "Where did that come from? Who knew those words were so deeply ingrained in my brain?"

And when you think about it, don't we have some awfully dumb songs ingrained in our brains? We have so many songs that so easily come to our minds and our lips about so many insignificant things. So many songs that really aren't worth remembering.

My friends, the song we will sing into eternity will celebrate the Lamb who was slain. This is a song that is worthy of getting stuck in our heads and in our hearts. This is a song we want to sing along with, a song we want to know the words to, a song we long to one day sing in perfect harmony around the throne. It's this longing we express when we sing:

> O that with yonder sacred throng we at his feet may fall;
> We'll join the everlasting song, and crown him Lord of all;
> We'll join the everlasting song, and crown him Lord of all.[5]

The four living creatures and all these redeemed people are singing their new song, and then the angels, all of the hosts of heaven, join in:

> Then I looked, and I heard around the throne and the living creatures and the elders the voice of many angels, numbering myriads of myriads and thousands of thousands, saying with a loud voice,
>
> > "Worthy is the Lamb who was slain,
> > to receive power and wealth and wisdom and might
> > and honor and glory and blessing!" (Rev. 5:11–12)

5   Edward Perronet, "All Hail the Power of Jesus' Name," 1780.

Can you just imagine the sound? Can you just feel the intensity and sincerity?

Notice that once again the emphasis is on the sacrificial death of Christ. This one of inestimable worth offered himself—a sacrifice valuable enough to redeem a people for God. Because he is all-powerful in conquering death, because he is the heir of all things, because he is all-wise and stronger than all of the forces of hell, he is worthy of all the honor, glory, and blessing that the hosts of heaven can shout to him.

But then the celebration grows even grander, reaching its crescendo. First it was cherubim and redeemed humanity, then the angels, and now:

> And I heard every creature in heaven and on earth and under the earth and in the sea, and all that is in them, saying,
>
> > "To him who sits on the throne and to the Lamb
> > be blessing and honor and glory and might forever and ever!"
>
> And the four living creatures said, "Amen!" and the elders fell down and worshiped. (Rev. 5:13–14)

Every creature and every person gives God and the Lamb the praise and glory they deserve. All of creation is unable to hold back from giving God and the Lamb unending applause.

Do you know what it is like when you see a performance, or someone says something significant and you can hardly wait to stand and applaud—when something is so amazing that you feel like you'll burst if you can't clap? That's the sense captured in this passage as every creature—every person on the earth, every cow in its stall, every moose in the forest, every bird in the air, every fish in the sea—joins in the roar of praise to Jesus!

Hearing and Keeping Revelation 4–5

John has given us entry into this heavenly scene where we have seen Jesus, seated with the Father on the throne at the heart of ultimate reality, surrounded by a grand celebration, worthy of being worshiped by all of creation. And I have to ask you: Does this heavenly scene and this magnificent Savior at the center awaken something deep inside you? Does it instill in you a yearning to sing this grand song too? Is your heart moved by the worthy-ness of Jesus, the worth-it-ness of Jesus?

Or, if you're honest, does it make you yawn and want to get on with your day?

Remember that blessing is promised to those who hear and keep what is written in this book. So what will it mean for us to hear and keep Revelation 4–5?

At the heart of what it means to hear and keep it must be the inability to resist the urge to join in. If there is no tug in our hearts, no longing to be a part of this grand celebration around the throne when Jesus finally receives all of the enthusiastic, thundering praise he deserves, maybe we need to ask ourselves some sober questions. Perhaps we need to ask: *What is it in my life that is getting the passion that belongs to Jesus?* Perhaps we need to pray and ask God to work in our lives, by his Spirit through his word, to awaken that kind of passion for his presence.

To hear and keep it is to allow the picture presented in this scene to capture our imaginations and shape what we consider to be beautiful, compelling, heartbreaking, worth celebrating, and worth longing for.

To hear and keep it means that there must be some correspondence in the way we worship with the way the Lamb is worshiped in heaven. Attending a worship service is one thing. It is really very easy to attend a worship service while never offering any whole-heart and whole-body worship that looks anything like the picture we're shown here. Does something need to change about the way we approach worship?

Finally, to hear and keep it is to direct our desire for glory toward the source of the only glory that will last. The human heart has a longing for glory. We are driven to attach ourselves to glory in the form of knowing a celebrity, being on the inside of power, and covering ourselves in the colors of our favorite sports teams. Yet these are merely tastes and glimpses of the glory for which we were made, the glory we will one day share and live in forever. Revelation 4 and 5 lift our eyes up from the attractions and derivative glories of this world and make us want to live lives that revolve around the most glorious being in the universe.

Jesus is worthy of our worship. Jesus is worthy of our trust. Jesus is worthy of our affections. Jesus is worthy of whatever may be required of us to live for him with patient endurance.

5

Blessed by Being Protected by Jesus

Revelation 6–7

EXPECTATIONS. Do you have some of those? We all do, don't we? Sometimes they are clear; sometimes we don't even realize we have them. Sometimes our expectations are based on what was promised to us, and sometimes they're based simply on what we hope for.

Sometimes our tastebuds are primed for a particular meal or treat, but it fails to deliver what we expected. Have you ever planned and saved for a vacation and found that the experience didn't live up to what you imagined it would be? The crowds were larger than you expected, the costs were more than you anticipated, or the company wasn't as enjoyable as you hoped? There are so many things in life we have expectations for. And sometimes our experience doesn't live up to our expectations.

How about the Christian life? Is the Christian life what you expected it would be?

Perhaps you started a journey with Jesus expecting that becoming a Christian would mean that life wouldn't be as hard as it had been, that it would become less complicated. Maybe you thought that prayer would be your resource for ridding your life of difficulty and conflict. Maybe you saw faith as the connection and prayer as the mechanism to secure a life in which hard, bad things are an aberration, way outside of the anticipated norm.

Most of us would never say that this is what we expected, but the evidence for or against it is how we respond when bad things happen. If we settle into a posture of anger or resentment toward God when he doesn't protect us from hard and painful things in this life, it reveals that our expectation was that he would keep things like cancer and car accidents and abuse and betrayal and loss away from us and our families since we belong to him.

So it is important that we know what has actually been promised to us; what we can rightly expect as we live our lives in this world as those who profess the name of Christ. And he hasn't left us in the dark regarding what we should expect. Right before his crucifixion John records that Jesus told the disciples that he was going away, and he told them exactly what they could expect in the time in between his ascension and his coming again. He told them that they were going to be hated and killed. "In the world you will have tribulation," he said. "But take heart; I have overcome the world" (John 16:33).

That's not exactly what we were hoping for, is it?

No one can ever say that Jesus was not honest about what those who are joined to him by faith can expect as we live our lives in this world for him. Anyone who tells you that you can have your best life now, and suggests that this is the message of the Bible, is lying to you. Jesus, however, is the faithful witness. Jesus tells us the truth about what we can expect as we live our lives in this world in this in-between time—this time in between his ascension and return.

In the Gospels and Acts we read about the ascension of Jesus from the perspective of those who were there when it happened. He blessed them and "he parted from them and was carried up into heaven" (Luke 24:51). That's the ascension of Jesus from earth into heaven from earth's perspective. In Revelation 5 we got to witness this event from heaven's perspective. Through the record of John's vision, we saw Jesus, as the Lamb who was slain, enter the heavenly throne room and take the scroll with seven seals from the right hand of the Father as the only one worthy to unseal it.

As we move into chapters 6 through 8, John describes for us what he saw in his vision as Jesus begins to open each of the seven seals. You'll remember that we said that the scroll contains God's sovereign plans for human history, particularly his plans for judgment and salvation. The scroll reveals how "the Lamb's victory is to become effective in establishing God's rule over the world."[1] We're going to see that the opening of each seal reveals something about what we can expect as history unfolds as we await the new creation. We don't have to wonder what we should expect our lives to be like in this in-between time as we wait for it. Revelation 6 and 7 tell us what to expect. So let's work our way through the opening of the seven seals and see what they have to tell us about what we can expect in this world as history unfolds under the direction and control of Jesus.

What We Can Expect

We can expect war, civil unrest, economic hardship and inequity, disease, and death.

The way John communicates the four connected realities revealed in the removal of the first four seals is unusual, but the realities themselves are painfully familiar and sadly ordinary.

> Now I watched when the Lamb opened one of the seven seals, and I heard one of the four living creatures say with a voice like thunder, "Come!" And I looked, and behold, a white horse! And its rider had a bow, and a crown was given to him, and he came out conquering, and to conquer. (Rev. 6:1–2)

Our task when we read this is to seek to rightly interpret what John is communicating through the symbols of horse and rider, bow and crown. And our first instinct when we read of this rider on a white horse may be to assume that this rider represents Christ, as many respected theologians do. In Revelation 19 Jesus will be represented as a rider on a white horse leading the armies of heaven to conquer. But if we read this

---

1 Richard Bauckham, *The Theology of the Book of Revelation* (Cambridge, UK: Cambridge University Press, 1993), 80.

passage in context of the other series of sevens to come (the seven trumpets and the seven bowls of wrath), as well as what Jesus himself said
about what believers should expect (Matt. 24; Mark 13; and Luke 21),
it becomes more likely that this horse and rider symbolize the many
power-hungry, self-glorifying warmongers who come out "conquering,
and to conquer" throughout history.[2] Think Pol Pot in Cambodia, the
Kim dynasty in North Korea, or Stalin in the Soviet Union.

Of course, many Bible teachers over the years have suggested that
when Jesus said that we would "hear of wars and rumors of wars" (Matt.
24:6), he was talking about something that will happen immediately
prior to the return of Christ. But has there ever been a time in human
history when there has not been "wars and rumors of wars"?

If you want to see how many wars are currently being fought around
the world right now, you can go to the Armed Conflict Location and
Event Data Project at ACLEDdata.com where you will find a world
map that highlights the conflicts around the world and breaks those
down into battles, violence against civilians, explosions, riots, and pro-
tests. And then you can break those down further under each of those
categories. On the day I checked the website, it stated that there were
currently 2,232 armed clashes taking place in the world. And that was
just one subset of the full picture.

Clearly we are not waiting for some future date in which there will
be wars and rumors of wars. This has always been a part of life in this
world in which nations and peoples and needs and agendas come into
conflict.

When he opened the second seal, I heard the second living creature
say, "Come!" And out came another horse, bright red. Its rider was

2   William Hendrickson provides a convincing case for this view in *More than Conquerors: An Interpretation of the Book of Revelation* (Grand Rapids, MI: Baker, 2015), 106–9. The same view is found in
Michael Wilcock, *The Message of Revelation: I Saw Heaven Opened* (Westmont, IL: InterVarsity Press,
1991), 74. Another view, which is affirmed by Jim Hamilton (James M. Hamilton, *Revelation: The
Spirit Speaks to the Churches* [Wheaton, IL: Crossway, 2012], 178), and G. K. Beale (G. K. Beale
with David H. Campbell, *Revelation: A Shorter Commentary* [Grand Rapids, MI: Eerdmans, 2015],
126–27), is that the rider on the white horse is a messianic pretender or satanic pretender.

permitted to take peace from the earth, so that people should slay one another, and he was given a great sword. (Rev. 6:3–4)

This horse is red. What has made this horse red? The blood of people killing each other. This isn't so much the bloodshed from the invasion of a foreign army but from civil unrest and conflict, insurrection and terrorism. If you watch local news, no matter where you live, there is sure to be the report of a murder or a conflict that has resulted in death nearly every day. People hate and kill one another. It has been a bitter reality of the world we live in ever since Cain killed his brother Abel.

When he opened the third seal, I heard the third living creature say, "Come!" And I looked, and behold, a black horse! And its rider had a pair of scales in his hand. And I heard what seemed to be a voice in the midst of the four living creatures, saying, "A quart of wheat for a denarius, and three quarts of barley for a denarius, and do not harm the oil and wine!" (Rev. 6:5–6)

This third seal speaks to scarcity and the resulting inflation so that a daily wage is just enough to buy food for that day. But notice that the oil and wine, the products enjoyed by the wealthy, are spared. So not only does this speak to scarcity of resources; it speaks to inequity of resources. It is a picture of the poor struggling to eat day by day while the rich enjoy their luxuries. It was the world the original recipients of this letter were living in. Many of the believers in the seven churches were marginalized so that when food was scarce, they would likely have been put at the end of the bread line. And, of course, this is the world we live in too.

When he opened the fourth seal, I heard the voice of the fourth living creature say, "Come!" And I looked, and behold, a pale horse! And its rider's name was Death, and Hades followed him. And they were given authority over a fourth of the earth, to kill with sword and with famine and with pestilence and by wild beasts of the earth. (Rev. 6:7–8)

This fourth horse is pale. Sickly. Maybe even the color of a corpse. We're told the name of the rider of this horse: Death. Death from warfare, famine, and disease. And Death is followed by Hades. Death is followed by the place of the dead. Notice that it isn't pervasive death. It is a quarter of the earth. We're going to see that, as we move through the seven seals, bowls, and trumpets, which are going to show us the same time period of history from different angles, the death and destruction are going to increase. The visions are going to increase in intensity.

None of these four realities of the world we live in should surprise any of us. But there is something surprising about what this vision reveals about these things. What may be surprising is where they come from. These things aren't presented to us as something God's enemy is doing in the world, but rather they come at the bidding of Jesus himself.

Not only are war, civil unrest, economic hardship and inequity, and disease and death summoned and sent from the throne room; notice that the conqueror is given a crown, the rider of the red horse is given a sword, and death is given authority over a fourth of the earth. Given by whom? Given by the Lamb who is seated on the throne.

How do we begin to wrap our minds around that?

Rather than seeing judgment only as something that will happen at the end of time, we need to see that even now a world that has rejected and rebelled against God is experiencing judgment. It's not yet the final judgment. That's coming, but this world is experiencing a measure of that judgment now.

When a religious leader goes on television after some sort of disaster and says that it is God's judgment at work, most of us cringe, usually because they connect the disaster to a particular sin, and usually it is someone else's sin and not their own. But they are at least partly correct. We can be sure that our world that has rejected the rule of God is, even now, experiencing his judgment. Paul put it this way in Romans: "For the wrath of God is revealed from heaven against all ungodliness and unrighteousness of men, who by their unrighteousness suppress the truth" (Rom. 1:18).

We're living in a world that is under the judgment of God for rebelling against him. The evils of war and unrest, economic desperation, and death are not uncontrolled or unguided. They are overseen and limited by the Lamb.

And while these hardships serve the purposes of judgment against those who have set themselves against the Lamb, they are intended to have a sanctifying purpose among all who belong to the Lamb. When the living creatures call these horses and riders to come, they're being called for the purpose of judgment on those who are destined for judgment, as well as for the purpose of purification and refining the faith of those who are destined for glory.

We can expect to be persecuted for our witness to Jesus Christ.

As the Lamb opened the first four seals, we heard the cry of the four living creatures, which Ezekiel says are angelic creatures (Ezek. 1:5; 10:7–8, 21). "When the fifth seal is opened, we hear a human cry."[3]

> When he opened the fifth seal, I saw under the altar the souls of those who had been slain for the word of God and for the witness they had borne. (Rev. 6:9)

John's attention is directed toward the altar that is in heaven, the altar written about by the writer of Hebrews on which Jesus offered himself as a sacrifice to secure redemption for his people. John saw the souls of those who shed blood for Christ and have been hidden and protected by the sacrifice of Christ. It seems like a visual demonstration of what Paul wrote about in Romans 8 when he asked the rhetorical question, "Who shall separate us from the love of Christ? Shall tribulation, or distress, or persecution, or famine, or nakedness, or danger, or sword?" which he answers by celebrating that nothing will be able to separate us from the love of God in Christ Jesus our Lord (Rom. 8:35–39). There were so many people John knew and loved who had been "slain

3   Peter J. Leithart, *Revelation 1–11* (Edinburgh: Bloomsbury, 2018), 276.

for the word of God and for the witness they had borne," people like Peter and James and Stephen and all the rest of the disciples who had all been killed for their allegiance to Jesus. John was able to look into heaven and see that tribulation and persecution and sword have not had the power to cut off these believers from Christ but instead have secured their place of protection with Christ.

Of course, Jesus had told them to expect to be persecuted. "Remember the word that I said to you," he said to his disciples in the upper room the night before he was crucified. "'A servant is not greater than his master.' If they persecuted me, they will also persecute you" (John 15:20).

But few of us really want to believe that, do we? We want to think that persecution is for people living in another time, in another place, under a different type of government. And sometimes we confuse being persecuted for our politics or our opinions or simply because of our personality with being persecuted for our clear witness to the kingship of Jesus. Many believers today seek to argue, legislate, or protest that persecution away. Often believers are more interested in demanding their rights and defending their position than in developing patient endurance in the persecution Jesus told us to expect. Revelation is written not as a guide on how to avoid persecution but rather as encouragement to endure persecution faithfully.

We can expect that our prayers for justice will be heard.

> They cried out with a loud voice, "O Sovereign Lord, holy and true, how long before you will judge and avenge our blood on those who dwell on the earth?" Then they were each given a white robe and told to rest a little longer, until the number of their fellow servants and their brothers should be complete, who were to be killed as they themselves had been. (Rev. 6:10–11)

Before we consider what these believers in heaven are praying for, we need to consider who they're praying to. They are praying to the God who is sovereign—sovereign over their suffering and death, sovereign over heaven and earth, sovereign over time and eternity. And he is the God who is holy and true. They are praying to a God whose holiness demands that evil be punished and a God who will be true to his promise to do so.

At the heart of their prayer is the cry, "How long?" And the response they receive to their question, "How long?" is "A little longer." There is a purpose given for the delay, though it must have been another difficult dose of reality for the original recipients of this letter, just as it should be for us today. They're told that there is a determined number of brothers and sisters in Christ who are going to have to face some of the same things they have faced. This is why those reading the letter are going to need patient endurance. The content of this letter that they've received from Jesus is not a promise that their suffering is going to decrease or disappear. Instead, this letter is intended to gird them for the fight of faith that is going to define the rest of their lives, and the rest of our lives.

As we read this over two thousand years after it was written, we can't help but wonder how this stretch of time could be considered "a little longer." G. K. Beale writes that "time in heaven may be reckoned differently than time on earth."[4] Waiting for God to act, waiting for him to set things right, can seem so very long that we're tempted to wonder if that day will ever really come. But, my friend, you can be assured that the day of justice is going to come. The question, "How long?" will one day be answered to the full satisfaction of every believer who has cried out to God with hot tears. God has set a day when he will set things right. The suffering of God's people has an expiration date. We have to wait a little longer. We have to wait for the day that is depicted in the opening of the sixth seal.

We can expect that a final judgment will come.

The opening of the sixth seal is a revelation of the final judgment day. It is the day that the saints under the altar have been praying for. If we've

---

4 Beale, *Revelation: A Shorter Commentary*, 136.

read the story of the Bible starting in Genesis, we know that there have been many precursors to this great final day of judgment. There were forty days of rain that destroyed all but Noah and his family. There was the day when sulfur and fire rained down on Sodom and Gomorrah and destroyed all but Lot and his family. There was the night when the Lord passed through Egypt and killed all of the firstborn except those hidden safely inside homes that were marked by the blood of a lamb. But all of those were just previews for the great and final day of judgment that the sixth seal reveals:

> When he opened the sixth seal, I looked, and behold, there was a great earthquake, and the sun became black as sackcloth, the full moon became like blood, and the stars of the sky fell to the earth as the fig tree sheds its winter fruit when shaken by a gale. The sky vanished like a scroll that is being rolled up, and every mountain and island was removed from its place. (Rev. 6:12–14)

John uses the same imagery that Isaiah, Ezekiel, Joel, and Jesus used to describe the final day of judgment (Isa. 13:10; Ezek. 32:7; Joel 2:31; Matt. 24:29). They all speak of the earth shaking, the sun darkening, the moon turning red, and the stars of the sky falling. It is as if the lights are being turned off in the universe because its day is done. They're all using symbolism to draw a picture for us of the terror of judgment day, the sense of everything of permanence being shaken. We're meant to feel the horror of this scene. We're meant to be filled with a sense that when this day comes, nothing will ever be the same again.

> Then the kings of the earth and the great ones and the generals and the rich and the powerful, and everyone, slave and free, hid themselves in the caves and among the rocks of the mountains, calling to the mountains and rocks, "Fall on us and hide us from the face of him who is seated on the throne, and from the wrath of the Lamb, for the great day of their wrath has come, and who can stand?" (Rev. 6:15–17)

Earlier we heard the martyrs in heaven praying. Here we hear humanity on earth praying, not to God, but to the mountains and rocks, begging them to fall and crush them. They would rather die than stand before the throne of the God that they have rebelled against. They would rather die than come face to face with the Lamb whose blood they have ridiculed and rejected. The day they laughed about and labeled as ridiculous will have become their inescapable reality. They will be desperate to find an answer to the all-important question that they should have sought an answer to far sooner. In light of facing the righteous Judge, they'll be asking, "Who can stand before a holy God who is angry over sin and survive? Who is able to withstand the blistering gaze of God? Is there anywhere to find protection in the storm of his judgment?"

No one need wait for that day to ask that question and have it answered. As we turn the page to chapter 7 of Revelation, an interlude before the seventh seal is opened, the question is answered as John is given a new vision of how God will keep believers spiritually safe in the final judgment.

All who have taken hold of Christ by faith can expect to be protected in the final judgment.

> After this I saw four angels standing at the four corners of the earth, holding back the four winds of the earth, that no wind might blow on earth or sea or against any tree. Then I saw another angel ascending from the rising of the sun, with the seal of the living God, and he called with a loud voice to the four angels who had been given power to harm earth and sea, saying, "Do not harm the earth or the sea or the trees, until we have sealed the servants of our God on their foreheads." (Rev. 7:1–3)

Four angels are standing at the four corners of the earth restraining the winds of destruction. Then another angel calls out to the angels who are preparing to accomplish the final judgment, telling them to put it on pause so that all who are servants of God can be marked for protection in the judgment.

When we read about being marked as belonging to God, marked for protection, it can't help but remind us of the night when the death angel went throughout Egypt. God told Moses what the Israelites needed to do to be protected from the judgment. Their homes had to be marked by the blood of an innocent lamb. According to Andrew Sach, that is a picture of what is happening here.[5] These servants are being marked by the blood of the Lamb so that they will not face the wrath of the Lamb.

> And I heard the number of the sealed, 144,000, sealed from every tribe of the sons of Israel:
>
> 12,000 from the tribe of Judah were sealed,
> 12,000 from the tribe of Reuben,
> 12,000 from the tribe of Gad,
> 12,000 from the tribe of Asher,
> 12,000 from the tribe of Naphtali,
> 12,000 from the tribe of Manasseh,
> 12,000 from the tribe of Simeon,
> 12,000 from the tribe of Levi,
> 12,000 from the tribe of Issachar,
> 12,000 from the tribe of Zebulun,
> 12,000 from the tribe of Joseph,
> 12,000 from the tribe of Benjamin were sealed. (Rev. 7:4–8)

We are learning that numbers in Revelation are symbolic. So when we come to the number 144,000 we know that we've got to interpret the symbolism. There were twelve tribes of Israel and twelve apostles. If you take 12 x 12, you have 144. Ten is another number of completeness. If you multiply 144 x 10 x 10 x 10, the sense of completeness is exponentially emphasized. This is the complete

---

5 Andrew Sach, "You've Heard of the Mark of the Beast," sermon, Grace Church Greenwich, London, January 17, 2021, https://www.greenwich.church/.

number of Old Testament saints who looked forward and put their faith in the Christ who was promised combined with those saints in the New Testament era who look back at the cross and resurrection and put their faith in Christ. This is the true Israel, the church across the ages. Everyone is accounted for. And they are all sealed for protection.

One reason we know that this is speaking of both Old Testament–era and New Testament–era believers in Christ is the way John lists the twelve tribes, which differs from other listings of the twelve tribes in the Bible. John begins his list with the tribe of Judah even though Judah is not the firstborn. Why begin with Judah instead of Reuben?

Judah is the one who was told by his father, Jacob, "The scepter will not depart from Judah, nor the ruler's staff from his descendants, until the coming of the one to whom it belongs, the one whom all nations will honor" (Gen. 49:10 NLT). What Jacob said would happen has finally happened. Jesus, the lion of the tribe of Judah, has come, and people of every nation are included in this number.

John's list also includes Joseph, while Ephraim and Dan are omitted. Why would that be? What is being communicated to us?

Remember that when the twelve tribes split into the northern and southern kingdoms under Rehoboam (1 Kings 12), the northern tribes had no temple and soon mixed the worship of the Baals with the worship of the one true God. Golden calves were erected in Dan and Ephraim. Evidently idolatry led these tribes away from God, and they never came to repentance. Dan and Ephraim aren't there. By listing the tribes in this way, John is demonstrating that not everyone who is part of the visible church on earth will prove to have received the mark of God that is given to all who embrace his covenant from the heart. It was true in the days of ancient Israel. It was true in Jesus's day, as we know that one of the twelve, Judas, was really a pretender. It was true in the first century, such as those in Ephesus who called themselves apostles and were found to be false (2:2). And it is true today.

It is interesting that after we've received this specific numbering of the sealed servants of God, it is as if John sees them from another angle, and from this perspective, it is a great multitude that no one can number. Logic makes us want John to say it is one way or the other— able to be numbered or unable to be numbered. But we are dealing with apocalyptic imagery, and both images communicate something significant about these sealed people. I like how Andrew Sach put it: "While the numbered list of tribes tells us that the number of those sealed is complete, this great multitude tells us that the number of those sealed will be vast."[6]

> After this I looked, and behold, a great multitude that no one could number, from every nation, from all tribes and peoples and languages, standing before the throne and before the Lamb, clothed in white robes, with palm branches in their hands, and crying out with a loud voice, "Salvation belongs to our God who sits on the throne, and to the Lamb!" And all the angels were standing around the throne and around the elders and the four living creatures, and they fell on their faces before the throne and worshiped God, saying, "Amen! Blessing and glory and wisdom and thanksgiving and honor and power and might be to our God forever and ever! Amen." Then one of the elders addressed me, saying, "Who are these, clothed in white robes, and from where have they come?" I said to him, "Sir, you know." And he said to me, "These are the ones coming out of the great tribulation. They have washed their robes and made them white in the blood of the Lamb." (Rev. 7:9–14)

When we read the words "a great multitude that no one could number," perhaps we're meant to think of God's promise to Abraham that he would have descendants as numerous as the stars in the sky and the sand on the seashore. Here is the fulfillment of that promise. God also told Abraham that he would be the father of a multitude of nations.

6   Sach, "You've Heard of the Mark of the Beast."

Here is a multitude made up of people from every nation, tribe, people, and language who are all true sons of Abraham.

They are all crying out with a loud voice saying, "Salvation belongs to our God!" It is interesting that they are not saying, "Salvation belongs to me!" They are on the other side of the final judgment and can see how God has preserved a people for himself through persecution and through judgment. They are praising God for the magnificence of his plans for history that have been executed through the opening of the seals. They know that their salvation is the result of having been marked by the blood of Christ, not by any worthiness in themselves. It's almost as if they don't have enough words to express all of the honor that is due to God for what he has done, so they pile them up into one long string of "blessing and glory and wisdom and thanksgiving and honor and power and might be to our God forever and ever! Amen."

Here are God's people protected and preserved through the final judgment. We read that they are "standing" before the throne (7:9). The question "Who can stand?" has been answered. We expect to see them ushered into the new Jerusalem at this point. But "Revelation is not ready at this early point in its dramatic development to expose fully God's plans for the new world."[7] We'll see the seventh seal opened in the next chapter, but we won't find a description of what it reveals. We're merely told that when it is opened, "there was silence in heaven for about half an hour" (Rev. 8:1). There is a sense of awe, of stunned silence, as heaven gazes into the wonder of what this world will one day become when it has been cleansed by the fire of God (8:5). But while we're not yet told everything that will be revealed to us about what life will be like for those have been protected in the final judgment, we are given a sense of its essence, its blessings:

Therefore they are before the throne of God,
    and serve him day and night in his temple;

7 Vern Poythress, *The Returning King: A Guide to the Book of Revelation* (Phillipsburg, NJ: P&R, 2000), 119.

and he who sits on the throne will shelter them with his
   presence.
They shall hunger no more, neither thirst anymore;
   the sun shall not strike them,
      nor any scorching heat.
For the Lamb in the midst of the throne will be their shepherd,
   and he will guide them to springs of living water,
and God will wipe away every tear from their eyes. (Rev. 7:15–17)

*We can expect to enjoy the presence and provision
of Christ forever in a cleansed creation.*

This is a poetic picture of what all who have been marked by the blood
of the Lamb, all who have been sealed to Christ by the Holy Spirit,
all who have patiently endured the tribulation of living for Christ in
a hostile world, can expect. We can expect that we will not only be
protected in the final judgment; we will enjoy the protective presence
of God for all eternity. Nothing and no one will be able to harm us.
All of our needs will be provided for. All the pain of the past will be
wiped away—not through an impersonal declaration but personally
and lovingly, as God himself will wipe away our tears. We'll be safely
in the fold of our shepherd, the Lamb.

Hearing and Keeping Revelation 6–7

So what are the implications for the heavy dose of reality provided for us
in Revelation 6 and 7? What is it going to look like for us to hear and keep
these chapters and thereby experience the promised blessing of this book?

As we look at all of the things Revelation 6 and 7 show us about what
we can expect in this life and the life to come, these chapters invite us
to examine our expectations to see how they line up with reality. Do
we expect to experience the hardships of war, civil unrest, economic
hardship and inequality, and disease and death, or deep down have
we really expected that being joined to Christ will somehow shield us
from these things? Do we expect that human effort should be able to

rid the world of these things, or are our expectations firmly on Christ to put an end to them?

When the fifth seal is opened, we see those who have been slain for their witness to Christ under the altar, and they are crying out to God, asking, "How long?" Most of us probably have times in life when we acutely long for Christ to return and set things right in this world. But how do our prayers compare to those of the saints here?

The Scriptures encourage us to pray for our own needs and for the needs of others. But if we were to survey most of the prayers that are included in the Bible, including this one, the priority of prayer always centers on the spread of the gospel of the kingdom, the preservation and strength of the church, the ministry of God's word, and the thwarting of godless and wicked powers in our world. So we should ask ourselves: Do I ever express in my prayers a longing for God to come in judgment, or are my prayers mostly about me and my little world? Do I ever pray for God to vindicate those who have been killed for their allegiance to Christ? Do I pray regularly for those facing intense persecution around the world, asking God to give them the grace to patiently endure? These are the prayers at the center of God's purposes, prayers that are treasured by him, prayers that have an effect that we would be completely unaware of were we not shown that effect in Revelation 6.

Perhaps the most important way we must hear and keep these chapters is to examine our lives for evidence that we have been sealed by God for God. Speaking to believers in Ephesus, Paul writes, "In him you also, when you heard the word of truth, the gospel of your salvation, and believed in him, were sealed with the promised Holy Spirit, who is the guarantee of our inheritance until we acquire possession of it" (Eph. 1:13–14). The Holy Spirit is the seal that God has placed upon all who have been washed in the blood of the Lamb. So that prompts us to examine ourselves, looking for evidence of the fruit of the Spirit in our lives. Is there fruit of being cleansed by the blood of Christ not only in living as someone who is forgiven of sin, but also as one who has come to hate sin? Is there evidence in the form of love, joy, peace,

patience, kindness, goodness, gentleness, faithfulness, and self-control
(Gal. 5:22–23)?

If so, you don't have to wonder what you can expect over these years
of your lifetime in this world as a Christian. You can expect hardship.
You can expect to be persecuted for your clear witness to the person
and work of Christ. You can expect that your prayers will be heard and
acted on in heaven. You can expect that justice will be done. You can
expect that when judgment falls, you will be protected in the judgment.
Though you may be mistreated in the here and now, you will have a
place of safety in your forever home. Though you may experience going
without in the here and now, you will be provided for there so that all
of your needs will be met forever. Though you may experience great
sorrow now, God himself is going to bless you with the comfort of his
presence as a shelter and a shepherd forever.

6

Blessed by Being on Mission for Jesus

Revelation 8–11

ABOUT SIX MONTHS AGO, the smoke detector outside our bedroom began to talk to us, relentlessly squawking and saying, "Fire! Fire!" Of course, this didn't happen in the middle of the day. It was in the middle of the night. David and I groggily worked our way through the house, finding no evidence of smoke or fire. We got a ladder and got close enough to the smoke detector to get the model number so we could look up the instruction manual online and try to figure out how to silence it. It didn't work. In the end, we unhooked it and went back to sleep. That began "The Great Guthrie Battle with the Smoke Detectors." Over the past six months or so, numerous other smoke detectors throughout the house have entered the fray. We've replaced batteries. We've gotten a different brand of batteries. We've reset them. We've even replaced some of them. The replacements started chirping and talking to us too. As I write, several of them are sitting on the kitchen counter with batteries out and wires exposed as we've taken a brief retreat from the battle to regroup and come up with another plan of attack. Or, really, another plan for peace.

When a smoke detector goes off in the middle of the night, you can't simply ignore it and go back to sleep. It is meant to rouse you. It is meant to warn you. It is meant to keep you from being burned and from having your house destroyed by fire.

In Revelation 8 through 11, we're going to read about seven trumpets—seven trumpets that are blown to announce the coming of the Lord to wage warfare against his enemies and the enemies of his people. They're meant to rouse a sleeping world to respond to the gospel in repentance and faith. Those who are awakened to the dire situation of being outside of Christ can find safety in him. Those who ignore these trumpet warnings will one day wake up to discover that the seventh trumpet has blown, and it is too late to find safety.

To rightly understand what is being communicated in the seven trumpets, we need to recall a previous time in the story of the Bible when seven trumpets were blown. Can you remember?

When Joshua led the nation of Israel into the promised land, they marched around the city of Jericho for seven days (Josh. 6). For seven days the people inside the walls of Jericho were warned of the coming judgment that God was going to accomplish as the trumpets blew and the Israelites marched around the city in silence. And when the seven trumpets sounded on the seventh day, the walls fell down and the Israelites entered the city.

So the story of the trumpets being blown and the walls falling down in Jericho provides some help to us in understanding the purpose of the trumpets—to announce the coming of the Lord to wage warfare against his enemies and the enemies of his people. It pictures for us the way in which the seventh trumpet will signal our entrance into the greater promised land that God has promised to us.

In our last chapter on the opening of the seals, we saw what believers can expect over the course of a lifetime of living in this world that is under a curse, under the judgment of God. We saw that while believers experience judgment in the sense of living in a world under judgment, they are sealed by God for protection and are therefore safe and secure from the harm of the final judgment. In this chapter, we're going to witness what the unsealed, "those who dwell on the earth," can expect to experience over the course of their lives lived on the earth and in the final judgment.

The first thing we need to settle, however, before we begin to work our way through the seven trumpets, is how what happens in the blowing of these seven trumpets relates to the opening of the seven seals in Revelation 6 and 7, and the pouring of the bowls in Revelation 16. Because we're used to events being presented to us in chronological order, we might assume that the seven trumpets depict events that transpire *after* the opening of the seven seals and *before* the pouring out of the seven bowls. But in actuality the events depicted in the seals, trumpets, and bowls take place over the same time period—the time between the first and second coming of Jesus. Revelation is showing us the same scene from different angles, and each angle helps us to see and understand a different aspect of what is taking place during the same period of time. Think of it as similar to watching a sporting event on television. Most major sporting events have numerous cameras covering the same action, and when something significant happens in the game, they often replay what happened from numerous camera angles. As we see it from different angles, the reality of what transpired becomes clearer to us.

That is what is happening in the book of Revelation. The seven seals of Revelation 6 and 7, the seven trumpets of Revelation 8 through 11, and the seven bowls of Revelation 16 each show us the same period of human history—the time between the life, death, resurrection, and ascension of Jesus, and the day he returns in glory to establish his kingdom on this earth and to usher in the new heaven and the new earth.[1]

Warning: Danger!

The blowing of the first four trumpets has some similarity to the opening of the first four seals. Like the first four seals were grouped together

---

1   To read more about the various sections of judgment as parallel descriptions of the same events, see G. K. Beale with David H. Campbell, *Revelation: A Shorter Commentary* (Grand Rapids, MI: Eerdmans, 2015), 22–24. Thomas Schreiner writes, "Some interpreters . . . think Revelation is a continuous narrative, and they do not see how the book is recursive and recapitulatory. John brings us to the end of history repeatedly in the book, and then he starts over again." Thomas Schreiner, *Hebrews–Revelation*, ESV Expository Commentary (Wheaton, IL: Crossway, 2018), 45. Similarly William Hendrickson writes, "A careful reading of the book of Revelation has made it clear that the book consists of seven sections, and that these seven sections run parallel to one another. Each of them spans the entire dispensation from the first to the second coming of Christ. This period is viewed now from one aspect, now from another." William Hendrickson, *More than Conquerors: An Interpretation of the Book of Revelation* (Grand Rapids, MI: Baker, 2015), 25.

to communicate what life will be like in this world in between the ascension and the return of Jesus, the first four trumpets speak to difficult realities in this world in this same time period. But while the first four seals portrayed difficulties that are experienced by everyone, the focus of the trumpets seems to be on how those who are not sealed, those who are not in Christ, those who "dwell on the earth," will experience life on earth during this time.

If we take the first four trumpets as a whole, they each seem to picture the impact of ongoing but not yet final judgment on the things in this world in which many people find their sustenance and security. These are not necessarily bad things. But they are vulnerable things. The trumpets are sounding an alarm, warning of the danger of having only this world and what it provides and promises to depend on for security and satisfaction.

> The first angel blew his trumpet, and there followed hail and fire, mixed with blood, and these were thrown upon the earth. And a third of the earth was burned up, and a third of the trees were burned up, and all green grass was burned up. (Rev. 8:7)

Burn, burn, burn. The first trumpet reveals a picture of one-third of the fields and trees that should be providing food burning up so that there is hunger that cannot be satisfied. Beale writes about this judgment by fire: "The fire is not literal, but figurative (as elsewhere in Revelation, most clearly in 4:5, but also in 1:14; 2:18; 10:1; 19:12)."[2] It pictures the way those who depend on this earth to sustain and satisfy them discover that it is limited in its ability to do so.

> The second angel blew his trumpet, and something like a great mountain, burning with fire, was thrown into the sea, and a third of the sea became blood. A third of the living creatures in the sea died, and a third of the ships were destroyed. (Rev. 8:8–9)

2   Beale, *Revelation*, 174.

"In Revelation, mountains speak of kingdoms, both good and bad, earthly and heavenly (14:1; 17:9; 21:10)."[3] Here with the second trumpet is a picture of the great kingdoms of the world that come crashing down, destroying the lives and livelihoods of those who lived in them. And, of course, we know that this has happened repeatedly throughout history.

> The third angel blew his trumpet, and a great star fell from heaven, blazing like a torch, and it fell on a third of the rivers and on the springs of water. The name of the star is Wormwood. A third of the waters became wormwood, and many people died from the water, because it had been made bitter. (Rev. 8:10–11)

The imagery with the third trumpet of a star falling from heaven blazing like a torch comes from Isaiah 14:12–15, where Babylon's guardian angel is pictured as a star cast down from heaven into a pit. Here in Revelation the star is called "Wormwood," which is based on Jeremiah 9:15 and 23:15, where God judges his disobedient people by giving them poisoned water to drink. This trumpet demonstrates that the very things in this world that people consume, expecting them to be life-giving, often end up poisoning them. It trumpets to those who think that their sins add to their lives that sin ruins everything; in fact, it will be their ruin.

> The fourth angel blew his trumpet, and a third of the sun was struck, and a third of the moon, and a third of the stars, so that a third of their light might be darkened, and a third of the day might be kept from shining, and likewise a third of the night. (Rev. 8:12)

At the fourth trumpet, the lights of heaven are all partially darkened. It's a picture of the failure of the world's wisdom and spirituality to truly enlighten, a picture of people going about their lives in darkness

---

3   Beale, *Revelation*, 174.

without the ability to see *what* is true and right and good, as well as *who* is true and right and good.

God intends to demonstrate his power over all the false gods people build their lives around that simply cannot supply them with the sustenance or security they crave. They sound a warning to all who dwell on the earth: *Don't put your trust in the things of this world! They're all vulnerable. They will all eventually fail you. Put your trust in the one who made the earth, the sun, moon, and stars. He can be trusted.*

Of course, earth dwellers are not inclined to come under the kingship of the true King because, whether they know it or not, they have given their allegiance to another king. And, sadly, he is not a good king. Rather than protecting his own, he torments his own.

Warning: Torment!

> And the fifth angel blew his trumpet, and I saw a star fallen from heaven to earth, and he was given the key to the shaft of the bottomless pit. He opened the shaft of the bottomless pit, and from the shaft rose smoke like the smoke of a great furnace, and the sun and the air were darkened with the smoke from the shaft. (Rev. 9:1–2)

"A star fallen from heaven to earth." That reminds us of Jesus's words when he said, "I saw Satan fall like lightning from heaven" (Luke 10:18). So we know who this "star" is. It is Satan or a demonic archangel. A bottomless pit that smokes—it isn't so hard to figure out what this is, is it? This is the pit of hell. William Hendrickson writes that this smoke is "the smoke of deception and delusion, of sin and sorrow, of moral darkness and degradation that is constantly belching up out of hell."[4]

> Then from the smoke came locusts on the earth, and they were given power like the power of scorpions of the earth. They were told not to harm the grass of the earth or any green plant or any tree, but only those people who do not have the seal of God on their foreheads. They

4 Hendrickson, *More than Conquerors*, 135.

were allowed to torment them for five months, but not to kill them, and their torment was like the torment of a scorpion when it stings someone. And in those days people will seek death and will not find it. They will long to die, but death will flee from them. (Rev. 9:3–6)

You knew we were eventually going to get to locusts in Revelation, right? We find them here in the fifth trumpet. We're seeing that John uses imagery from the Old Testament to describe heavenly and earthly realities. So it is Moses and the prophets who help us to understand what John describes in the fifth trumpet. In Joel 1 and 2, the prophet uses the imagery of a locust plague along with military imagery to describe the demonic army set against God and his people on his great day. John seems to draw upon this imagery while adding gruesome features to the creatures presented in Joel's vision.

When we read that these locusts with the poisonous power of scorpions come from the bottomless pit, we are able to rightly interpret that these are demons from the pit of hell. The one who holds the keys to this place, who, we remember from Revelation 1, is Jesus, has allowed this door to be opened. These demons are not out of his control. In fact, he sets parameters, or limits, to what and who these demons can harm. These demons tempt and deceive, making evil appear virtuous and attractive. But in the end they sting. In the end those who come under their power experience not freedom and joy but torment, the torment of guilt and regret, slavery to sin, and sickness of soul. These demons, however, can only harm those who do not have the protective seal of God, as believers have been freed from guilt and slavery to sin. While these demons can torment those outside of Christ only for a limited period of time, that torment will be unbearable. It will make the unsealed wish that they were dead.

In appearance the locusts were like horses prepared for battle: on their heads were what looked like crowns of gold; their faces were like human faces, their hair like women's hair, and their teeth like lions' teeth; they had breastplates like breastplates of iron, and the noise of their wings was like the noise of many chariots with horses rushing into battle. They have tails and stings like scorpions, and their power to hurt people for five months is in their tails. They have as king over them the angel of the bottomless pit. His name in Hebrew is Abaddon, and in Greek he is called Apollyon. (Rev. 9:7–11)

Notice John's repeated use of "like" to provide a vivid sense of these demonic creatures that bring a spiritual plague of misery upon humanity. It's as if John is struggling a bit to describe what he is seeing in a way that will communicate the reality of their demonic nature. We know they're demonic because we're told where they come from and who is king over them. These demons appear commanding, invulnerable, seductive, and cunning. But they sting and hurt and torment. The power to hurt people is in their tails, in devastation left behind after the fun has been had. And doesn't this seem to reflect the reality that so many things that seem so empowering, so natural, and so enjoyable on the surface actually end up bringing misery? Reveling in supposed freedom to indulge, so many people find themselves enslaved to things that are quite literally killing them. So many people indulge in things that they think will add to their lives but really only take and take from their lives. That's because they come from the pit of hell, from the one who "comes only to steal and kill and destroy" (John 10:10). John gives us his name here in Revelation in both Hebrew and Greek, both of which mean "destroyer."

Certainly, there are many people in the world who have rejected Christ as their king who would never admit to having this Abaddon or Apollyon as their king. They can't see it. They think that they are in charge of their own lives and their own destinies. But John can see, from the perspective of heaven, that all who are not sealed, all who have refused the offer of grace from the true King, all who dwell on the earth have a king who only wants to destroy them. He wants to destroy their happiness. He wants to destroy their families. He wants to destroy their futures.

Warning: Wounding!

When the fifth trumpet blew, demons emerged from the bottomless pit. When the sixth trumpet is blown, a voice from the throne says, "Release the four angels who are bound at the great river Euphrates" (Rev. 9:14). This can be confusing because we're told that these are four angels, so we immediately assume they are four of God's holy angels. But "good angels aren't released; but are commissioned or sent,"[5] and they don't breathe fire, smoke, and sulfur. So, these four angels are clearly fallen angels, or demons.

Demons emerge again, breathing fire and smoke and sulfur, but this time they emerge from being bound "at the great river Euphrates." Repeatedly in the Old Testament, the armies that brought destruction on Israel came from the region of the Euphrates (e.g., Isa. 7:20; 8:7–8; Jer. 46:2, 6, 10). G. K. Beale explains that John uses "Euphrates" here not as a geographical reference but as a spiritual reference to "where Satan will marshal his forces against God's people."[6]

The demons are portrayed as troops on horses, and two times we're told that plagues of fire, smoke, and sulfur come out of the mouths of these horses (9:17–18). The threat is in what they say, the false teaching that originates with them. John is using apocalyptic language to describe something we don't always see as scary or troubling—deception and false teaching. Here, however, we get to see what false teaching looks like from the vantage point of heaven, which enables us to see just how deadly it is.

We know from chapters 2 and 3 of Revelation that false teaching was a problem for many of the original recipients of this letter. Of course, it is a problem in our day as well, though many Christians have a very cavalier attitude about it. Many Christians view teaching that distorts who Jesus is, what he offers, and what he requires as simply a difference of opinion, interpretation, or approach. This picture, however, shows us that the deception of false teachers and the promotion of alternative

5   Schreiner, *Hebrews–Revelation*, 640.
6   Beale, *Revelation*, 190.

gods aren't merely human phenomena; they are actually empowered by demonic spirits. This apocalyptic imagery draws back the curtain of heaven so we can see false teaching and deception as God sees it so we will see the real danger in it. Deception leads to spiritual and physical death.

Notice, however, that these horses don't just kill; they wound. There is something about that word, *wound*, that gets me. And if you have known anyone who has embraced conspiracy theories, prosperity-gospel teaching, universalism, or the popular notion that heaven is for good people who do good things and avoid doing really bad things, then you get that false teaching wounds people. It damages them. It corrupts and contaminates the way that they think and feel, what they value, what they fear, what makes them angry, and what they anticipate in the future.

Oh, how we wish that those who have been wounded by the way false teachers repeatedly deceive them would turn to find healing and truth from the only God who can provide it to them. But human hearts can be so very hard.

> The rest of mankind, who were not killed by these plagues, did not repent of the works of their hands nor give up worshiping demons and idols of gold and silver and bronze and stone and wood, which cannot see or hear or walk, nor did they repent of their murders or their sorceries or their sexual immorality or their thefts. (Rev. 9:20–21)

Two times we read that they did not repent. They witness death and destruction on a massive scale, yet their hearts are as hard as a rock. "They refuse to turn from the very things that ruin their lives."[7] The trumpets have been blasting in the form of preliminary and partial judgments, warning them of the final judgment, but they love their lives and their lies, their hate and their evil, and their sexual freedom

---

7   James M. Hamilton, *Revelation: The Spirit Speaks to the Churches* (Wheaton, IL: Crossway, 2012), 216.

and pursuit of wealth too much to turn toward Christ in repentance and faith.

Warning: Witnesses!

The purpose of these six trumpets has been to warn a pagan and idolatrous world that judgment is coming. Every possible chance for repentance has been given. But it doesn't work. Which raises questions: How will anyone be brought to repentance in a world filled with so much disappointment, destruction, and death? Is it even possible? What are citizens of the kingdom of heaven to do during this in-between time in a world that seems to have no hope? The answer is found in chapters 10 and 11.

The blowing of the six trumpets has led us up to the moment of final judgment, but here in chapter 10 a pause has been put on the drama as John sees "another mighty angel" (v. 1) coming down from heaven, with " a little scroll open in his hand" (v. 2), who says that when the seventh trumpet is sounded, "the mystery of God would be fulfilled, just as he announced to his servants the prophets" (v. 7). What is this mystery that the Old and New Testament prophets wrote about that is about to be fulfilled? It is the mystery of the way in which God's promise to Abraham, that in him all the nations would be blessed (Gen. 18:18; cf. Gal. 3:8), would be fulfilled. It's the mystery Paul described as "the mystery of his will, according to his purpose, which he set forth in Christ as a plan for the fullness of time, to unite all things in him, things in heaven and things on earth" (Eph. 1:9–10). It's the mystery of the gospel (Eph. 6:19).

Then the voice that I had heard from heaven spoke to me again, saying, "Go, take the scroll that is open in the hand of the angel who is standing on the sea and on the land." So I went to the angel and told him to give me the little scroll. And he said to me, "Take and eat it; it will make your stomach bitter, but in your mouth it will be sweet as honey." And I took the little scroll from the hand of the angel and ate it. It was sweet as honey in my mouth, but when I had eaten it my stomach was made bitter. And I was told, "You must again prophesy about many peoples and nations and languages and kings." (Rev. 10:8–11)

How is it that amongst all of the hard-hearted people of the world that God will create a people for himself from many peoples and nations and languages and kings? Evidently the warnings of the trumpets are not enough. Fear of judgment is not enough to make a spiritually dead person spiritually alive. But in his wise plan, God has ordained to use the gospel witness of ordinary people who have found satisfaction and security in Christ. They have faced disaster and evil and death in this life, but instead of being destroyed by it, they have been sanctified by it. Instead of living as a slave to a king who is bent on tormenting them, they live as sons and daughters of a king who is committed to treasure and protect them. And they just can't keep from talking about it.

This good news of the gospel is what nourishes and sustains them. It works its way through them and can't help but pour out of them to anyone and everyone who will listen. It is a message of comfort and assurance to those who believe. But it is a message of bitter consequences for those who refuse to embrace it. And those who are witnessing to them feel this bitterness. They take no pleasure in the coming destruction of those who reject the gospel.

> Then I was given a measuring rod like a staff, and I was told, "Rise and measure the temple of God and the altar and those who worship there, but do not measure the court outside the temple; leave that out, for it is given over to the nations, and they will trample the holy city for forty-two months. And I will grant authority to my two witnesses, and they will prophesy for 1,260 days, clothed in sackcloth." (Rev. 11:1–3)

Earlier John described the church on earth like an army of 144,000 and the church in heaven as a great multitude that can't be counted. In these verses, 11:1–3, he describes the church again, this time in terms of the people of God as the temple. He is told to measure the temple, which is similar to the earlier counting and sealing. It is an indication of God's protection over his people.

He also sees those outside the temple, those outside of Christ, who are not neutral regarding Jesus and his people. They will do everything they can to silence these witnesses. According to this vision, they will do so for forty-two months, or 1,260 days (11:2–3), which represents the entire time in between the ascension and return of Christ. Rather than read this as a literal number of months or days, we should recognize that John is actually communicating what this time will be like, not how long it will last. He's saying that the entire time in between Jesus's ascension and his return will be a time of persecution.

We've seen that John leans heavily into the story of Israel in the Old Testament and in the prophets. So it shouldn't surprise us that Israel's story might help us to interpret his meaning here. If we consider that Israel journeyed in the wilderness for two years before they were judged for disobedience and told that they would spend forty years wandering, we see that God's people spent forty-two years journeying from Egypt to the promised land, a time of testing. Later we discover that when Elijah prayed for the heavens to be shut over Israel because of idolatry, there was no rain for three and a half years (Luke 4:25). "This period seems to be associated with a time of rebellion during which God's faithful people are protected in the midst of trials."[8] This same time period of three and a half years is also significant in the book of Daniel, as it is the period of time given for the tribulation of the Jews under Antiochus Epiphanes, an intense period of suffering through which God's people emerged victorious. So whenever we read about forty-two months or 1,260 days, or three and a half years in Revelation, we should think of it as a period of testing or suffering, which is overseen and limited by God and from which God's people will emerge as overcomers.

Who are these two witnesses who will prophesy during this time? They are those Jesus spoke of at his ascension when he said to his

8   Richard D. Phillips, *Revelation*, Reformed Expository Commentary (Phillipsburg, NJ: P&R, 2000), 313.

gathered disciples: "Repentance for the forgiveness of sins should be proclaimed in his name to all nations, beginning from Jerusalem. You are witnesses of these things" (Luke 24:47–48). Why are there two? Because in John's day testimony was confirmed by having two witnesses.

> These are the two olive trees and the two lampstands that stand before the Lord of the earth. And if anyone would harm them, fire pours from their mouth and consumes their foes. If anyone would harm them, this is how he is doomed to be killed. They have the power to shut the sky, that no rain may fall during the days of their prophesying, and they have power over the waters to turn them into blood and to strike the earth with every kind of plague, as often as they desire. (Rev. 11:4–6)

The two witnesses and the two olive trees and the two lampstands all refer to the same thing—the church, those who have experienced new life in Christ and faithfully testify to it. These witnesses are telling the truth that the world needs to hear.

When he describes fire from their mouths and rain not falling, John is likely alluding to what happened in 2 Kings 1:10–14 when the prophet Elijah called down fire from heaven to consume soldiers who had been sent to arrest him. Here is heaven's perspective on the power of the gospel we proclaim. It may seem weak or foolish, but in reality the word of God proclaimed by the witnesses has incredible power.

> When they have finished their testimony, the beast that rises from the bottomless pit will make war on them and conquer them and kill them, and their dead bodies will lie in the street of the great city that symbolically is called Sodom and Egypt, where their Lord was crucified. For three and a half days some from the peoples and tribes and languages and nations will gaze at their dead bodies and refuse to let them be placed in a tomb, and those who dwell on the earth will rejoice over them and make merry and exchange presents, because

these two prophets had been a torment to those who dwell on the earth. But after the three and a half days a breath of life from God entered them, and they stood up on their feet, and great fear fell on those who saw them. Then they heard a loud voice from heaven saying to them, "Come up here!" And they went up to heaven in a cloud, and their enemies watched them. (Rev. 11:7–12)

The world will find the witness of the church a torment. They won't want to hear it—so much so that they will do the same thing that was done to Jesus to those who testify to him. They will kill them. Then they'll celebrate the fact that the witnesses are dead. But that won't be the end, because resurrection day will come. The day will come when "a breath of life from God" will enter into all who have died in Christ and for Christ.

Can you see that John has gone out of his way to make the story of these witnesses sound like the story of Jesus? They suffer like Jesus and are raised to heaven like Jesus. The intended message to those in the first century who heard Revelation read to them and the message to us is the same. We should expect to suffer like Jesus. But we can also expect to be raised like Jesus.

We know that what John saw in this apocalyptic vision is exactly what the churches in Asia were about to experience. They would be given great power to witness, and they would be trampled for it, fed to the lions for it, and lit on fire as torches for it. But we also know that rather than silencing the church, this persecution invigorated the church and her witness so that early church father Tertullian would write in the second century that "the blood of the martyrs is the seed of the church."[9]

At that hour there was a great earthquake, and a tenth of the city fell. Seven thousand people were killed in the earthquake, and the rest were terrified and gave glory to the God of heaven. (Rev. 11:13)

9   Quintus Septimius Florens Tertullianus, *Apologeticus*, L.13.

Isaiah, Amos, and the writer of 1 Kings write about events in which a tenth, or seven thousand people, were spared when the judgment wiped out the majority. John seems to have this in mind but flips it on his head, writing that only a tenth suffer judgment while the rest are terrified and give glory to God.

It may be that what John witnessed when he sees "the rest" who are terrified and give glory to the God of heaven is simply what Paul wrote about when he says that "every knee should bow . . . and every tongue confess that Jesus Christ is Lord, to the glory of God the Father" (Phil. 2:10–11). Paul seems to be describing a day when every human will bow before Jesus regardless of whether or not they have called upon him for salvation. In other words, it may be that mention of those giving glory to the God of heaven here in Revelation 11 is an acknowledgment of God's rule that comes too late. Nowhere else in Revelation do we find anything that appears to be a conversion of many believers immediately prior to Christ's coming.

But throughout the book of Revelation, giving God glory refers to a right response to God of true worship. So it seems more likely that this reflects the effective outcome of the trampling and testimony of the witnessing church. While many will refuse to repent as they experience the precursors of the final judgment in the first six trumpets, there will be some who will listen to the message of the gospel declared by the witnessing church. The threat of judgment by itself won't be enough to cause rebellious people to repent, as the judgments themselves do not convey God's gracious willingness to forgive those who repent. Fear of judgment must be met with the truth of the gospel. The Spirit uses that declared word to go to work on hard hearts, replacing them with hearts of flesh that are responsive to the grace of God.

Some people say that talk is cheap, meaning that it is easy to say something instead of doing something. But clearly this talk is not cheap. The gospel declaration of these witnesses is costly. They pay for their words with their lives. But their witness is also profitable. There is a return on the investment of their gospel witness in the form of repentance and faith by some who listen to their message. Another thing people sometimes say is, "Preach the gospel, and if necessary use words," a quote that is falsely attributed to Saint Francis of Assisi. But the book of Revelation will have nothing to do with that. The gospel cannot be declared without words. The gospel is an announcement of what Jesus Christ has done in history to make it possible for the worst of sinners, the most dedicated of idolaters, to be given new spiritual life.

What is amazing is that while most of the world will not heed the warnings presented in the precursors to the final judgment, represented in the first six trumpets, some will listen to ordinary people who are willing to be trampled as they offer a clear testimony to the person and work of Christ in their generation.

In John's day, and in our day as well, the church often looks weak, backward, compromised, and sometimes just like the world around it. But amazingly the church is God's instrument for calling a dying world to a place of safety. And while it may appear at times that the church has been silenced and defeated, those apparent defeats are only temporary because of God's resurrection power, which is what we see when the seventh trumpet is blown.

Warning: Destruction!

Then the seventh angel blew his trumpet, and there were loud voices in heaven, saying, "The kingdom of the world has become the kingdom of our Lord and of his Christ, and he shall reign forever and ever." And the twenty-four elders who sit on their thrones before God fell on their faces and worshiped God, saying,

"We give thanks to you, Lord God Almighty,
     who is and who was,
for you have taken your great power
     and begun to reign.
The nations raged,
     but your wrath came,
     and the time for the dead to be judged,

and for rewarding your servants, the prophets and saints,
  and those who fear your name,
  both small and great,
and for destroying the destroyers of the earth."

Then God's temple in heaven was opened, and the ark of his covenant was seen within his temple. There were flashes of lightning,
rumblings, peals of thunder, an earthquake, and heavy hail. (Rev.
11:15–19)

Just as the trumpets on the seventh day brought down the walls of
Jericho so that God's people could take possession of the land that God
was giving to them (Josh. 6:20), when the seventh trumpet of heaven
blows, the pilgrimage of God's persecuted people will be complete. We
will take possession of the land that God has promised to us. He will
have cleansed his land and destroyed its destroyers. His enemies will
have experienced his wrath, and his servants will receive their reward.
The ark of his covenant, which throughout the Old Testament has
always represented his presence, will be within his temple. In other
words, he will come to dwell among his people.

All of those who ignored the warnings, who raged against the God
of heaven, who hardened their hearts against the God of grace, who
rejected and sought to silence the gospel of grace declared by God's
people, will finally and fully receive what they rightly deserve. And all
who have come under King Jesus will enter into the blessing that Jesus
deserves yet has been granted to us by grace.

Hearing and Keeping Revelation 8–11

So what are the implications of these seven trumpets for you and me?
What is it going to look like for us to hear and keep these chapters and
thereby experience the promised blessing of this book?

If you are outside of Christ, the most important response to the
blowing of these trumpets of warning is to respond to that warning by
running to Christ. Don't be one of those people who spends a lifetime

ignoring the warnings of God's judgment as well as the witness of God's people to the grace and mercy to be found in Christ.

If you are in Christ, recognize that all of the partial precursors to the final judgment presented in the first six trumpets are not falling on you. You don't have to be afraid of what is presented in them. And the reason you don't have to be afraid is that you have a source of security and satisfaction that "those who dwell on the earth" simply don't have. If you are in Christ, then by definition you no longer belong to the world. You no longer expect that it will satisfy and sustain you. You have a resource for resisting the devil and a source of truth in your life that will protect you from his deception. You have been sealed to Christ by the Holy Spirit, and as you resist the devil, you will find that he flees from you (James 4:7).

If you are in Christ, you have a calling, a purpose, and a reason to keep getting up in the morning in a dark world. We have good news to share with people who have no hope of escaping the grip of the deception of the devil and the false promises of the world apart from the power of the gospel.

We have good news of a king who entered into this world with its legions of demons and exercised his power over them. Jesus encountered a legion of demons inhabiting a man, tormenting him so intensely that the man lived among the tombs and cut himself to try to find relief from the torment. A short time later the same man was clothed instead of naked, calm instead of crazed, at peace instead of in agony. This is what Jesus offers to all who are tormented by the power of sin. He restores. He heals.

Here is the good news we have to declare to a hard-hearted world: *When the world seems to be falling down around you, you can enjoy complete security. You can escape the grip of evil that only torments and takes from you. You can come under a king who will love and bless you rather than deceive and wound you. He will take away your hard heart and give you a new heart that is soft and responsive to his offer of grace and mercy.*

The world may or may not listen to us. It may trample on all of our good intentions and carefully chosen and presented words. But while some will seek to silence us, others will listen to us. Some will repent. Some will come to fear the God of heaven and give him glory. And when the final trumpet blows, they too will find themselves among the servants, the prophets, and the saints who fear his name and will enjoy his presence forever.

Whenever we are tempted to give way to fear as the world around us threatens to trample us, we have a refuge. We find refuge in the one who allowed this world to trample him, who gave himself over to death. After three days the breath of life entered into him. He rose from the dead and ascended into heaven where he sits at the right hand of God the Father. He has walked this road before us. He will walk this road with us. He will breathe his resurrection life into us. He will come to reign with us and to reward us. When the seventh trumpet blows, we will not regret what our witness for him might have cost us. We will forever enjoy what our witness for him will have gained for us. We will find ourselves forever blessed by his reward given to us and his presence with us.

7

Blessed by Living and Dying in Jesus

Revelation 12–14

IT WAS PAINFUL and in some ways perplexing to read, a social media post by someone who had pastored a large church and written a number of best-selling books:

> I have undergone a massive shift in regard to my faith in Jesus. The popular phrase for this is "deconstruction," the biblical phrase is "falling away." By all the measurements that I have for defining a Christian, I am not a Christian. Many people tell me that there is a different way to practice faith and I want to remain open to this, but I'm not there now.[1]

I pray this is not the end of the story. But it is the story of so many people in our day. Of course, it has been the story of many people over the centuries, but our share-everything-on-the-Internet age seems to make it more visible and in some ways more acceptable, even admirable, affirmed for its "authenticity" and "courage."

What causes a person who has called him- or herself a Christian to fall away? Often it's because his or her confidence in the Bible as the

1 Josh Harris (@harrisjosh), "I have undergone a massive shift in regard to my faith in Jesus." *Instagram*, July 26, 2019, https://www.instagram.com.

word of God has come into question. Sometimes it is because of doubts about the Bible's teachings about hell, offense over penal substitutionary atonement, unsatisfying answers to questions about the suffering in the world, and disgust or disagreement with the institutional church. But according to one Pew study, the vast majority—71 percent—of people who leave the faith of their childhood today do so because "they gradually drifted away."[2] There weren't huge barriers to belief. They weren't angry with God. They didn't have huge intellectual objections to Christian beliefs and practices. They just drifted away.

It is into this reality that the book of Revelation speaks. Through John's vision in Revelation, we're able to see what is really underneath and behind our culture's encouragement of doubt, its questioning of the Bible's teaching and the Bible itself, as well as what seems to be a natural tendency to drift. Actually, there is something or someone supernatural at work. Underneath and behind it all is an enemy. And not just *an* enemy, *your* enemy.

In Revelation 12 through 14, the curtain is drawn back for us so that we can see the unseen reality of a war that took place in heaven, and a war taking place right now in this world and in your life, whether you realize it or not. You see, you have an enemy who is engaged in a war for your soul. His goal is to alienate you from Christ and claim you as his own. It's not that he cares about you. He has no good intentions toward you. He simply wants to use you in his futile attempt to defeat God.

Your enemy wants to convince you that Jesus really isn't worth your allegiance or obedience. He wants to convince you that the things and experiences and ideologies of this world are what will make you happy. Of course, his promises of pleasure and comfort have an expiration date. They're limited to this lifetime. What happens beyond that, he'd rather not talk about. That's part of his scheme—to convince people that this life is all there is so they should make the most of it.

These chapters in Revelation include a repeated refrain for those of us who are under constant attack from this enemy, a repeated call

2   "Faith in Flux," Pew Research Center, April 27, 2009 (rev. February 2021), https://www.pew forum.org.

intended to keep us alert, to keep us in the fight against the schemes of our enemy. It is a call to endurance and faith.

As soon as we hear it, we realize we've heard it before in this letter. It was there in the first chapter when John described himself to those he was writing to as their "brother and partner in the tribulation and the kingdom and the patient endurance that are in Jesus." In the letters to the seven churches, we heard him affirm those who were patiently enduring. And, if you will remember, in the first chapter I suggested that if someone were to ask you what the book of Revelation is about, you could tell them that Revelation is a call to patient endurance of tribulation as we await the coming of Christ's kingdom in all of its fullness. In this interlude between the seven trumpets and the seven bowls, John is coming back to the primary aim of his letter—to call believers to patient endurance. Or we could say that here in the middle of the book, he is connecting his call to patient endurance to what makes this call necessary: the significant pressure being placed on us by the enemy of our souls to keep us from it. He wants us to understand what we're up against and what is at stake if we become complacent, indifferent, or casual about our allegiance to Jesus. He wants us to see the tactics our enemy uses to seek to untether us from Christ and, in the process, to woo us to himself.

Of course, none of us think we're vulnerable to transferring our allegiance to Satan. But, you see, most who have given their allegiance to him are completely unaware that is what they've done. They would never describe it in those terms. They think of themselves as non-religious, good neighbors, patriots, committed professionals, change agents in their churches, and truth tellers in society. They don't recognize that primary allegiance to anything other than Christ, to be defined by and supremely devoted to any cause or organization or ideology other than Christ, is to be marked by that beast rather than marked and sealed for Christ by the Holy Spirit.

We might not be able to see this. That's why we need Revelation. John was allowed to see what is taking place in the world from the vantage point of heaven and told to write it down for us. He was allowed to see what we can't see with our human eyes so that we will know and reckon with the reality of the cleverly disguised evil in the world and its intentions for us.

Your Enemy

By this point, we shouldn't be surprised that John uses figurative symbolism to expose the true nature of our enemy. And we also shouldn't be surprised that the Old Testament is our guide to rightly interpreting his symbolism.

> A great sign appeared in heaven: a woman clothed with the sun, with the moon under her feet, and on her head a crown of twelve stars. She was pregnant and was crying out in birth pains and the agony of giving birth. (Rev. 12:1–2)

The sun, the moon and stars. Have we heard this somewhere before in the Bible—a dream or vision that included the sun, the moon, and stars that might help us to determine who this woman is? How about the dream that Joseph had in which the sun, the moon, and eleven stars, which represented his father, mother, and brothers, were bowing down to him? This was the family that became the twelve patriarchs. So who is this woman? This woman represents the covenant community, the twelve tribes out of whom is born the messianic Savior.

> Another sign appeared in heaven: behold, a great red dragon, with seven heads and ten horns, and on his heads seven diadems. His tail swept down a third of the stars of heaven and cast them to the earth. And the dragon stood before the woman who was about to give birth, so that when she bore her child he might devour it. (Rev. 12:3–4)

Notice that this dragon has seven heads and ten horns and seven diadems on his heads. This is telling us that he is powerful and has a universal reach. Richard Phillips says, "These are not like the laurel crown of victory worn by the woman but are crowns of his usurped earthly dominion. His crowns are the iron crowns of tyranny."[3] The identity of the dragon is made clear in 12:9, where we read that the dragon is "that ancient serpent, who is called the devil and Satan."

This dragon is pictured hovering around the woman, who is about to give birth, with the intention of devouring the baby as soon as it is born. We immediately think of Mary. And certainly there is a sense in which Mary is being pictured here. But there is more to this. We should probably think first of Eve. Remember what God said to the ancient serpent in the garden of Eden after he deceived Eve and seduced Adam into sin? He said he would put enmity, or conflict, between the offspring of the woman and the serpent but the outcome of the conflict would never be in doubt (see Gen. 3:15). An offspring of this woman would one day crush the head of the ancient serpent. When Cain killed Abel, it was Satan at work (Gen. 4:8). When Pharaoh gave the order for all of the Hebrew children to be drowned in the Nile River (Ex. 1:16), he was simply an instrument of Satan, hovering and seeking to devour. As Saul chased after David, Satan was energizing his murderous jealousy (1 Sam. 18–24). When Haman sent out the edict that on a certain day all of the people in the kingdom were to rise up and kill the Jews throughout the Persian Empire (Est. 3:6), he was simply an agent of the dragon seeking to destroy the offspring of the woman. And when Herod considered the report of the wise men seeking "he who has been born king of the Jews" (Matt. 2:2), and ordered that all of the male children born in Bethlehem should be killed, it was Satan-inspired slaughter. Ever since Eden, Satan has sought to destroy the promised child before that child puts an end to his dominion of evil.

> She gave birth to a male child, one who is to rule all the nations with a rod of iron, but her child was caught up to God and to his throne, and the woman fled into the wilderness, where she has a place prepared by God, in which she is to be nourished for 1,260 days. (Rev. 12:5–6)

3 Phillips, *Revelation*, 346.

John writes that this child is the "one who is to rule all the nations with a rod of iron." And that phrase should sound familiar. It comes from Psalm 2, which speaks of God's king, God's Son, to whom God will give the nations and the ends of the earth. So this single sentence of Revelation 12:5–6 traces the events from Jesus's birth all the way to his resurrection and ascension and through to the throne in heaven and his reign from heaven until he returns to this earth, which John symbolizes using 1,260 days (which is the same as the three and a half years and forty-two months used elsewhere to refer to this same period of time). During this period of time God's people will be cared for, or nourished, as they await his return.

Next John comes back to what Jesus accomplished in his death and resurrection. And we realize that in those events, something was happening, not simply on a hill outside of Jerusalem but in heaven itself:

> Now war arose in heaven, Michael and his angels fighting against the dragon. And the dragon and his angels fought back, but he was defeated, and there was no longer any place for them in heaven. And the great dragon was thrown down, that ancient serpent, who is called the devil and Satan, the deceiver of the whole world—he was thrown down to the earth, and his angels were thrown down with him. And I heard a loud voice in heaven, saying, "Now the salvation and the power and the kingdom of our God and the authority of his Christ have come, for the accuser of our brothers has been thrown down, who accuses them day and night before our God. (Rev. 12:7–10)

Speaking about his coming death on the cross, Jesus had said, "Now will the ruler of this world be cast out" (John 12:31). And that's exactly what happened when Jesus made his declaration from the cross, "It is finished" (John 19:30). In Colossians, Paul describes the connection between what happened at Calvary and what took place in heaven as "God canceling the record of debt that stood against us with its legal demands. This he set aside, nailing it to the cross. He disarmed the rulers and authorities and put them to open shame, by triumphing over them in him" (Col. 2:14–15). Jesus's atoning death put an end to Satan's right to stand in the throne room of heaven and list out all of the reasons why you and I deserve to be punished for our sins. On that day the accuser was thrown out, ejected from heaven.

Now maybe the idea that Satan was ever in the throne room of heaven sounds strange to you. But think back to the book of Job. What happened there at the beginning of his story? We read that "there was a day when the sons of God came to present themselves before the LORD, and Satan also came among them" (Job 1:6). What was Satan there to do? He was there to accuse. His accusation that day was essentially, "Your servant Job doesn't really love you for you. He's only using you to get all of the comforts you provide to him. If you take those away, he will curse you to your face."

There's a sense in which, if we're honest, we realize that it makes perfect sense that someone would be before the throne of God pointing out the evil deeds of humanity. We know what humanity has done throughout the ages. More than that, we know what we have done throughout our lifetimes. The devil had a good argument and ground to stand on until Jesus dealt with the very real guilt of the elect at the cross. From then on, the accuser had no case. He's been barred from any future appearances, thrown out of the courts of heaven.

His weapon of condemnation has been taken away. His power has been limited. Or, as we'll read later in Revelation, he has been bound (20:2). But he is on a very long leash. He still has a measure of power that God has granted to him in the realm to which he has been relegated. He has no more influence in heaven but plenty of influence on this earth. He's still a roaring lion, still seeking to devour (1 Pet. 5:8). His focus has turned away from devouring Jesus and toward devouring Jesus's people. He has declared war on all who have been joined to Christ by faith. If that is you, you are on his hit list. He's out to destroy you. He wants to fill you with doubts about the reliability of the Bible and about the work of Christ. He wants to turn things upside down so that what is evil will appear to be morally good and right, and what is holy and just will appear to be outdated, irrelevant, ridiculous, even immoral. And if that doesn't work, he wants to deaden you to the things of God so that you will simply drift away.

But that doesn't have to happen. He can be conquered:

> And they have conquered him by the blood of the Lamb and by the word of their testimony, for they loved not their lives even unto death. Therefore, rejoice, O heavens and you who dwell in them! But woe to you, O earth and sea, for the devil has come down to you in great wrath, because he knows that his time is short! (Rev. 12:11–12)

"And they have conquered him." I wonder how these words hit the friends of Antipas in the church in Pergamum when they heard them. Earlier in Revelation 2, John was told to write to the church in Pergamum, "I know where you dwell, where Satan's throne is. Yet you hold fast my name, and you did not deny my faith even in the days of Antipas my faithful witness, who was killed among you, where Satan dwells" (Rev. 2:13). Did they think to themselves, "Is that what you mean by conquering? Because when he was killed, it seemed like defeat."

The message of Revelation to them and to you and me is this: Yes, doing battle against the devil may mean that you lose a lot in this life. You might lose your reputation, your friends, your job. You might even lose your life. But to live and die in the Lord will turn out for your blessing. To live your days on this earth all out for Christ, no matter what assault the devil sends your way, is true victory, not defeat. You won't regret it. Your life won't be over. You will awake to find yourself among the many who have laid down their lives for the gospel before you. Jesus himself will comfort and reward you.

> And when the dragon saw that he had been thrown down to the earth, he pursued the woman who had given birth to the male child. But the woman was given the two wings of the great eagle so that she might fly from the serpent into the wilderness, to the place where she is to be nourished for a time, and times, and half a time. The serpent poured water like a river out of his mouth after the woman,

to sweep her away with a flood. But the earth came to the help of the woman, and the earth opened its mouth and swallowed the river that the dragon had poured from his mouth. Then the dragon became furious with the woman and went off to make war on the rest of her offspring, on those who keep the commandments of God and hold to the testimony of Jesus. And he stood on the sand of the sea. (Rev. 12:13–17)

Here's the picture: the woman is carried on the wings of an eagle into the wilderness to be nourished. This is the people of God living as strangers and aliens in this world in the time between the ascension and the return of Christ. They haven't been abandoned. Jesus promised when he left that he would be with them (Matt. 28:20). And he is keeping the promise. He is with them, nourishing them for "a time, and times, and half a time" (which equals three and a half years, forty-two months, and 1,260 days). This symbolizes the entire time between the ascension and the return of Jesus, when Jesus provides spiritual protection for his people who are enduring tribulation and persecution. During this time, the Spirit will be at work in and through them.

The picture also includes the dragon standing on the edge of the sea. Throughout the Bible the sea is a place of chaos and evil. And here is the dragon, standing on the sand of the sea, preparing to bring evil out of the sea in the form of a beast:

And I saw a beast rising out of the sea, with ten horns and seven heads, with ten diadems on its horns and blasphemous names on its heads. And the beast that I saw was like a leopard; its feet were like a bear's, and its mouth was like a lion's mouth. And to it the dragon gave his power and his throne and great authority. (Rev. 13:1–2)

This imagery of a beast is strange to us, but it shouldn't be unfamiliar if we know our Bible. It certainly would not have been strange to John's first readers. The prophet Daniel wrote about four beasts that represented consecutive world powers over history—the empires of

Babylon, Persia, Greece, and then Rome (Dan. 7:1–8). Like Daniel's fourth beast, which represented imperial Rome, the beast here in Revelation has ten horns (Dan. 7:7). John is portraying the Roman Empire as a grotesque monster whose authority has been granted by Satan.

While the imagery of beasts may have been familiar to John's first readers, they might not have seen the Roman Empire in this way at this point in time. Some of the churches had seen the beastly nature of Rome up close, but other churches in cities such as Laodicea and Thyatira likely enjoyed being part of the empire. They had made themselves at home in the empire and were enjoying its perks. They couldn't see the evil lurking underneath. They needed to have the curtain drawn back so they could see its true nature and intentions. They needed to see that Rome was demanding the kind of loyalty that belongs to God alone and that becoming too comfortable with all that Rome had to offer would lure them into spiritual compromise. By using the imagery of a beast to refer to Rome and its rule over the world, John showed that "from God's vantage point, [Rome] was a ravaging and idolatrous animal, and its power comes from Satan."[4]

Of course, when we read about this beast, we should see that it also represents world systems and governments in our own day that are hostile to the people of God. The devil's tactics are similar in every age. Just think of what it is like today to be identified with Christ under the governments of North Korea, China, or Iran. There are many parts of the world in which the governmental system is clearly beastlike. But perhaps it isn't just out there somewhere. The beast is out to divert our loyalties away from Jesus as our only hope and toward the state and its policies and programs as our best and only hope. Perhaps we should be willing to recognize this power at work closer to home. This first beast represents governmental tyranny throughout history working against Christ and his church. It is political and governmental powers demanding the loyalty that belongs to Christ alone. Because this beast is so devious, we don't always recognize the work of the beast for the

4   Thomas Schreiner, *The Joy of Hearing* (Wheaton, IL: Crossway, 2021), 29.

tyranny it is. Sometimes the evil of political, social, and economic entities is subtle. Instead of appearing beastly, it appears beautiful. Instead
of outright persecution, its ideas and actions are much more subtle,
yet equally as evil. They are beastlike in the way they demand loyalty
to their philosophies, language, sexual ethics, priorities, and methods.

> One of its heads seemed to have a mortal wound, but its mortal
> wound was healed, and the whole earth marveled as they followed the
> beast. And they worshiped the dragon, for he had given his authority
> to the beast. (Rev. 13:3–4a)

This beast has a wound that is healed. The dragon has given him authority. It sounds something like the experience of Jesus and the relationship between God the Father and the Son, doesn't it? The devil is not
original. Satan, or the dragon, is preeminently a counterfeit of God
the Father while the beast from the sea presents himself to the world
as a counterfeit Christ. He is an unholy warrior opposed to Christ, the
holy warrior. Vern Poythress writes:

> He has a counterfeit resurrection in the form of a mortal wound that
> was healed (Rev. 13:3). . . . The dragon gives the beast "his power and
> his throne and great authority" just as the Father gives the Son his
> authority (John 5:22–27). Worship of the dragon and the beast go
> together (13:4), just as worship of the Father and the Son go together
> (John 5:23). The beast claims universal allegiance from all nations
> (13:7), just as Christ is Lord over all nations (7:9–10).[5]

By presenting the person and work of Satan in this way, John is
setting before his first readers the question, Which one will you serve?
From which will you draw your life, your identity, your satisfaction,
your security? He's setting the question before us too. We would like
to think that we can add some Christian faith on top of our ordinary

5 Vern Poythress, "Counterfeiting in the Book of Revelation as a Perspective on Non-Christian
Culture," *Journal of the Evangelical Theological Society* 40/3 (1997): 411–18.

middle-class life. But we can't. We want to think that we can have a consuming loyalty to our country or party or tribe while maintaining our supreme loyalty to Christ. But we can't. Either we follow the Lamb wherever he goes, or we will end up following the beast. This is what the people of the earth do in this vision.

> They worshiped the beast, saying, "Who is like the beast, and who can fight against it?" (Rev. 13:4)

This is an interesting response to the beast on several accounts. First, we're a bit surprised that the beast would be worshiped. He seems grotesque. Yet we know that "the most despicable tyrants have often been extremely popular and have elicited virtual worship from their people."[6] Clearly the beast has a blinding power so that people are blinded to his evil and at the same time blinded to the beauty of Christ.

The second interesting aspect of the response of the people to the beast is their sense of inevitability. "Who can fight against it?" they ask (13:4). There's no use putting up a fight. Of course, that's exactly what the beast wants us to think. Whenever we're battling against sin, he whispers in our ear, "Resistance is useless. This is just who you are. You were made this way. You can't help it. Besides, it's not that big of a deal." This is when we simply must listen to another voice, the voice of the Scriptures in which we're told, "Submit yourselves therefore to God. Resist the devil, and he will flee from you. Draw near to God, and he will draw near to you. Cleanse your hands, you sinners, and purify your hearts, you double-minded" (James 4:7–8).

> And the beast was given a mouth uttering haughty and blasphemous words, and it was allowed to exercise authority for forty-two months. It opened its mouth to utter blasphemies against God, blaspheming his name and his dwelling, that is, those who dwell in heaven. Also

6   Phillips, *Revelation*, 368.

it was allowed to make war on the saints and to conquer them. And authority was given it over every tribe and people and language and nation, and all who dwell on earth will worship it, everyone whose name has not been written before the foundation of the world in the book of life of the Lamb who was slain. If anyone has an ear, let him hear:

> If anyone is to be taken captive,
>   to captivity he goes;
> if anyone is to be slain with the sword,
>   with the sword must he be slain.

Here is a call for the endurance and faith of the saints. (Rev. 13: 5–10)

We would really like for this to read differently. We don't particularly like it when we read that the beast, "was allowed to make war on the saints and to conquer them." We want to conquer, not be conquered. And Revelation has been making some hefty promises to those who conquer. So what do we do with that?

What we must understand is that the way we as believers conquer is by laying down our lives. Everything in this world and even the internal voice we have inside us tells us to preserve our lives at all costs. This is why we need this revelation, this word from Jesus to us. The Lamb is calling us to love him more than we love our own lives. He's calling us to endure to the end, whether that end is a peaceful death in our bed at home surrounded by our loved ones or a violent death at the hands of a Satan-inspired persecutor.

So we've seen two members of an unholy trinity, the dragon and the beast from the sea. Now we see the third, the beast from the earth, who is a counterfeit Holy Spirit:

> Then I saw another beast rising out of the earth. It had two horns like a lamb and it spoke like a dragon. It exercises all the authority of

the first beast in its presence, and makes the earth and its inhabitants worship the first beast, whose mortal wound was healed. It performs great signs, even making fire come down from heaven to earth in front of people, and by the signs that it is allowed to work in the presence of the beast it deceives those who dwell on earth, telling them to make an image for the beast that was wounded by the sword and yet lived. And it was allowed to give breath to the image of the beast, so that the image of the beast might even speak and might cause those who would not worship the image of the beast to be slain. (Rev. 13:11–15)

We could think of this beast from the earth as the deceitful propaganda machine for the beast from the sea. "Whereas the first beast relied mainly on power, the second beast supports him with lies."[7] His lies produce false religion. And not just religion as we might define it, but also the political and social ideologies that have essentially become a religion to so many. We are surrounded by the voice of this beast in government, media, and entertainment that touts progress beyond the narrow thinking of the Bible, the God of the Bible, its message of salvation and judgment, and its call to holy living.

Notice that this land beast speaks like the great red dragon introduced in chapter 12. In other words, he speaks with authority, but what he says isn't true. He deceives. He tells people to give allegiance to the beast from the sea. He uses his words and his seemingly miraculous signs to make the first beast seem believable and credible. He gives religious backing to political entities that are actually out to diminish and destroy the things and people of God. Whenever a pulpit is used to point to the state as our hope and salvation rather than Christ alone as our hope and salvation, we're hearing the voice of this beast. Whenever a pulpit is used to encourage compromise with culture so that our Christianity will be accepted or even applauded, we're hearing the voice of this beast.

7 Phillips, *Revelation*, 376.

Remember that he is a counterfeit of the Holy Spirit. We know that the Spirit uses his power to seal us to Christ. Similarly, this land beast seeks to seal or mark people, to bind them to and identify them with the first beast. And with this, we've finally come to this image in Revelation that has created so much confusion, speculation, and anxiety for so many—the mark of the beast. Yet when we read it in context of the whole of Revelation, isn't it abundantly clear what is being communicated to us? Numerous times we've already been shown those who are in Christ being sealed or marked. We read in chapter seven about the servants of God being sealed on their foreheads (7:3), and in chapter nine we read that those who could not be harmed by demonic powers on the earth were those who have the seal of God on their foreheads (9:4). And because we understand that John is writing in symbolic language, we haven't interpreted this as an actual physical mark but as a spiritual mark or seal.

In fact it isn't just in Revelation that we read that those set apart for God have God's name on their foreheads. If we go all the way back to the book of Exodus, we read that the attire of the priests who entered into the presence of God included a turban on which a plate of pure gold was placed, and engraved on it were the words "Holy to the LORD" (Ex. 28:36). This mark or sign worn on the priests' foreheads distinguished them as belonging to, being identified with, set apart for, and in service of the Lord. In the New Testament, those who take hold of Christ and become part of "a holy priesthood" (1 Pet. 2:5) are marked not physically but spiritually. They offer spiritual, not physical, sacrifices. What was physical for the Old Testament–era priests helps us to understand what is spiritual for all who become priests in the new temple of the new creation (which is everyone in Christ). We are sealed or marked as set apart for God by the Holy Spirit. The mark of the beast is figurative language for what marks a person who has a very different loyalty, identity, belonging, and purpose. Their lives reflect, or we could say they are marked by, having given themselves over to this counterfeit trinity.

> Also it causes all, both small and great, both rich and poor, both free
> and slave, to be marked on the right hand or the forehead, so that
> no one can buy or sell unless he has the mark, that is, the name of
> the beast or the number of its name. (Rev. 13:16–17)

In John's day, slaves, soldiers, and devotees of various religions were tat-
tooed, indicating that they were owned by or solely devoted to another.
The mark of the beast is an apocalyptic symbol for belonging as well
as "the state's political and economic 'stamp of approval,' given only
to those who go along with its religious demands."[8] Notice that the
mark is on the hand or the forehead. This is telling us it is about how
these people think, what they value, and what they do with their lives
that marks them out as belonging to the beast instead of the Lamb.
This mark is not a chip implanted in a person's body; it's about their
internal character and commitments being lived out in such a way that
they are marked by them. And what becomes obvious is that there is
no love for Christ and no pursuit of holiness; there's only love for self
and a pursuit of everything this world has to offer.

Notice that verse 16 says that the land beast "causes *all*, both small
and great, both rich and poor, both free and slave, to be marked." Every
person who has ever lived is marked one way or another. Either we are
marked by our belonging and allegiance to Christ, or we are marked by
our belonging and allegiance to his imitator, his counterfeit, the beast.
We would like to think that there is some sort of middle ground, a
way of neutrality for nice but unconvinced people. But there just isn't.

This beast exercises his power not only through government and
religion but also through business. In John's day, it was evidenced in
the requirement of involvement in feasts to idols in order to be in the
trade guilds. For us it may look more like being required to wear a pride
shirt or pin at our workplace or having our business defamed because
of our refusal to give money to certain causes that the beast insists are
good and even moral. For the short term, being identified by, connected

8   G. K. Beale, *The Book of Revelation: A Commentary on the Greek Text*, New International Greek
     Testament Commentary (Grand Rapids, MI: Eerdmans, 1999), 715.

to, or having allegiance to the beast is useful. It will help us network. It will help us fit in. It will help us to keep our job, keep our house, and keep our kids in school and in the latest sneakers. It will put food on the table. So what are we to do when the pressure is on? John tells us:

> This calls for wisdom: let the one who has understanding calculate the number of the beast, for it is the number of a man, and his number is 666. (Rev. 13:18)

To navigate life in a world in which the true nature of governments, politicians, businesses, technologies, organizations, and ideologies is veiled, a world in which an evil power is at work to deceive and a counterfeit savior is demanding allegiance, we need wisdom. In fact, that almost seems like an understatement. We desperately need wisdom. This is why we're so glad to have and to be reading and studying the book of Revelation. In this book, Jesus is pulling back the curtain for us so we can see behind the façade of worldly insight and attractiveness into the true nature of things, so we can see the foolishness and ugliness of this world's systems. We have to "calculate the number of the beast." In other words, we need to evaluate things and ideas carefully. If something is truly of God, it would have to be numbered 777, perfection to the *nth* degree. We need to look and listen carefully in order to recognize what is off, what falls short of the glory of God, what is merely, in fact infinitely, human, which would symbolically be numbered 666.

We also need to look at where being marked by the beast or being marked by Christ will take us, which is where John's vision goes next.

Your Refuge

> Then I looked, and behold, on Mount Zion stood the Lamb, and with him 144,000 who had his name and his Father's name written on their foreheads. And I heard a voice from heaven like the roar of many waters and like the sound of loud thunder. The voice I heard was like the sound of harpists playing on their harps, and they were singing a new song before the throne and before the four living

creatures and before the elders. No one could learn that song except the 144,000 who had been redeemed from the earth. It is these who have not defiled themselves with women, for they are virgins. It is these who follow the Lamb wherever he goes. These have been redeemed from mankind as firstfruits for God and the Lamb, and in their mouth no lie was found, for they are blameless. (Rev. 14:1–5)

Mount Zion, a fortress of safety and security. A place of beauty and joy. A refuge from the inevitable attacks anywhere outside of it. And who is going to live there? Not those whose lives are defined by their love and allegiance to the world, but those whose lives are defined by their love for Christ. The bride who has loved Christ, the bridegroom, exclusively and faithfully, which is what is meant by "have not defiled themselves with women." Those who have followed the Lamb wherever he has taken them, which for many will be down the same path he walked, the path that leads to a cross. Those gathered in Mount Zion will be the "firstfruits" for God. In other words, those who live and die in the Lord are gathered to Christ to await a great and final harvest to come. And as those firstfruits are being gathered, God continues to warn and call those who are tempted to listen to the false gospel of the beast.

> Then I saw another angel flying directly overhead, with an eternal gospel to proclaim to those who dwell on earth, to every nation and tribe and language and people. And he said with a loud voice, "Fear God and give him glory, because the hour of his judgment has come, and worship him who made heaven and earth, the sea and the springs of water." (Rev. 14:6–7)

The hour of judgment coming might not sound like good news. But anyone who has experienced significant injustice, endured living under a corrupt government or in an abusive home, or had their livelihood or innocence taken from them should recognize the incredibly good news that the hour of judgment is truly coming. And there is more good news:

Another angel, a second, followed, saying, "Fallen, fallen is Babylon the great, she who made all nations drink the wine of the passion of her sexual immorality." (Rev. 14:8)

The source of all the ugliness, perversion, and unsatisfying consumerism and consumption that wrecks so many lives will, on that day, lose all of its allure. No longer will it be able to deceive and destroy.

And another angel, a third, followed them, saying with a loud voice, "If anyone worships the beast and its image and receives a mark on his forehead or on his hand, he also will drink the wine of God's wrath, poured full strength into the cup of his anger, and he will be tormented with fire and sulfur in the presence of the holy angels and in the presence of the Lamb. And the smoke of their torment goes up forever and ever, and they have no rest, day or night, these worshipers of the beast and its image, and whoever receives the mark of its name." (Rev. 14:9–11)

What a contrast—verses 1 through 5 showed those who have been marked by Christ enjoying perfect security in Mount Zion, singing and celebrating. And here, in verses 9 to 11, we see all who have been marked by the imposter, all who believed his false promises and fell for his charm, gagging and spitting as they drink the wine of God's wrath. Rather than being comforted by the Lamb, they'll be tormented in the presence of the Lamb. And the torment will never end.

John, by inspiration of the Holy Spirit, pleads with us to live and die in such a way that we can be sure that we will experience the comfort of the Lamb, saying:

Here is a call for the endurance of the saints, those who keep the commandments of God and their faith in Jesus. (Rev. 14:12)

Because of the warnings we've heard from these angelic messengers as well as the promise the Spirit gives to us from heaven, we're prepared, once again, to hear and heed this call to endure, to keep on trusting the promises of God, to keep on pursuing glad obedience to God, to keep on declaring and living out our allegiance to Christ.

> And I heard a voice from heaven saying, "Write this: Blessed are the dead who die in the Lord from now on." "Blessed indeed," says the Spirit, "that they may rest from their labors, for their deeds follow them!" (Rev. 14:13)

This blessing is promised to those who "die in the Lord." And for a person to "die in the Lord" requires that they lived in the Lord. This blessing is for those who wake up every day and live out each day, facing whatever comes, determined to keep trusting in the promises of God in the person of Jesus Christ. The blessing is not that their lives will be comfortable or easy in the here and now. This blessing is far greater than that and will last far longer than that. The promised blessing is that they are going to be gathered by Jesus to Jesus. All of the struggles of this life, everything it costs them to stay in the fight, to remain faithful in their allegiance to Jesus Christ, will have proved worthwhile. The battle with the enemy is likely to rage throughout their lifetime, but it will come to an end. The day will come when they rest and enjoy their reward in the presence of their King.

Your Redeemer

Every cycle we've witnessed so far has taken us through the span of redemptive history leading up to the final judgment and salvation of God's people, and this one is no different. Here in Revelation 14, it is presented to us through the imagery of two harvests. First, the grain harvest:

> Then I looked, and behold, a white cloud, and seated on the cloud one like a son of man, with a golden crown on his head, and a sharp sickle in his hand. And another angel came out of the temple, calling with a loud voice to him who sat on the cloud, "Put in your sickle,

and reap, for the hour to reap has come, for the harvest of the earth is fully ripe." So he who sat on the cloud swung his sickle across the earth, and the earth was reaped. (Rev. 14:14–16)

We immediately know who this person seated on the cloud is, this one "like a son of man, with a golden crown on his head." We remember that these are the words Daniel used to describe the Christ, the words that Jesus used to refer to himself, and words that John used at the beginning of Revelation to describe the risen and glorified Jesus who appeared to him on Patmos. And we remember that Jesus often spoke of harvest. He told his disciples that "the harvest is plentiful, but the laborers are few" (Matt. 9:37–38). In particular he used the harvest as imagery for what will happen at the end of the age. Acknowledging that there were weeds among the wheat (or false believers amongst the true church), Jesus said, "Let both grow together until the harvest, and at harvest time I will tell the reapers, 'Gather the weeds first and bind them in bundles to be burned, but gather the wheat into my barn'" (Matt. 13:30). Here in Revelation 14, we see that is exactly what's happening. Harvesttime has come, and the Lord of the harvest is gathering his own to himself.

But there is also another harvest taking place. Not a harvest of grain, but a harvest of grapes:

Then another angel came out of the temple in heaven, and he too had a sharp sickle. And another angel came out from the altar, the angel who has authority over the fire, and he called with a loud voice to the one who had the sharp sickle, "Put in your sickle and gather the clusters from the vine of the earth, for its grapes are ripe." So the angel swung his sickle across the earth and gathered the grape harvest of the earth and threw it into the great winepress of the wrath of God. And the winepress was trodden outside the city, and blood flowed from the winepress, as high as a horse's bridle, for 1,600 stadia. (Rev. 14:17–20)

The grapes are not being gathered to Christ; they are being gathered to go into the winepress of the wrath of God. This winepress is not inside the safety of the city of Mount Zion, but outside the city. It is not a fine cabernet that is being produced; it is punishment being executed. The picture is bloody; even disturbing. But remember that it is here as a warning to all, a call to all to run to Christ.

In chapter 15 our attention is drawn away from the blood of those who have reaped the result of their rebellion against God by being reaped in the grape harvest to those who have been gathered to Christ. They're standing beside the sea of glass that surrounds God's throne. And they're singing. And the song sounds a bit familiar, yet also new:

> And I saw what appeared to be a sea of glass mingled with fire—and also those who had conquered the beast and its image and the number of its name, standing beside the sea of glass with harps of God in their hands. And they sing the song of Moses, the servant of God, and the song of the Lamb, saying,
>
>> "Great and amazing are your deeds,
>>   O Lord God the Almighty!
>> Just and true are your ways,
>>   O King of the nations!
>> Who will not fear, O Lord,
>>   and glorify your name?
>> For you alone are holy.
>>   All nations will come
>>   and worship you,
>> for your righteous acts have been revealed." (Rev. 15:2–4)

Back in Exodus 15 we read the story of how God gathered his people from Egypt and brought them safely across the Red Sea while bringing judgment on the armies of Pharaoh. And when they were safely delivered, they sang. Here, once again, the redeemed people of God—those who welcomed the wisdom of God so that they could rightly calculate the number of the beast and thereby resisted his allure—are singing. But their song is about a much greater deliverance than the deliverance of Israel from Egypt. This is the deliverance not of one nation but of a people from every nation, a deliverance accomplished not by Moses but through the work of the Lamb. The latter-day Pharaoh— the dragon and his army—has been defeated. The King of the nations has executed perfect justice and righteousness and is properly feared, glorified, and worshiped.

Contemplating this vision and imagining singing this song in this gathering must have filled first-century believers with a desire to patiently endure, to conquer the beast, and to one day join in this song of victory. Does it do the same for you?

Hearing and Keeping Revelation 12–14

We've had the curtain drawn back to see into the true nature of so much that influences the world we live in, the voices we hear, the temptations we face. We've needed to see it. So what will it mean for us to hear it, heed it, and live in light of it?

First and foremost, we must heed the repeated call to endure in spite of the enemy's powerful allure and deceitful lies. To endure doesn't mean we don't examine our faith. In fact, we interrogate our faith. But we don't interrogate it apart from the Scriptures, using human reason and values. Instead we search the Scriptures and bring our questions, opinions, and doubts to the Scriptures to find answers, correction, and insight. Rather than drift, we cling to Christ, to his word, to his people. We stop expecting that we can be casually committed to him in a way that will enable us to enjoy all that life in this world has to offer with a little Christ added in. Instead, we reckon with the reality that overcoming or conquering may look like being conquered. Allegiance to Christ may cost us a great deal in this life. But when we enter the gates of Mount Zion, we won't regret anything we have let go of in the here and now to take hold of Christ.

When we really believe that we conquer through the blood of the Lamb and the word of our testimony so that we love Christ more than we love our own lives—even to losing everything in this life, perhaps even life itself—it shifts our focus away from protecting ourselves to being willing to risk ourselves—risk everything—for the cause of the gospel. When our job or our place in the group or the family is threatened, we're able to say, "What is the worst that can happen if I am bold about Christ being the only hope for sinful people? I'll lose my job? I have an eternal inheritance that is awaiting me. I'll lose some friends and family? I have a family made up of brothers and sisters in Christ. I'll lose my comfortable life? I know I can't hold on to it forever anyway. In fact, I really believe what Jesus said: 'Whoever seeks to preserve his life will lose it, but whoever loses his life will keep it' (Luke 17:33)."

Hearing and keeping these words means that we want to be marked by what marks the redeemed in this passage. Did you notice what distinguishes them? True spirituality. A rigorous pursuit of personal holiness. Uncorrupted, uncompromised, undefiled spirituality. They are "free from intercourse with the pagan world system."[9] They are obedient as they follow the Lamb, who is also their shepherd, and are corrected by his rod and protected by his staff. They're willing to submit even when it is costly. And there is something about the way they talk. "In their mouth no lie was found" (Rev. 14:5). They don't listen to or repeat half-truths or outright falsehoods. Their words have weight because they are consistently truthful. And not just generally truthful, but truthful about the costs and benefits of following the Lamb even when the beast is breathing down their neck and pitching a much more attractive message.

Oh, don't we want this to be what distinguishes us in the world—that we as individuals, and as the church, would be known not for compromise but for purity, not for charting our own course but for following the Lamb, and not for embracing conspiracy theories or our culture's mantras but for being committed to the truth, even when that truth is costly and inconvenient?

Maybe you wonder if there is anything here for you if you don't experience the kind of persecution for your faith that is pictured in this book. Hopefully there is at least one type of suffering you are

---

9   Leon Morris, *The Revelation of St. John: An Introduction and Commentary,* Tyndale New Testament Commentaries 20 (Grand Rapids, MI: Eerdmans, 1969), 177.

experiencing out of love for Christ—the suffering that comes from a daily battle against sin. There is inherent suffering in dying to oneself, saying no to fleshly desires, not just once but again and again over the long haul. This is at the very heart of endurance and faith. Don't discount it. Pursue it. As you do, receive the assurance that is given in Revelation and anticipate the promises in this book that are given to all who overcome. As you overcome your appetites for the things that do not take you closer to Christ, and as you overcome your propensity to always put yourself first, and as you overcome your fear of what other people will think if you identify with Christ, you can be sure that all that is promised in this book to those who overcome—life and reward and blessing—will be yours when you see Christ face to face.

Revelation 12:11 describes those who have conquered the dragon "by the blood of the Lamb and by the word of their testimony," saying that "they loved not their lives even unto death." Oh, don't we want it to be said of us? Don't we want to hear and respond to this call to endure? Perhaps you will want to pray this prayer along with me, inserting your own name in place of mine: *Lord, may it be said of me, "Nancy conquered the devil by the blood of the Lamb and by the word of her testimony, for she loved not her life even unto death."*

8

Blessed by Being Ready for the Return of Jesus

Revelation 15–16

SOMETIMES WHEN I find myself flipping channels as I look for something worth watching on television, I think back to my childhood, when we only had three or four channels to choose from. How can I have access to so many channels and yet find so little I actually want to watch?

I heard recently about The Puppy Channel, a short-lived cable television channel. Twenty-four hours a day you could turn to The Puppy Channel and watch video footage of puppies. Puppies playing. Puppies chewing. No talk; just instrumental music. Who wouldn't want to watch puppies? Evidently not enough of us, as it went off the air after about three or four years.

In my search to be entertained, there are plenty of things I flip past because I have no desire to see what is being shown. And sometimes I find myself watching a TV program or movie that includes scenes that are too violent or gory for me. When that happens, I put my hand in front of my eyes with my fingers ever so slightly parted so I don't have to see what I don't want to see, but can see enough to know when the scene is over, and I can start watching again.

I wonder if some of us may have a tendency to try something similar with the Bible. There may be parts of the Bible, aspects or actions of the God of the Bible, that make us uncomfortable, and we'd rather not look too closely. Perhaps there is a part of us that wants to put our hands up to certain parts of the Bible so that we won't have to see them, so that just the parts we feel good about slip through the cracks.

The Bible reveals a God who, throughout history, has poured out wrath on his enemies. To some, that seems rather primitive, perhaps inconsistent with a God who is love. Perhaps we think the descriptions of his wrath are too harsh, too black and white, or too vindictive, or that some who experience his wrath don't really deserve it. We'd rather ignore it, soften it, perhaps even scrub it.

But here we are in Revelation, and it simply won't let us ignore it. In fact, Revelation, particularly Revelation 15 and 16, is going to challenge us to think very differently about the wrath of God. It is going to invite us to stop shielding ourselves from this aspect of God's character and plan and begin, instead, to gaze intently into it. As we gaze into the wrath of God presented in this passage, we're going to see that the wrath of God flows out of his excellencies and perfections.

We're also going to see that the inhabitants of heaven are not at all embarrassed by God's wrath. Quite the opposite—they celebrate it. It seems to add to God's worthiness of honor and worship, not detract from it. So what do they know that we don't know? What has shaped the perspective they have on this world and the evil in it that needs to shape our perspectives?

We've actually already been witnessing the wrath of God being poured out in previous chapters, haven't we? As the seals were opened, we saw a measure of wrath poured out over the entire age between the first and second coming of Christ, culminating with the seventh seal corresponding to Christ's return and the final judgment. If you remember, the seal judgments impacted one quarter of the earth. Similarly, we saw wrath revealed in the trumpets, which served to warn the nations of final judgment, depicted by the final trumpet heralding the kingdom of Christ putting an end to the kingdoms of this world. The trumpet judgments impacted one-third of the earth. The seven bowls presented in Revelation 15 and 16 are more comprehensive and final. They serve to answer the question, What happens when the trumpet judgments, which were intended to rouse rebellious sinners toward repentance, fail to do so?

When we came in the last chapter to the first few verses of Revelation 15, we heard the singing of those "who had conquered the beast and its image and the number of its name" (v. 2). It says that they were singing "the song of Moses, the servant of God, and the song of the Lamb" (v. 3). In other words, they're singing the song the people of God sang after they crossed the Red Sea and saw the walls of water wash over the Egyptian army (Ex. 15). But it is also "the song of the Lamb." Evidently John wants us to see what he's about to present to us in light of what happened in Egypt. So perhaps we should review that history a bit.

We read in Exodus that the people of Israel were groaning because of their slavery and because their sons were being systematically killed upon birth by being thrown into the Nile River to drown. Exodus 2:23 says that their cries for rescue came up to God. Do you see a similarity in the situation of many of the churches John was writing to? In the pages of Revelation we have also read about the cries of God's people who were being killed, not by Egyptians but by Roman oppressors.

In response to the cries of the Israelites in Egypt, God remembered his covenant and sent a deliverer, Moses. As Moses lifted up his staff, God sent a series of plagues on Egypt that were intended to make his glory known, expose the false gods of Egypt, and call Pharaoh to repentance. But over and over, Pharaoh's heart was hardened. In Revelation 15 and 16, we're going to see that God hears the cries of those being persecuted and sends a series of plagues on their persecutors that are intended to make his glory known, expose their false gods, and call them to repentance. And we're going to see that the hearts of the persecutors are also hardened.

At the Red Sea, God drove back the sea so that the people of Israel passed through on dry ground. But when the Egyptians went after them on that dry ground, the water came back upon them and destroyed them. Moses writes, "Thus the LORD saved Israel that day from the hand of the Egyptians, and Israel saw the Egyptians dead on the seashore" (Ex. 14:30). The Israelites recognized that it was God's judgment against their enemies that provided their deliverance, and it moved them to sing a song that celebrated the Lord's triumph. And this is what we have in Revelation 15: the Lord's people, standing on the far side of the persecution of the beast of the sea, singing a song that celebrates the Lord's triumph over their enemies because they recognize that this is what has provided their deliverance. They're not embarrassed by the wrath of God poured out on their persecutors; they revel in it. They see the wisdom, goodness, and covenant love of God in it. From their vantage point they can see that the pouring out of wrath on those who persecuted them is a glorious demonstration of how great, amazing, just, true, and altogether righteous God is. So they sing:

> Great and amazing are your deeds,
>   O Lord God the Almighty!
> Just and true are your ways,
>   O King of the nations!
> Who will not fear, O Lord,
>   and glorify your name?
> For you alone are holy.
>   All nations will come
>   and worship you,
> for your righteous acts have been revealed. (Rev. 15:3–4)

They are not afraid to look squarely and deeply at the wrath of God because they can see clearly that it is just and true. His holiness demands it. It is part of what makes him worthy of worship by the whole world. It is the epitome of his "righteous acts being revealed." And if that is the case, we need to see it too. So let's work our way through four things revealed in the wrath of God. (And I really wish

I had come up with seven because that would have been apropos, don't you think?)

Four Things Revealed in the Wrath of God

1. Pouring out his wrath is God's glorious way
of preparing a place for his people.

Remember that the tabernacle or temple was the place where the presence of God—notably his holiness—dwelt. So it is significant that John sees these seven plagues or bowls of the wrath of God coming from out of "the sanctuary of the tent of witness in heaven":

> After this I looked, and the sanctuary of the tent of witness in heaven was opened, and out of the sanctuary came the seven angels with the seven plagues, clothed in pure, bright linen, with golden sashes around their chests. And one of the four living creatures gave to the seven angels seven golden bowls full of the wrath of God who lives forever and ever, and the sanctuary was filled with smoke from the glory of God and from his power, and no one could enter the sanctuary until the seven plagues of the seven angels were finished. Then I heard a loud voice from the temple telling the seven angels, "Go and pour out on the earth the seven bowls of the wrath of God." (Rev. 15:5–16:1)

Seven angels clothed in pure bright linen that reflects the holiness of their mission emerge from the place where God's holiness dwells. This tells us that what these angels are doing is an expression of God's holiness, not the irrational rage of an egotistic, capricious deity. The wrath of God is the righteous, pure, and perfectly appropriate expression of his justice toward evil.

These seven angels are carrying seven golden bowls. Earlier in Revelation 5 we read about golden bowls in the sanctuary. They were "golden bowls full of incense, which are the prayers of the saints" (Rev. 5:8). What were those saints praying for? They were crying out for justice, for those who had put them to death to experience God's justice. Now these same golden bowls are coming out of the sanctuary, and they are filled with God's wrath, which tells us that what is about to happen is in response to the prayers of the saints.

John writes, "No one could enter the sanctuary until the seven plagues of the seven angels were finished." The wrath of God accomplishes something so that God's people will finally be able to enter his sanctuary. When the angels come out of the sanctuary with bowls of wrath poured out on the earth, into the sea, into the rivers, on the sun, on the throne of the beast, on the river Euphrates, and into the air, it cleanses all of creation, making it a sanctuary in which God intends to dwell with his people forever. And this is such good news! You and I don't want to have to live forever in a world tainted by evil, rebellion, idolatry, and immorality. And we won't have to. God is determined to get all of the ugliness and evil cleaned out before we enter into our forever home. Pouring out his wrath is God's glorious way of cleansing and preparing a home for us.

2. Pouring out his wrath is God's just way of giving those who have rejected his mercy and persecuted his people what they rightly deserve.

In chapter 16, the seven angels begin to pour out their seven bowls or plagues. The first four bowls are poured out on different spheres of nature: the earth (16:1), the sea (16:3), the rivers and springs (16:4), and the sun (16:8). But their impact is on people. We sometimes say that God hates the sin but loves the sinner. And it is true that God loves sinners. But "God does not divorce sin from sinners. Sin is not an impersonal activity; it is the action of a creature against the Creator."[1] And, likewise, judgment for sin will not be an impersonal activity. It will be visited upon people who persist in rebellion and rejection of the grace and mercy of God.

So much of Revelation has required us to use our visual imagination. But in these bowls of wrath, it seems that John is asking us to use our sensory imagination to grasp the reality of the wrath of God. And in this first bowl, we can close our eyes and almost feel the physical pain of judgment:

---

1 Andrew Jones, "The Whore, the Beast, the Lamb and His People," sermon, St. Helen's Bishopsgate, London, September 30, 2001, https://www.st-helens.org.uk/.

> So the first angel went and poured out his bowl on the earth, and harmful and painful sores came upon the people who bore the mark of the beast and worshiped its image. (Rev. 16:2)

The first bowl of wrath that inflicts painful sores reminds us of the sixth plague on Egypt that caused boils to break out in sores on all of the people and animals of Egypt (Ex. 9:9). We should remember that every one of the plagues on Egypt served to expose the weakness of various Egyptian gods. The plague of boils exposed the weakness of the goddess that Egyptians believed had power over disease and the goddess that they credited with healing. So in the same way, each bowl of wrath represents God's judgment against the idols humanity has worshiped in place of God. With this first bowl, God exposes the idol of physical health and medical breakthroughs. It reminds those who worship immortality that they are mere mortals. And "just as the magicians of Egypt could not protect the Pharaoh or his people, so now the mark of the beast not only fails to protect those who serve the dragon, it actually identifies them as objects of God's wrath."[2]

> The second angel poured out his bowl into the sea, and it became like the blood of a corpse, and every living thing died that was in the sea. (Rev. 16:3)

Now God strikes the sea so that the water becomes thick and coagulated like blood, which kills every living thing in it. Nothing survives. Once again, let's use our sensory imagination. Most of my life I've had a policy of eating fish away from our home, because I hate how cooking fish and disposing of the unused portions make my house smell. (Don't you hate it when you have fish one night and forget to run the dishwasher, and you come into the kitchen the next morning and the whole room smells?) Now imagine the smell of rotting, dead fish everywhere you turn. You can't escape it. It permeates everything.

2 Kim Riddlebarger, "The Place Called Armageddon," sermon, The Riddleblog, accessed August 18, 2021, http://kimriddlebarger.squarespace.com.

In the same way, the stench of idol worship and God's judgment for it permeates everything around those who engage in it.

Consider also that in John's day the sea was the center and source of commerce. If every living thing in the sea died, it would be an economic disaster. This is a judgment on everything we place our confidence in to sustain us apart from God alone. It is a defeat of the idol of finding our sufficiency in our bank account or business success.

Next, God makes the source of life a source of death:

The third angel poured out his bowl into the rivers and the springs of water, and they became blood. (Rev. 16:4)

There is no fresh water to be found, but only blood to drink. Can you just feel the desperate thirst of those on whom this judgment is poured out? It is disgusting and distressing for us to think about. But it is cause for celebration in heaven:

And I heard the angel in charge of the waters say,

"Just are you, O Holy One, who is and who was,
    for you brought these judgments.
For they have shed the blood of saints and prophets,
    and you have given them blood to drink.
It is what they deserve!" (Rev. 16:5–6)

Back in Revelation 6:10 we heard the cry of God's people asking, "O Sovereign Lord, holy and true, how long before you will judge and avenge our blood on those who dwell on the earth?" Here is their answer. When the people of the first century first read Revelation, it must have been a great comfort to hear that those who had spilled the blood of the saints would be forced to drink blood. The punishment fits the crime. It must have given God's persecuted people the strength to keep on trusting that "vengeance is mine," says the Lord (Deut. 32:35; Rom. 12:19).

And I heard the altar saying,

"Yes, Lord God the Almighty,

true and just are your judgments!" (Rev. 16:7)

Perhaps John anticipated that those who heard his letter read might have some of the same questions we as modern people have about whether or not the wrath of God is truly just, and so he addresses those potential objections in advance by assuring them and us of the justice of his judgments.

As I was working on this chapter, I read yet another news report of someone exonerated by DNA evidence of a crime they'd been convicted of years before. Except this person was executed before that DNA evidence emerged. The justice system got it wrong. It is a reminder that so much justice as executed in this world is flawed. But God never has and never will get it wrong. His judgments are always true and just. We can trust him. God will get it right. No one will experience his wrath who does not justly deserve it.

Earlier in the fourth trumpet judgment, the light of the sun, moon, and stars was diminished by one-third. This fourth bowl brings not diminished light but a massive intensification of the sun's heat:

The fourth angel poured out his bowl on the sun, and it was allowed to scorch people with fire. They were scorched by the fierce heat, and they cursed the name of God who had power over these plagues. They did not repent and give him glory. (Rev. 16:8–9)

Once again, the description of these judgments awakens our senses to what is ahead for those who reject Christ, in this case, the scorching pain of a sunburn for which there is no relief, and the hunger and thirst from food sources being burned up and water sources being dried up.

What is interesting is that the agony of this situation doesn't result in people calling out to God for relief or in repentance; they just double down. They curse God and continue in their refusal to repent. We see clearly in this fourth bowl that God's wrath doesn't fall on innocent people who are basically good and simply haven't yet had the chance to repent. It falls on hardened people who vigorously refuse God to the very end.

The first four bowls have been poured out on various parts of creation. The content of the fifth bowl is more narrowly targeted:

> The fifth angel poured out his bowl on the throne of the beast, and its kingdom was plunged into darkness. People gnawed their tongues in anguish and cursed the God of heaven for their pain and sores. They did not repent of their deeds. (Rev. 16:10–11)

Darkness. Have you ever been in utter darkness? And can you remember what that feels like? Inherent in darkness is utter uncertainty, fearfulness, and a desperate aloneness. Whether it is physical, psychological, or both, this judgment clearly brings torment and anguish on those who use their power and influence in opposition to God and his people. Yet those who experience it do not suffer in silence. They're too busy cursing God.

I wonder if at this point in his vision, John thought of what he had written in his Gospel: "Light has come into the world, and people loved darkness rather than the light because their works were evil" (John 3:19). Here, the judgment of darkness falls on people who love the darkness, which seems like the ultimate "be careful what you wish for."

3. Pouring out his wrath is God's proven way of gathering his enemies for destruction.

Now the scene shifts from various judgments on the earth and its inhabitants to the final battle, which is portrayed here and in several other places in Revelation (11:7–11; 19:19–21; 20:8–10). This will be the final struggle in which God will emerge victorious over Satan, preserving all who have placed their faith in him. God will not be caught by surprise in this battle. All of his enemies may think they are gathering together to destroy the saints, but, in fact, they are being gathered by God for their own destruction.

> The sixth angel poured out his bowl on the great river Euphrates, and its water was dried up, to prepare the way for the kings from the east. (Rev. 16:12)

Water drying up. That reminds us of the Red Sea drying up. The people of God got across, and the dried-up riverbed became the place where the Egyptian army met their doom. When they heard of water being dried up, surely the first hearers of this book would have thought of the armies of Egypt facing destruction in the dried-up Red Sea. But they also would have thought of ancient Babylon. Isaiah and Jeremiah prophesied that when God brought judgment on Babylon, it would involve the drying up of the Euphrates River along its border to the east (Isa. 11:15; 44:27–28; Jer. 50:38; 51:36). And the prophecy was fulfilled when Cyrus came from the east and diverted the waters of the Euphrates, which allowed his army to cross the shallow waters and defeat the Babylonians. It was Cyrus's victory against Babylon that led to Israel's release from captivity (Isa. 44:26–28; 45:13). By referring to the drying up of the river Euphrates, John presents this historical event as a picture or preview of what is going to happen to the latter-day Babylon. Greg Beale explains it this way:

> The idea here is that God, as He did in the days of Cyrus, will dry up the waters of the river protecting and nurturing Babylon to allow for the kings of the earth, under immediate demonic influence but ultimately under God's sovereign control, to gather together in order for Babylon to be defeated and for His eternal kingdom and the reign of His saints to be established.[3]

God sets the stage for the battle. And then his enemies assemble on the stage God has set:

> And I saw, coming out of the mouth of the dragon and out of the mouth of the beast and out of the mouth of the false prophet, three

---

3   G. K. Beale with David H. Campbell, *Revelation: A Shorter Commentary* (Grand Rapids, MI: Eerdmans, 2015), 341.

unclean spirits like frogs. For they are demonic spirits, performing signs, who go abroad to the kings of the whole world, to assemble them for battle on the great day of God the Almighty. (Rev. 16:13–14)

John sees the unholy trinity: the dragon, the beast of the sea, and the beast of the earth, who for the first time here is called "the false prophet." Notice that each of them has something coming out of its mouth. Evidently what they have to say is as unclean and disgusting as the croaking of frogs. We're probably meant to think also of all those piles of dead, stinking frogs in the second plague on Egypt. What comes out of their mouths is equally disgusting, defiling, and destructive. They're deceiving the kings of the world into gathering for what they think will be a victory over the kingdom of God.

When we read that the kings of the whole world are being assembled, we're not meant to think of modern geopolitical entities. It's more likely John is alluding to an Old Testament event, a scene from 1 Kings 22 in which King Ahab was enticed by lying spirits in the mouths of his prophets to go to battle where he met his death. John is portraying a similar scene in which world powers set against Christ are enticed by the deception of these demonic voices to gather for war against Almighty God and the Lamb, not knowing that it will bring about their own demise. Deceived into thinking that they are gathering to exterminate the saints, they are really being gathered together to be exterminated by King Jesus, who is going to show up for this battle unexpectedly.

At this point in John's record of his vision, something interesting happens. Jesus interrupts John's recounting of his vision to speak directly to his people. He says:

Behold, I am coming like a thief! Blessed is the one who stays awake, keeping his garments on, that he may not go about naked and be seen exposed! (Rev. 16:15)

We've read about Jesus coming "like a thief" before (Matt. 24:42–43; cf. 1 Thess. 5:2; 2 Pet. 3:10). How will his coming be "like a thief"?

Thieves don't send advance notices of their arrival. They come when they are not expected. Jesus is reminding his own that his coming will be unexpected. He wants us to know that we cannot become lulled into thinking that things will continue as they are forever. He wants us to live each day anticipating that this could be the day of his return. Earlier in Revelation, Jesus told the Laodiceans that they didn't realize that they were naked and counseled them to buy white garments from him so they could clothe themselves (3:17–18). Here, once again, he is calling people who may be in the church but have not genuinely been joined to him to clothe themselves in his righteousness. Instead of being caught naked through self-sufficiency and the pursuit of money, sex, and power, we are to be clothed in the righteousness of Christ, clothed in humility, love, and the full armor of God. In this way we'll be ready for his coming, whenever it is.

Now back to the battle:

> And they assembled them at the place that in Hebrew is called Armageddon. (Rev. 16:16)

Armageddon in Hebrew is literally "Mount of Megiddo." Megiddo is the place where righteous Israelites were attacked by wicked nations (Judg. 5:19; 2 Kings 23:29; 2 Chron. 35:20–22), and where kings who oppressed God's people were defeated (Judg. 5:19–21). It's where false prophets were destroyed (1 Kings 18:40). It's the place where the destruction of "all the nations that come against Jerusalem" was prophesied to take place (Zech. 12:9–12). Beale writes that "Megiddo became proverbial in Judaism as the place where righteous Israelites were attacked by evil nations."[4] Because John's original readers would have been familiar with the imagery of Megiddo as Israel's consummate battlefield where her enemies had been defeated, it makes complete sense that John would choose Megiddo to symbolize the location of the final battle of the Lord against the forces of darkness. They would have

4   Beale, *Revelation*, 346.

heard John saying, "All who have set themselves against Christ and his people are going to be utterly defeated, just as many other enemies of God have been defeated in the past."

According to Kim Riddlebarger, "The reference to Armageddon is not a description of a literal military battle in which men in tanks and airplanes fight against God. Instead, we have an apocalyptic image of the kings of the earth being gathered together by the dragon to wage war against Mount Zion, which is symbolic of the church of Jesus Christ."[5] This is a spiritual battle, not a military one. John is giving us an apocalyptic vision of Satan's final assault on the church, an assault that is crushed by Jesus Christ upon his return to earth.

4. Pouring out his wrath is God's consummate way of putting an end to evil.

Finally, we come to the seventh bowl, which is poured into the air. Remember that Paul called Satan "the prince of the power of the air" (Eph. 2:2). This means that when the seventh bowl is poured into the air, we recognize that this final bowl is being poured out on the entire corrupt world system in service to Satan and opposition to Christ. When the seventh bowl is poured out, it will be the end of evil and its impact on this world. This is not a day to dread; this is the day we are longing for. This will be the end of sin, the end of suffering, the end of conflict:

> The seventh angel poured out his bowl into the air, and a loud voice came out of the temple, from the throne, saying, "It is done!" (Rev. 16:17)

There's something about this voice saying, "It is done!" that sounds familiar, isn't there? John is the one who recorded the final words of Jesus on the cross: "It is finished" (John 19:30). It is hard to imagine that he wouldn't intend for us as readers to make that connection. He wants us to see that everything accomplished on the cross will come

---

5 Riddlebarger, "The Place Called Armageddon."

to its full fruition on the day of Christ's return. While the head of the serpent was crushed in his death and resurrection, the ancient serpent will be destroyed for good on the day of his return. With the seventh bowl John tells us that the wrath of God is finished. The justice of God has been fully satisfied. It has been exhausted either on his Son or on unrepentant sinners.

> And there were flashes of lightning, rumblings, peals of thunder, and a great earthquake such as there had never been since man was on the earth, so great was that earthquake. (Rev. 16:18)

Throughout Revelation thunder, lightning, and earthquake symbolize the arrival of the end (6:12; 8:5; 11:13, 19; 19:6). And that is certainly what is pictured here.

> The great city was split into three parts, and the cities of the nations fell, and God remembered Babylon the great, to make her drain the cup of the wine of the fury of his wrath. And every island fled away, and no mountains were to be found. (Rev. 16:19–20)

John is using a bit of irony when he references "the great city." This is the city of man that has always been about building a reputation for greatness, ever since it was founded and first called Babel. John uses Babylon as a symbol of a world that is absorbed with its own greatness and refuses to acknowledge the greatness of God. And when this final bowl is poured out, that city, that ethos, that rebellion and resistance toward God, collapses for good.

John says that Babylon is made to "drain the cup of the wine of the fury of his wrath." This cup contains the full vehemence and fierceness of God's holy wrath poured out against all sin. It is "fire and sulfur and a scorching wind" concentrated in a cup (Ps. 11:6). We have read about this cup before in the Old Testament. Isaiah 51:17 puts this cup in God's extended hand, calling it "the cup of his wrath," and for those who drink from it, "the cup of staggering." The psalmist writes that when God pours this cup, "all the wicked of the earth shall drain it down to the dregs" (Ps. 75:8).

But it is not just in the Old Testament that we've read about this cup. We read about it in the Gospels. This is the cup that Jesus prayed he would not have to drink. On the night before he was crucified, Jesus prayed, "My Father, if it be possible, let this cup pass from me; nevertheless, not as I will, but as you will" (Matt. 26:39). But, of course, he did drink it. Jesus drank the cup of God's wrath in all of its fiery intensity.

Hearing and Keeping Revelation 15–16

So what are the implications of these bowls of wrath for you and me? What is it going to look like for us to hear and keep these chapters and thereby experience the promised blessing?

If all of this wrath and misery have fueled some fear on your part, the truth is, you are right to be afraid of the wrath of God. No person in his or her right mind wouldn't fear that wrath. But you don't have to live in that fear. There is a place of safety, a place of protection that is open to you. It is the place where the bowl has already been poured out, where the wrath has already been absorbed and thereby extinguished. That is in the person of Jesus.

The wrath of God was poured out upon Christ so that something very different can be poured out on all who are connected to him by faith: his love and mercy and grace and forgiveness. The good news of the gospel in light of the reality of the bowls of wrath is spelled out in 1 Thessalonians 5:9 where we read, "God has not destined us for wrath, but to obtain salvation through our Lord Jesus Christ."

So the first and foremost way to hear and keep Revelation 15 and 16 is to flee to the place of safety in the person of Christ. Drink the cup of salvation that he holds out to you, made possible because he drank "the cup of the wine of the fury of his wrath" in your place.

And if you have fled to him, you must stay alert in looking for him. This is where the promised blessing is, in refusing to be lulled into complacency, thinking that life is about the things this world has to offer and what the world says really matters rather than living in anticipation and readiness for Jesus to return to judge and cleanse this world. Jesus's message in Revelation 16:15 is simply: *Stay awake and trust me. Live in me and for me as you wait for me to come again.*

Hearing and keeping these chapters must also mean that we refuse to be embarrassed by, to diminish, or to disregard his wrath. Surely it means that we warn those who are vulnerable to it, inviting them into the place of safety that we have found. Instead of holding up our hands trying not to see it, we can open our hands to welcome it.

Jesus taught us to pray, "Deliver us from evil" (Matt. 6:13). He does that for us day by day. And one day he's going to do that in an ultimate and final way. His pouring out of wrath will be the answer to our prayers. We pray, "Your kingdom come," and on that day we can be sure that his kingdom is going to come in an ultimate and final way as well. When his kingdom comes, it will mean the utter destruction of every kingdom in opposition to his. When his kingdom comes we won't be embarrassed by the true and just judgment that is poured out on all who have opposed him. We'll lift our hands to celebrate and praise him for it.

One day it will become perfectly clear that God's wrath was not the problem, but the solution this world is desperate for, the answer to all of those who ask, "Why doesn't God do something about the evil and suffering in the world?" Right now, in his kindness, he is delaying his justice to provide an opportunity for sinners to repent. It's not slowness on his part. It is grace and mercy being poured out on all who will repent and believe.

9

Blessed by Being Prepared as a Bride for Jesus

Revelation 17:1–19:10

MY FIRST DATE with David was on New Year's Eve. And when he left at 3 a.m. on that first day of 1986, I blissfully fell asleep. I knew I had found him, the one. When Valentine's Day weekend came around a little more than a month later, I didn't like it that he was talking about renewing his lease on his apartment because I didn't want him to be tied up there and unable to get a place with me. When I flew to Oregon with him in April to meet his family, I took some postcards with me that I could use to write notes to some of my friends on the return flight in the event that he decided to pop the question on Cannon Beach or at Black Butte and we got engaged. But I brought the postcards back home with me. In fact, I might still have them.

Then in June he picked me up to go out for dinner. He made some sort of excuse to stop by his apartment. There on the door was a hand-drawn sign that said "Chez Dave" (French for "at the home of Dave") where he said we were going to have dinner. He gave me a rose (which I still have pressed in a book) and a card that had the words of Psalm 34:3 written in it: "Glorify the LORD with me; let us exalt his name together" (NIV). And the "together" part was underlined. I said yes.

The next day we went to a jewelry store in Waco and bought a ring. And Sunday I wore it to church. I remember sitting in the choir loft admiring its sparkle under the lights. And then the next day we got busy getting ready for the wedding. There was so much to do: pick a date, send out invitations, get a dress, plan a reception. And I loved it all because I loved him. I could hardly wait, not just for the wedding but for the marriage.

If you know a couple who is engaged to be married and getting ready for a wedding, you know how busy they are, how focused they are on preparations, how happy they are as they look forward to that day and the life together that will come after that day.

Actually, if you are in Christ, you are the person who is engaged to be married. You are preparing for a wedding. Perhaps you've never thought of yourself and your relationship to Christ in this way. But clearly the Bible intends for us to view it that way. From the very beginning of the Bible, God speaks of his relationship with his people in terms of a marriage. Since the very beginning in Eden, when God presented a bride, Eve, to his son, Adam, and everything went terribly wrong with this bride and groom, God has been at work to present a bride to his Son, Jesus. It has been a very long engagement. But the wedding day is coming. In light of this coming wedding day, the questions we need to consider are these: Are we preparing ourselves for it? Are we remaining faithful to our bridegroom as we wait for him to come for us?

As we turn to Revelation 17:1–19:10, it may not appear to you on first blush that what we're reading has anything to do with this marriage. But it does. Revelation as a whole is a call to patient endurance as we wait for our king, the Lamb, our bridegroom, to come. And inherent in that patient endurance is faithfulness. To wait is going to require that we refuse the advances of any other lovers who seek to seduce us. In Revelation 17 we're presented with a seductress who has every intention of having us for herself. She doesn't want us to hold out for our holy bridegroom. She is portrayed as alluring and exciting. She appears wealthy and promises uninhibited pleasure. But that is just how she appears from an earthly and human perspective. In Revelation we're being shown reality from heaven's perspective, from the vantage point that reveals all things as they truly are. And she is not what she seems.

Revelation 17 through 19 shows us four things we must do if we're going to be prepared as a bride for our bridegroom. And the first is this: *We can't allow ourselves to be seduced by a love that won't last.*

The Seductress

> Then one of the seven angels who had the seven bowls came and said to me, "Come, I will show you the judgment of the great prostitute who is seated on many waters, with whom the kings of the earth have committed sexual immorality, and with the wine of whose sexual immorality the dwellers on earth have become drunk." And he carried me away in the Spirit into a wilderness, and I saw a woman sitting on a scarlet beast that was full of blasphemous names, and it had seven heads and ten horns. The woman was arrayed in purple and scarlet, and adorned with gold and jewels and pearls, holding in her hand a golden cup full of abominations and the impurities of her sexual immorality. And on her forehead was written a name of mystery: "Babylon the great, mother of prostitutes and of earth's abominations." And I saw the woman, drunk with the blood of the saints, the blood of the martyrs of Jesus. (Rev. 17:1–6)

Here is Babylon, which is a symbol for the city of man, humanity intent on living apart from God, portrayed as a woman, but not just a woman; she's a prostitute. In fact, she's not just a prostitute; she's the "mother of prostitutes." The picture John paints is so vivid that you can almost see her profile picture and bio on the app she uses to find sexual partners to hook up with. She's dressed in the latest designer clothes. No costume jewelry for her; it's all real gold and jewels and pearls. In her photo she's holding a golden cup. She must be rich. We might imagine there is fine wine in the cup, but we'd be wrong. Inside the cup is the blood of those who have refused her, those who have seen her for what she is and exposed her. In the cup is the blood of those she has put to death who were patiently enduring her persecution while waiting for the true bridegroom. Also inside the cup is the evidence of the disgusting and degrading things she's done to obtain all of her nice clothes, expensive jewelry, and sexual conquests. She's had way too much to drink from this cup, and she's intoxicated.

Across her photo in large letters is the name she has given to herself: "Babylon the great." And when we read it, we realize that we've heard of this family. She comes from a long line of Babylons. She is a daughter of Babel, that ancient people who sought to build a tower to the sky to invade God's glory and take it for themselves. They intended to build a city and make a name for themselves. But their project came to a destructive end. She's a daughter of that ancient city that dragged the people of God into exile, the city led by Nebuchadnezzar, who said, "Is not this great Babylon, which I have built by my mighty power as a royal residence and for the glory of my majesty?" (Dan. 4:30). We can see the family resemblance.

This woman represents the world in opposition to God and his people. She looks appealing. Most people would look at her and think that she's beautiful. In fact, John seems quite taken with her:

> When I saw her, I marveled greatly. But the angel said to me, "Why do you marvel?" (Rev. 17:6–7)

It seems as if John has fallen under her spell. Clearly she's attractive. She seems fun. She seems powerful. She seems like the kind of person you'd want to post a selfie with to show how well connected you are. But the angel is about to reveal to John, to the seven churches in Asia, and to us, what may not be obvious from the way she presents herself:

> I will tell you the mystery of the woman, and of the beast with seven heads and ten horns that carries her. The beast that you saw was, and is not, and is about to rise from the bottomless pit and go to destruction. And the dwellers on earth whose names have not been

written in the book of life from the foundation of the world will marvel to see the beast, because it was and is not and is to come. (Rev. 17:7–8)

Here's the truth about her, the angel tells John. She gets all of her power and presence, all of her allure and accoutrements, from the beast. And we remember the beast from chapter 13 of Revelation. This is the beast that rises from the sea, the counterfeit Christ, the imitation savior, the governmental, ideological, and political force that is set against Christ and his people. This beast is the one propping up the woman, whispering in her ear, providing her funding, empowering her evil. John writes that her identity and intentions aren't immediately evident on the surface. To grasp who she is and what she is determined to do requires us to look closely and think deeply.

> This calls for a mind with wisdom: the seven heads are seven mountains on which the woman is seated; they are also seven kings, five of whom have fallen, one is, the other has not yet come, and when he does come he must remain only a little while. As for the beast that was and is not, it is an eighth but it belongs to the seven, and it goes to destruction. And the ten horns that you saw are ten kings who have not yet received royal power, but they are to receive authority as kings for one hour, together with the beast. These are of one mind, and they hand over their power and authority to the beast. They will make war on the Lamb, and the Lamb will conquer them, for he is Lord of lords and King of kings, and those with him are called and chosen and faithful. (Rev. 17:9–14)

This woman is seated on seven mountains. John's first readers would have immediately recognized that John was talking about Rome, as the city of Rome was built on seven hills. Rome glittered with an abundance of wealth. She flexed her muscles of power. She was attractive and alluring, and everybody who was anybody was engaged with her. From what we read in the letters to the seven churches in Revelation 2 and 3, we know that many Christians in the first century were attracted to the luxuries, significance, power, and access she dangled in front of them. Of course, Rome was also the place where Christians would soon be lit on fire as human torches or fed to the lions. Every Babylon turns violent toward those who resist and expose her true ugliness.

But certainly John is using the symbol of the great prostitute to refer to more than first-century Rome. The fact that he doesn't say explicitly that this is Rome makes the vision timeless. Throughout history we've seen a succession of Babylons or Romes—regimes that have attracted the masses, declared their own greatness, rejected any need for God, and oppressed those who are "called and chosen and faithful."

What is so sad about this woman is that she doesn't realize that the satanic source of her ideas and values, the beast she rides on, doesn't really love her. In fact, he hates her. And the day is coming when all of her lovers will hate her too:

> And the angel said to me, "The waters that you saw, where the prostitute is seated, are peoples and multitudes and nations and languages. And the ten horns that you saw, they and the beast will hate the prostitute. They will make her desolate and naked, and devour her flesh and burn her up with fire, for God has put it into their hearts to carry out his purpose by being of one mind and handing over their royal power to the beast, until the words of God are fulfilled. And the woman that you saw is the great city that has dominion over the kings of the earth." (Rev. 17:15–18)

Her picture might look good on the screen at this point. But the day is going to come when her pimp, the beast, will turn on her, and she will be made desolate. Her beautiful clothes will be gone, and she'll be left naked and exposed. Instead of feasting on the finest of foods herself, she's going to become a feast for the beast. He's going to devour her. She's going to get burned. More than that, she is going to burn. And all who have joined themselves to her by committing spiritual adultery with her are in danger of being burned too.

Then I heard another voice from heaven saying,
"Come out of her, my people,
    lest you take part in her sins,
lest you share in her plagues;
for her sins are heaped high as heaven,
    and God has remembered her iniquities." (Rev. 18:4–5)

Here is a voice from heaven speaking to us, his people, calling us to come out of this city of Babylon, away from this wicked woman, so we won't be seduced into living like her and vulnerable to burning up with her. There is an urgency to his voice. He's warning us to flee from the evil city before it's too late. We've seen where association with her will lead; it's time to get out. So how are we going to do that?

We live in Babylon. It is ubiquitous, everywhere. Are we supposed to follow in the steps of the Essenes in the second century who went out to live in the desert, or the monks in the medieval era who moved into monasteries, or the Amish in our day and time who live out in the country avoiding modern technology? I don't think so.

If only changing our address would accomplish what we're being called to do here. This is going to require far more than a change of address. It will require a radical change of heart, a change in our affections and interests and desires. It means that we have to figure out how to live in Babylon as citizens of the new Jerusalem, as aliens and strangers. We're going to have to figure out what it will mean for us to refuse to make ourselves at home here. What we're being called to here is not separatism but distinctiveness. What we hear in this voice from heaven is a summons to refuse to become entangled with the world, to refuse to make our home here spiritually in terms of allegiance and loyalty.

As we take note throughout this chapter of Babylon's materialism and consumption, we realize that to come out of her is going to mean resisting the seductive nature of her advertising, starving the greed of always wanting more and better.

And as we begin to think it through, we realize that if we are going to be prepared as a bride for our bridegroom, there is something else we are going to have do: *We have to break up with all of our old lovers.*

The Breakup

We're going to have to delete the world's number from our phones. No more late-night conversations. We can't keep up the flirtation. We can't think that we can stay close to the world, enjoying all it has to offer, giving our heart and affections to it, and still be faithful to our bridegroom. It simply won't work.

In a way, Revelation 18 is John seeking to shake some sense into our heads about what we might have seen as a harmless infatuation. He wants us to know that if we refuse to come out of Babylon, if we refuse to give up our dalliances with the world, we're going to be destroyed with her. She seems so in control, so self-confident. Our interactions with her seem so natural, not dangerous. And we can't imagine that she will ever be anything except beautiful and powerful. But John shows us, one day, in a single day, everything will change:

> "I sit as a queen,
> I am no widow,
>> and mourning I shall never see."
> For this reason her plagues will come in a single day,
>> death and mourning and famine,
> and she will be burned up with fire;
>> for mighty is the Lord God who has judged her. (Rev. 18:7–8)

The great prostitute boasts, saying in essence, "I'll never lose this power. I'll never lose affection and adulation. I'll never lose." But from his vantage point, John can see that she's going to lose everything. And everyone who has joined themselves to her is going to lose everything too. On the day when Babylon gets her due, everyone who has made their home there, their fortune there, finds their identity and meaning there, will lose everything they thought made them happy, everything that provided their security, everything that gave their lives meaning. John wants us to hear from them. He wants us to hear agony in their cries.

And the kings of the earth, who committed sexual immorality and lived in luxury with her, will weep and wail over her when they see the smoke of her burning. They will stand far off, in fear of her torment, and say:

"Alas! Alas! You great city,
    you mighty city, Babylon!
For in a single hour your judgment has come." (Rev. 18:9–10)

Everyone whose power was an extension of the beast's power, every-one who was seduced by her into committing spiritual adultery with her, everyone who went to her summits and conferences, they're going to watch in fear as she burns because they know that her torment is going to become their torment:

And the merchants of the earth weep and mourn for her, since no one buys their cargo anymore, cargo of gold, silver, jewels, pearls, fine linen, purple cloth, silk, scarlet cloth, all kinds of scented wood, all kinds of articles of ivory, all kinds of articles of costly wood, bronze, iron and marble, cinnamon, spice, incense, myrrh, frankincense, wine, oil, fine flour, wheat, cattle and sheep, horses and chariots, and slaves, that is, human souls. (Rev. 18:11–13)

Everyone who has profited from her corruption, enjoying a standard of living made possible at the expense of men, women, and children in the sweatshops of the world, will lose it all:

The fruit for which your soul longed
    has gone from you,
and all your delicacies and your splendors
    are lost to you,
        never to be found again! (Rev. 18:14)

The merchants of these wares, who gained wealth from her, will stand far off, in fear of her torment, weeping and mourning aloud:

> Alas, alas, for the great city
> that was clothed in fine linen,
>   in purple and scarlet,
> adorned with gold,
>   with jewels, and with pearls!
> For in a single hour all this wealth has been laid waste.
>   (Rev. 18:14–17a)

All of the delicacies that they once fed on are going to turn sour in their stomach. All of their collections are going into the dumpster. All of their fine clothes are going to become rags. All of their bank accounts and stock portfolios and insurance policies and investment properties are not going to be able to secure their future like they thought they would. It will be gone in one day, and they will be reduced to weeping and wailing:

> All shipmasters and seafaring men, sailors and all whose trade is on the sea, stood far off and cried out as they saw the smoke of her burning,

> "What city was like the great city?"

> And they threw dust on their heads as they wept and mourned, crying out,

> "Alas, alas, for the great city
>   where all who had ships at sea
>   grew rich by her wealth!
> For in a single hour she has been laid waste." (Rev. 18:17b–19)

It was their connections in and to the great city that filled the lives of these shipmasters and sailors not only with wealth but with significance.

They loved her. One minute she is gleaming and bright, and the next minute she's just gone. For good.

Then we hear the angel call to those who were not seduced by Babylon, those who made a clean break from her. They had prayed, "How long before you will judge and avenge our blood on those who dwell on the earth?" (6:10). And in the destruction of Babylon, their prayers for vindication have been answered. Rather than lament, they're called to rejoice:

> Rejoice over her, O heaven,
>   and you saints and apostles and prophets,
> for God has given judgment for you against her! (Rev. 18:20)

The destruction that brings great sorrow to those who loved Babylon brings great joy to the bride. The bridegroom has put an end to Babylon's cruelty toward the bride that he loves. He has given Babylon what she deserves. Never again will she seduce. Never again will she become drunk on their blood. In fact, a mighty angel begins to recount all of the things that will never again take place in Babylon:

> Then a mighty angel took up a stone like a great millstone and threw
> it into the sea, saying,
>
> > "So will Babylon the great city be thrown down with violence,
> >   and will be found no more;
> > and the sound of harpists and musicians, of flute players and
> >   trumpeters,
> >   will be heard in you no more,
> > and a craftsman of any craft
> >   will be found in you no more,
> > and the sound of the mill
> >   will be heard in you no more,
> > and the light of a lamp
> >   will shine in you no more,

and the voice of bridegroom and bride
>   will be heard in you no more,
for your merchants were the great ones of the earth,
>   and all nations were deceived by your sorcery.
And in her was found the blood of prophets and of saints,
>   and of all who have been slain on earth." (Rev. 18:21–24)

No more culture and creativity. No more industry. No more purpose or meaning. No more light. No more love. Everything that brought richness and beauty to life will be gone for good. What a contrast to the "no mores" we read about in the new Jerusalem—no more tears, no more death, no more mourning or crying or pain (21:4).

Finally, we get to hear the bride speak. Instead of crying out "Alas! Alas!" she's crying out, "Hallelujah!" This is what she's been waiting for! All of her resistance to the world's seduction and all of her years of waiting for her bridegroom have proved worthwhile:

After this I heard what seemed to be the loud voice of a great multitude in heaven, crying out,

>   "Hallelujah!
> Salvation and glory and power belong to our God,
>   for his judgments are true and just;
> for he has judged the great prostitute
>   who corrupted the earth with her immorality,
> and has avenged on her the blood of his servants."
> Once more they cried out,
> "Hallelujah!
> The smoke from her goes up forever and ever."

And the twenty-four elders and the four living creatures fell down and worshiped God who was seated on the throne, saying, "Amen. Hallelujah!" And from the throne came a voice saying,

"Praise our God,
all you his servants,
you who fear him,
small and great."

Then I heard what seemed to be the voice of a great multitude, like the roar of many waters and like the sound of mighty peals of thunder, crying out,

"Hallelujah!
For the Lord our God
the Almighty reigns.
Let us rejoice and exult
and give him the glory,
for the marriage of the Lamb has come,
and his Bride has made herself ready;
it was granted her to clothe herself
with fine linen, bright and pure"—
for the fine linen is the righteous deeds of the saints.
(Rev. 19:1–8)

She has been preparing for this day, and the day is finally here. After all of the waiting, it is finally time for the wedding. And she is ready. And in this she shows us the third way we must prepare ourselves for our wedding day: *we have to say yes to the dress.*

The Dress

The wording John uses here is important. We read, "It was *granted her* to *clothe herself* with fine linen, bright and pure." And there is part of us that wants to say in response, "Which is it? Was the wedding dress given to her, or did she provide it herself?" And the answer is yes.

We can't get ourselves ready for this wedding on our own. We're being prepared as a bride *for* Jesus *by* Jesus. To be dressed appropriately for this wedding is going to require that we are provided with the perfect righteousness of another, the righteousness of Christ given to us as a gift. This grace given to us will also go to work in us so that we will be able to "put on then, as God's chosen ones, holy and beloved, compassionate hearts, kindness, humility, meekness, and patience, bearing with one another. . . . And above all these put on love, which binds everything together in perfect harmony" (Col. 3:12–14). We'll be empowered by this grace to live in a way that brings honor to our bridegroom. And when we fail, we can be sure that as we turn from our sin toward him in repentance, he will "forgive us our sins and . . . cleanse us from all unrighteousness" (1 John 1:9). We'll be provided with what we need to work out our salvation with fear and trembling (Phil. 2:12). The righteousness of our groom is going to work in and through our lives in such a way that his righteousness will be evident. It's going to purify us and beautify us and satisfy us.

> And the angel said to me, "Write this: Blessed are those who are invited to the marriage supper of the Lamb." And he said to me, "These are the true words of God." (Rev. 19:9)

The joy of our lives, the blessing of our lives, now and into the future is that we've been invited to the marriage supper of the Lamb, not simply as a guest, but as the bride. We've already been sealed to our bridegroom with the promised Holy Spirit (Eph. 1:13). He is going to show up right on time. We can count on it. So we must prepare for it. In fact, there's one more thing to do to prepare for it. But this isn't one of those things to put on your to-do list. It's one of those things brides who are in love with their bridegroom can't keep from doing, even if everyone around them wishes they wouldn't. Brides who are in love can't stop talking about the bridegroom. This is how we know we really are prepared for the wedding: *we find that we can't keep from talking about our bridegroom.*

Our Bridegroom

> Then I fell down at his feet to worship him, but he said to me, "You must not do that! I am a fellow servant with you and your brothers

who hold to the testimony of Jesus. Worship God." For the testimony of Jesus is the spirit of prophecy. (Rev. 19:10)

John is so overcome with the glory and beauty of what the angel has shown to him about our future marriage that, in a moment of wonder, he falls down to worship the angelic messenger and is quickly corrected. The angel is just the messenger with the good news, like John is and like we are to be. Love for your bridegroom Jesus means that you "hold to the testimony of Jesus." You simply can't stop talking about him to anyone who will listen.

I hate to put you on the spot, but I have to ask: Who was the last person you talked to about your bridegroom? Did she sense in you a longing for the wedding day, a longing for this eternal marriage?

The wedding day itself isn't actually in our passage in Revelation. We have to skip ahead to catch a glimpse of it. We find it in Revelation 21:2–3, where we read:

> I saw the holy city, new Jerusalem, coming down out of heaven from God, prepared as a bride adorned for her husband. And I heard a loud voice from the throne saying, "Behold, the dwelling place of God is with man. He will dwell with them, and they will be his people, and God himself will be with them as their God.

Finally, we'll have the relief and joy of being together, enjoying the marriage we were meant for, the happiest marriage of all time, the marriage that will never end.

Hearing and Keeping Revelation 17–19

Revelation 17 through 19 has shown us a vivid picture of what this world is like and what all who love this world can expect if they refuse to leave her. So what is it going to look like for us to hear and keep these chapters and thereby experience the promised blessing in it?

We live in Babylon. We shop in her supermarkets, wear her clothes, and benefit from her privileges. Perhaps the most important thing we must do is step back to get perspective on our lives and ask ourselves some questions:

- Have I allowed myself to be seduced by her?
- What does she offer me that threatens to entice me away from Christ?
- Are there areas in which I've compromised or made accommodation?
- Have I been too afraid of losing my job or losing customers or losing friends if I refuse to make the compromises the world applauds?
- Have I become so attached to certain luxuries that I would resent God for taking them away?
- Have some of the pleasures of life in this world, the enjoyment of things like sports and entertainment and food, morphed into idols that have become too important to me so that I have little time left for the things of God?
- What ideas, images, and dreams of the world have become so much a part of my thinking and feeling and dreaming that I don't even recognize them as worldly?

Perhaps a test of whether or not we've given our heart away to Babylon is how we respond when her luxuries, her benefits, are taken away from us now. In Revelation 18 we see the response of those who are closely entangled and dependent upon her. They mourn. But we also see the response of those who are called and chosen and faithful. They celebrate. They have taken the long view. They are so convinced that the world and its desires are passing away that when they see the world and its trinkets proving to be fleeting, instead of saying "Alas! Alas!" they say, "Hallelujah!" They recognize that God is answering their prayers. His kingdom is coming. His will is being done on earth as it is in heaven. They are rejoicing, but they're not gloating. They're rejoicing that evil will not have the final word in this world. Instead, this world's system of oppression, exploitation, greed, and violence will collapse under the judgment of God.

John wants us to see the world for what it is. What he communicates through this vision in Revelation, he states more clearly in his earlier letter: "Do not love the world or the things in the world. If anyone loves the world, the love of the Father is not in him. For all that is in the world—the desires of the flesh and the desires of the eyes and pride of life—is not from the Father but is from the world. And the world is passing away along with its desires, but whoever does the will of God abides forever" (1 John 2:15–17).

My friend, are you living like you really do believe that "the world is passing away"? The people in the churches who first received John's letter likely would have found it difficult to envision a day when Rome would fall. But that day came, just as it has come for so many world powers since then. Similarly, today, we have a hard time believing that governments that persecute God's people such as Burma, China, India, Iran, Nigeria, North Korea, Pakistan, Russia, Saudi Arabia, Syria, and Vietnam will ever be reduced to nothing. In fact, it is not merely the governments we consider to be set against Christ that will one day come to an end. Every human government has a limited shelf life. One day all of the many *isms* that have such a grip on the many cultures of the world—classism, racism, materialism, consumerism, egoism, hedonism, humanism—will no longer rule the day. Every kingdom will one day give way to the true kingdom.

Hearing and keeping this passage must mean that day by day and year after year we're finding that love for our true bridegroom is squeezing out any lingering love of the world. We're growing in wisdom and in our ability to see things as they are. We're better able to see what will last, where true security can be found.

Whenever we gather with fellow believers to come to the Lord's Table, we are, in a very real sense, coming away from Babylon. We're demonstrating our desire for our bridegroom, our longing for the greater feast that this feast points to. We're demonstrating that we don't expect that this world will ever satisfy us like Christ satisfies us. We believe what he said when he told us that he is coming soon. And so we're talking about him, preparing for him, waiting for him.

When I think about being prepared as a bride, it makes me think back to what it was like when David and I were engaged. We were already planning and merging our lives together, and as our wedding day got closer, it got harder and harder to go home to my little apartment at night. We wanted to be together. When we returned from our honeymoon and drove up to our apartment, David said what he had said many times during our engagement: "It is getting late, I guess I better drive you home." And we looked at each other and celebrated that we didn't have to be separated anymore.

One day, after all of the preparing for the wedding, our bridegroom will come for us. All of the waiting will be over. The wedding will give way to the marriage, an eternity of togetherness with the one who loves us. Until then, let's keep ourselves pure for him, let's talk about him, let's love him with all of our souls, all of our strength, and all of our minds.

Blessed by Sharing in the Resurrection of Jesus

Revelation 19:11–20:15

"THE RIGHT SIDE OF HISTORY" or "the wrong side of history." We hear these phrases bandied about in relation to all kinds of political and social issues and positions. What do people mean when they talk about being on the wrong side of history? I think they mean that the dominant opinion amongst people in a future era will judge a particular action or attitude to be proven wrong. But there is an assumption to that, isn't there? It assumes that history is a moral force in and of itself, and that this world is always progressing toward what is good and beautiful and true. It assumes that the majority opinion at any given time is what determines these things. And I think we know better than that, don't we?

But there is some value in considering what it will mean to be on the right side of history, not merely next year or in the next decade or century but at the end of human history as we know it. It is a worthy consideration, because to be on the wrong side of where history is headed has significant consequences. Eternal consequences.

Actually, it is not difficult to know what it will mean to be on the right or wrong side of history when human history as we know it comes to an end. Anyone who has read the third chapter of Genesis knows exactly where the problems we have in this world come from and exactly how our problems are going to be resolved. Genesis 3:15 is like a neon sign declaring to anyone who will heed its wisdom exactly how to be on the right side of history. Genesis 3:15 says that an offspring of the woman is going to one day crush the head of the offspring of the serpent. He's going to put an end to evil. Until that day, there is going to be conflict between the offspring of the serpent and the offspring of the woman. But there is no question who will be the ultimate victor.

To be on the right side of history is to be on the side of the victor, the offspring of the woman, the Lamb, the King, the one who, according to the passage at hand, is called "Faithful and True," "The Word of God," the "King of kings" and the "Lord of lords." And to be on the wrong side of history is to be in league with the offspring of the serpent, the dragon, the beast and the false prophet, the accuser, the deceiver, the devil.

Revelation 19:11 through 20:15 depicts in vivid detail how the conflict that began in the garden and has raged throughout human history will come to its final climax and conclusion. In fact, we've been witnessing the crushing of the offspring of the serpent in the chapters leading up to these. In chapter 17 we saw the great prostitute destroyed. In chapter 18 we witnessed the fall of Babylon. In chapters 19 and 20 we're going to witness the final destruction of the unholy trinity we met back in chapters 12 and 13—the dragon, the beast, the false prophet— and all who have given their allegiance to him. We might be tempted to think these things are taking place sequentially because they follow each other in John's account. But more likely John is simply moving the camera to shoot the same scene from various angles so that we can see the various aspects of the final defeat of evil. When this happens, all who have overcome the world, the flesh, and the devil by becoming joined to Christ will undisputedly prove to have been on the right side of history, even as we begin an eternity of enjoyment of the King, living forever in his kingdom.

In his sermon on Revelation 20, Andrew Latimer applies this idea of being on the right or wrong side of history to what John presents here, which I will borrow to work through Revelation 19 and 20.[1] What will it mean to be on the right side of history, according to Revelation 19 and 20? Let's work our way through it to find out.

Sharing in the Victory

Being on the right side of history will mean sharing in the victory of King Jesus instead of sharing in the defeat of the beast and the kings of the earth.

> Then I saw heaven opened, and behold, a white horse! The one sitting on it is called Faithful and True, and in righteousness he judges and makes war. His eyes are like a flame of fire, and on his head are many diadems, and he has a name written that no one knows but himself. He is clothed in a robe dipped in blood, and the name by which he is called is The Word of God. And the armies of heaven, arrayed in fine linen, white and pure, were following him on white horses. From his mouth comes a sharp sword with which to strike down the nations, and he will rule them with a rod of iron. He will tread the winepress of the fury of the wrath of God the Almighty. On his robe and on his thigh he has a name written, King of kings and Lord of lords. (Rev. 19:11–16)

We ended the last chapter with the bride waiting for her bridegroom to come for her, and in this passage we see that he has come. But he doesn't seem dressed for the wedding. That's because there is something he must do first, something he must take care of in order to begin his marriage to his bride. He has to deal with evil. That's what he is dressed for. He arrives on the scene dressed like a warrior. This is the warrior Messiah that the Old Testament prophets wrote about, the one so many were looking for in his first coming. He came the first time as a shepherd

---

1 Andrew Latimer, "Don't Find Yourself on the Wrong Side of History," sermon, Grace Church Greenwich, May 9, 2021, https://www.greenwich.church/.

king who laid down his life for his sheep. But here is a picture of his second coming. He is "riding a white stallion, wielding a sword to slay the enemies of his church."[2]

He is coming to make war. This will be a perfectly just war, a war waged for the purpose of establishing shalom on the earth. It will also be a bloody battle. We see the evidence on the warrior's clothing, a picture that immediately reminds us of Isaiah 63 in which Isaiah sees a divine warrior arriving from enemy territory with crimsoned garments, saying that the lifeblood of his enemies has spattered on his garments.

History is replete with wicked tyrants who have perverted justice and wielded the sword for personal gain and power. But not this warrior king. Jesus comes asserting the power that emanates from his own being as he who is Faithful and True. When he comes to make war on his enemies, it will be a perfectly righteous war. It will be the execution of perfect justice.

Jesus will "tread the winepress of the fury of the wrath of God." When we think about a winepress, we may have idyllic images in our minds of barefoot men and women happily crushing grapes with their feet. This picture is not that. There is no joy in this scene. These are people being crushed, and while it is figurative, it is a depiction of a reality that should terrify those who have set themselves against this good king. In the end evil must be crushed and destroyed. And it will be.

When Jesus comes, he will be accompanied by the armies of heaven, which will include his mighty angels (2 Thess. 1:7) and also all who have bowed the knee to him as King. But he will not be merely another king on the scene vying for power or territory. He will be the King over every king.

In the last chapter we read about the marriage supper of the Lamb. Here we read about another supper, but it could not be more different.

Feasting at the Marriage Supper

Earlier in Revelation 19:9 John writes that those who are invited to the marriage supper of the Lamb are blessed. But then a few verses later

---

2   Richard D. Phillips, *Revelation*, Reformed Expository Commentary (Phillipsburg, NJ: P&R, 2000), 543.

he describes a very different kind of supper, a gruesome supper. Being on the right side of history will mean feasting at the marriage supper of the Lamb instead of being feasted on by the birds at the great supper of God:

> Then I saw an angel standing in the sun, and with a loud voice he called to all the birds that fly directly overhead, "Come, gather for the great supper of God, to eat the flesh of kings, the flesh of captains, the flesh of mighty men, the flesh of horses and their riders, and the flesh of all men, both free and slave, both small and great." And I saw the beast and the kings of the earth with their armies gathered to make war against him who was sitting on the horse and against his army. And the beast was captured, and with it the false prophet who in its presence had done the signs by which he deceived those who had received the mark of the beast and those who worshiped its image. These two were thrown alive into the lake of fire that burns with sulfur. And the rest were slain by the sword that came from the mouth of him who was sitting on the horse, and all the birds were gorged with their flesh. (Rev. 19:17–21)

Notice the inclusiveness of this horror—"all men, both free and slave, both small and great." Status or lack thereof isn't going to make a difference on this day. The only thing that will matter is whether a person's guilt has been dealt with. And there are only two ways guilt can be dealt with. If our guilt has not been dealt with at the cross of Christ, it will be dealt with on the battlefield of Armageddon.

The beast and the false prophet are captured and thrown alive into the lake of fire. All who have aligned themselves with the beast are slain by the sword in one swift motion. And then the vultures show up to feast on them—such an inglorious end to so many who certainly seemed so impressive. Such a contrast to the glorious end of so many who may have seemed unimpressive to the world but were known and loved and saved by Christ, those who are clearly on the right side of history, who will be welcomed to feast at the marriage supper of the Lamb.

Reigning with Christ

Being on the right side of history will mean reigning with Christ in heaven rather than tormented with Satan in the lake of fire and sulfur.

Let's take stock of the targets of God's anger dealt with so far. Babylon: fallen. Beast and false prophet: thrown into the lake of fire. Humanity that has refused the grace and mercy of Christ in favor of being in league with the beast: slain by the sword. There's only one more member of the unholy alliance to be dealt with:

> Then I saw an angel coming down from heaven, holding in his hand the key to the bottomless pit and a great chain. And he seized the dragon, that ancient serpent, who is the devil and Satan, and bound him for a thousand years, and threw him into the pit, and shut it and sealed it over him, so that he might not deceive the nations any longer, until the thousand years were ended. After that he must be released for a little while. (Rev. 20:1–3)

When we read, "Then I saw . . ." at the beginning of chapter 20, we are tipped off that John is presenting a new "camera angle" on events that don't necessarily follow the events of chapter 19 chronologically.[3] John sees another vision. He sees an angel coming down from heaven with two things in his hands: the key to the bottomless pit and a great chain (and, of course, we're remembering that these things are symbols). This angel is on a mission from God to bind up Satan and lock him into the pit. A key question for us to ask and answer is, "When did or does this happen?" And we realize that actually we've read before about the binding of Satan in each of the Gospels.

In Matthew 12 and Mark 3 Jesus is being challenged by the Pharisees after casting demons out of a man who was blind and mute. The Pharisees say that only Beelzebub, the prince of demons, can cast out demons. And Jesus says to them, "How can someone enter a strong

---

3   A detailed case for the events of Revelation 20 not following the events of Revelation 19 chronologically is made by Anthony Hoekema, *The Bible and the Future* (Grand Rapids, MI: Eerdmans, 1994), 227–38.

man's house and plunder his goods, unless he first binds the strong man? Then indeed he may plunder his house" (Matt. 12:29). Clearly Jesus is saying that he has bound "the strong man," and is therefore able to "plunder his house" by casting out these demons.

In Luke 10 the seventy-two followers that Jesus sent two by two into towns ahead of him have returned, saying, "Lord, even the demons are subject to us in your name!" And [Jesus] says to them, "I saw Satan fall like lightning from heaven" (Luke 10:17–18). I've often heard it taught that Jesus is referring here to what happened when Satan first rebelled against God. But Jesus is responding to what has just happened in the ministry of his emissaries. "Jesus saw in the works his disciples were doing an indication that Satan's kingdom had just been dealt a crushing blow—that, in fact, a certain binding of Satan, a certain restriction of his power, had just taken place."[4] Satan has fallen because the demons are losing their grip on their tools of deception and destruction as the word of Christ goes out and Christ's kingdom claims new territory in the hearts and lives of those who repent and believe.

In the days leading up to his crucifixion Jesus said, "Now is the judgment of this world; now will the ruler of this world be cast out. And I, when I am lifted up from the earth, will draw all people to myself" (John 12:31–32). In Jesus's crucifixion and resurrection from the dead, Satan will be cast out and bound so that he can no longer deceive the nations. This will free "all people," in other words, people from every tribe, tongue, and nation, from Satan's deception so that they will embrace Christ by faith.

One more, from Paul. In Colossians, Paul writes that in nailing the record of debt that stood against us with its legal demands to the cross, "he disarmed the rulers and authorities and put them to open shame, by triumphing over them" (Col. 2:15). These passages point to the disarmament or binding of Satan that took place in the life, death, resurrection, and ascension of Christ.

4   Hoekema, *The Bible and the Future*, 229.

So rather than seeing the binding of Satan as an event that will take place at or near the end of the age we're living in, it makes more sense to understand it as Satan being bound and restricted through the life, death, and resurrection of Jesus, and that he is bound or restricted even now.

John writes that Satan will be bound for one thousand years. And as soon as we hear it, we are reminded that the numbers throughout Revelation have consistently been used to symbolize realities. If ten represents completeness in the human experience or dimension, one thousand represents 10 x 10 x 10, the ultimate completion. That's how we understand the symbolism of this number when it appears elsewhere in Scripture.[5] For example, when we hear God speaking in Psalm 50:10, saying, "Every beast of the forest is mine, the cattle on a thousand hills," we don't insist that there are literally one thousand hills that contain the cattle that God owns. Likewise, here, one thousand years means a complete period of time, the length of which is known only by God. We don't know how long it will be until Satan is loosed for a brief time before Jesus returns. But we know it will be the right time.

We can't help but wonder, however, how Satan can be bound in the time we are living in and still have so much power and do so much damage in the world. The answer is that binding doesn't necessarily mean total restraint. Satan is bound in a specific way. He is restricted and limited but not totally confined. He still prowls around like a roaring lion seeing to devour (1 Pet. 5:8). He still oversees "the spiritual forces of evil" at work against believers (Eph. 6:12). We can think of him as being on a leash, a very long leash.

Satan is bound in this way for a specific purpose—so that his lies about the goodness of God and the hope found in the gospel will not

---

5   The Bible's use of the number ten includes ten "God said" statements at creation, the Ten Commandments, ten plagues, ten virgins, and ten lepers. It's use of one thousand includes Num. 10:36, "Return, O LORD, to the ten thousand thousands of Israel"; Deut. 7:9, "the faithful God who keeps covenant and steadfast love with those who love him and keep his commandments, to a thousand generations"; Ps. 84:10, "For a day in your courts is better than a thousand elsewhere"; Ezek. 47:3–5, referring to the measurement of the new temple in Ezekiel's vision, "the man measured a thousand cubits"; and 2 Pet. 3:8, "with the Lord one day is as a thousand years, and a thousand years as one day."

have the power to deceive the nations. Yes, some people, many people, are deceived. But not like they were before the death, resurrection, and ascension of Jesus and the sending of the Holy Spirit.

If we go back to the Old Testament, we remember that after we read about the promise to Abraham, that through him "all the families of the earth shall be blessed" (Gen. 12:3), there was not an immediate huge influx of the nations taking hold of the covenant promises of God. We read about individuals or particular tribes joining themselves to the people of God in the worship of Yahweh in the Old Testament, but it is limited. And then everything changes with the coming of King Jesus into the world and the sending of his Spirit upon his ascension. We read in the Gospels how Jesus reached outside the fold of the Jews with the gospel so that Gentiles began to take hold of him by faith. We read in Acts how Pentecost ushered in an era of the gospel being preached in Jerusalem, Judea, Samaria, and to the ends of the earth so that the word was spreading and believed. We read in the Epistles about churches being formed throughout the known world. What changed? Satan was bound through the life, death, resurrection, and ascension of Jesus so that the nations were no longer deceived, and they began coming in. Satan remains bound until all who were chosen in Christ for salvation from every people group of the world are safely in the fold.

John has seen a vision of what is happening on earth during the period between the first and second coming of Jesus in regard to Satan's limitations. Next he sees what is happening in heaven during this same period of time.

Sharing in the Resurrection

Being on the right side of history will mean sharing in the resurrection of Jesus rather than succumbing to the second death:

> Then I saw thrones, and seated on them were those to whom the authority to judge was committed. Also I saw the souls of those who had been beheaded for the testimony of Jesus and for the word of God, and those who had not worshiped the beast or its image and

had not received its mark on their foreheads or their hands. They came to life and reigned with Christ for a thousand years. The rest of the dead did not come to life until the thousand years were ended. This is the first resurrection. Blessed and holy is the one who shares in the first resurrection! Over such the second death has no power, but they will be priests of God and of Christ, and they will reign with him for a thousand years. (Rev. 20:4–6)

John sees thrones. And we need to ask, where are these thrones located? Throughout revelation the thrones have been in heaven. So we know right off that this scene is a heavenly scene, not something taking place on earth. He sees souls, not people who are body and soul. These are the souls of people who held to their testimony of Jesus to their final breath. And for them, that last breath was simply a passageway into reigning with Christ in heaven.

Imagine the comfort it must have been to those believers in the seven churches who had watched as people they loved had been put to death for their allegiance to Jesus, to feast their eyes and their hearts on this picture of those saints reigning with Christ in heaven. It would have emboldened them in their own witness, as they recognized that suffering on earth for Jesus results in reigning with Christ in heaven.

John describes the raising of the souls of believers into the presence of Christ to reign with him as "the first resurrection," indicating that a second or final resurrection is coming. When Jesus returns to this earth, the souls of those gathered to him in heaven are going to come with him. He is going to call the dust of our bodies out of their graves, and from that dust he is going to fashion for us glorious bodies like his own glorious body. Right now, there is only one human being who has a glorified body. But he is just the first. The day is coming when we will once again be body and soul, but this time with bodies that can never die.

Those who are not in Christ never experience that first resurrection of soul into the presence of Christ. They will be raised only once, at the coming of Jesus, to stand before him in judgment. And on that day it will be very clear what it will mean to be on the right side of history.

Preserved through the Fire

Being on the right side of history will mean being preserved through the fire instead of consumed by the fire.

The thousand years during which the saints have reigned and the devil has been held in check will end with the release of Satan from his prison or binding for a brief period of time in which he will be able to deceive the nations for the express purpose of gathering his army of followers for a final but futile battle against Jesus and his church:

> When the thousand years are ended, Satan will be released from his prison and will come out to deceive the nations that are at the four corners of the earth, Gog and Magog, to gather them for battle; their number is like the sand of the sea. And they marched up over the broad plain of the earth and surrounded the camp of the saints and the beloved city, but fire came down from heaven and consumed them, and the devil who had deceived them was thrown into the lake of fire and sulfur where the beast and the false prophet were, and they will be tormented day and night forever and ever. (Rev. 20:7–10)

We've already read about this war and its outcome a couple of times from different angles earlier in Revelation. This is the same battle as Armageddon presented in the sixth bowl in chapter 16 and as the war on the Lamb presented in chapters 17 and 19. In each of these battle scenes, the defeat is too final for these passages to be anything other than varied descriptions of the same event—the last battle of history. Each portrayal of this battle has shown us unique aspects so that we will live now and witness now and rest now in light of it.

Here's how Paul wrote about this same final battle: "Then the lawless one will be revealed, whom the Lord Jesus will kill with the breath of his mouth and bring to nothing by the appearance of his coming" (2 Thess. 2:8). Jesus merely puffs out a breath, and evil is gone for good. Here in Revelation, John portrays this final battle as a blast of fire. No prolonged battling back and forth with onlookers wondering who will get the upper hand in the end. In a moment, the Creator of the heavens and the earth will bring an end to the conflict that has been raging ever since he put enmity between the offspring of the woman and the offspring of the serpent.

The chapter ends with the final event that must transpire to deal with the world's evil so that the new creation can be ushered in.

Rewarded

Being on the right side of history will mean being rewarded instead of condemned by what is written in the books:

> Then I saw a great white throne and him who was seated on it. From his presence earth and sky fled away, and no place was found for them. And I saw the dead, great and small, standing before the throne, and books were opened. Then another book was opened, which is the book of life. And the dead were judged by what was written in the books, according to what they had done. And the sea gave up the dead who were in it, Death and Hades gave up the dead who were in them, and they were judged, each one of them, according to what they had done. Then Death and Hades were thrown into the lake of fire. This is the second death, the lake of fire. And if anyone's name was not found written in the book of life, he was thrown into the lake of fire. (Rev. 20:11–15)

As we consider this description of the final judgment, there are several questions we want to ask and answer: (1) Who will be judged in this judgment? (2) On what basis will they be judged? (3) What will be the results of the judgment?

So, first, who will be judged in this judgment? Some say that the only people facing this judgment are those who are spiritually dead—those who have lived and died outside of Christ. But more likely this is a picture of all who have died physically—saints and sinners—appearing before God's judgment throne. In numerous passages elsewhere in the Bible we've been told that all people appear before this divine judge. Paul writes in Romans 14:10–12, "We will *all* stand before the judgment seat of God. . . . Each of us will give an account of himself to God." In 2 Corinthians 5:10 he writes, "We must *all* appear before the judgment seat of Christ, so that *each one* may receive what is due for what he has done in the body, whether good or evil." What Paul stresses in these verses is *each* and *every* and *all*.

So if we will all be judged, on what basis will we be judged? According to this passage we'll be judged on the basis of what is written in the books. But notice that here in Revelation 20:11–15 there are "the books" and there is "another book," which is "the book of life." The key to understanding what this passage means for your future is understanding the difference between "the books" and "the book."

The books contain a record of the life of every person who has ever lived. It is stunning that so many people think this is going to work out well for them. We know "there is none who does good, not even one" (Ps. 14:3). No one will be able to stand before God solely on the basis of the record of his or her deeds. What is written in the books will condemn them.

"The book" is quite different from "the books." Elsewhere (Rev. 13:8; 21:27), this book is called "the Lamb's book of life," meaning that it is a list of all whose sins have been covered by the blood of the Lamb. The book is a record of the names of all those God calls his own. It is a list of all those who know him and love him, all those whom God chose in him before the creation of the world to be holy and blameless in his sight (Eph. 1:4). All those "he predestined . . . for adoption to himself as sons through Jesus Christ, according to the purpose of his will" (Eph. 1:5). It is the list of names that make up the bride, the elect, those who were once spiritually dead and have been made alive by becoming joined to Christ.

Moses knew about this book. In pleading for God to spare the sinful Israelites he said, "But now, if you will forgive their sin—but if not, please blot me out of your book that you have written" (Ex. 32:32).

Jesus referred to this book too, telling the disciples who were bragging about their ability to overpower demons, "Nevertheless, do not rejoice in this, that the spirits are subject to you, but rejoice that your names are written in heaven" (Luke 10:20).

The presentation of both the book of life and the books does beg the question, If your name is in the book of life, is the record of your life in the books irrelevant? No, it isn't.

In his sermon "We Will All Stand before the Judgment of God," John Piper explains that what is written in the books is condemnation for those who are not connected to Christ, but it will be confirmation for all who are joined to him by faith.[6] What is written there will confirm that they are connected to Christ in a saving, transforming way. If you are in Christ, the books will show how you threw yourself on his mercy and welcomed his forgiveness, how your appetites and affections changed as his Holy Spirit was at work in you, and it became evident in how you lived your life. The books will provide an accounting of all the things God's grace in your life has empowered you to do and become because of your connectedness to Jesus.

And what will be the result of this judgment? Those who have nothing to plead but their own fleshly works will find that all of their efforts are woefully inadequate to protect them from the second death, the death of the soul. It is hard to read the words that describe what the result will be for those who have rejected Christ and therefore are missing that crucial deed of calling upon his mercy. But as hard as it is to read the words "thrown into the lake of fire," the reality behind the words is utterly unbearable.

Revelation 20 doesn't tell us specifically what the result of this judgment will be for those who have overcome the world and clung to Christ, but other passages do. Jesus said, "The Son of Man is going to come with his angels in the glory of his Father, and then he will repay each person according to what he has done" (Matt. 16:27). And in the very last chapter of Revelation Jesus puts it this way: "Behold,

6   John Piper, "We Will All Stand before the Judgment of God," sermon, Bethlehem Baptist Church, Minneapolis, MN, October 30, 2005, https://www.desiringgod.org/.

I am coming soon, bringing my recompense with me, to repay each one for what he has done" (Rev. 22:12). What follows judgment for the believer is reward. In what form? I don't know. But whatever it is, I want it; don't you?

> What no eye has seen, nor ear heard,
>   nor the heart of man imagined,
> what God has prepared for those who love him. (1 Cor. 2:9)

Whatever it is, it will prove to define what it means to be blessed.

Hearing and Keeping Revelation 19:11–20:15

We've been considering what it will mean to be on the right or wrong side of history when human history as we know it comes to an end. And Revelation 19 and 20 have presented to us two starkly different destinies. To be on the right side of history will often mean being out of step with the prevailing attitudes, values, and power brokers in our day. But on the final day of history, while many will regret their loyalty to the current regime, no one who has sided with Jesus will have an ounce of regret.

These chapters in Revelation have shown us that those who serve in the army of the King, those who share in the resurrection of Christ, those who are safe inside the camp of the saints, those whose names are found in the book of life, will prove to have been on the right side of history. So to hear and keep what is written in these chapters is most significantly to run to Jesus and become joined to him in his death so that you will share in his resurrection, make your home in the camp of the saints, and become washed in the blood of the Lamb. The most urgent issue of life is whether or not King Jesus is your king.

If it is true (and it is!) that Satan has been bound so that he can no longer deceive the nations with his lies about the benefits of Christ, it means that we can invest ourselves in sharing the gospel with people who have never heard it before, confident that some will be able to hear it, understand it, and respond to it in repentance and faith. Sometimes we are so pessimistic about the possibility that someone we share the gospel with will really make that turn toward Christ. But the good news we've seen in Revelation 20 is that Satan with his lies is the one who is limited and disadvantaged, not Christ and his truth.

If it is true (and it is!) that when we die, an eternal life of reigning with Christ will have only begun, we don't have to be afraid of being marginalized, persecuted, hated, or harmed in the short number of years of this life. We don't have to be afraid of the unknowns of death because of what has been revealed clearly about this life after death.

And that is good news because of what we're shown here about the ultimate release of Satan to wage war immediately before Jesus comes to doom him to eternal torment. This means that we can expect not less but more apostasy, false teaching that will deceive many, and persecution, making it more challenging to persevere in the truth. But it also means that for the rest of our lives we can live with confidence that the devil's final defeat and destruction are sure. He will not tyrannize the church with his evil schemes forever.

As we consider what the coming judgment of humanity means for us, it means that how we live out the ordinary days of our lives matters for all eternity. One day we will give an account of how we have used what God has entrusted to us for a return for his kingdom, and everything we've done for the glory of God will add to our eternal joy.

We will find ourselves on the right side of history, not because we were smart or savvy, but because in grace our king revealed himself to us, called us to himself, and intends to share his victory with us for all eternity.

11

Blessed by Living in the New Creation with Jesus

Revelation 21:1–22:5

HAVE YOU EVER experienced something or done something that made you think to yourself, *I was made for this?* I remember feeling that way when I got my first job as a publicist at a Christian publishing company. Because I was musical, I had originally pursued a job hoping to find a place in the record and music side of the company. But the open position was for a publicity assistant in the book publishing side. I loved books, so I went for it. And it didn't take me long to recognize that I had landed in a job I was made for.

I suppose some people have this sense when they discover that they have a body made for running fast, or a mind made for numbers, or a flare for cooking or decorating. I was not made for any of those things.

Perhaps the opposite of having a sense of "I was made for this" is a sense of "This is not the way it should be." And most of us have felt that way at one time or another. Achieving what we hoped for shouldn't be this hard. Relationships shouldn't be this fragile. Governments shouldn't be this corrupt. Bodies shouldn't be this vulnerable. Losses shouldn't be this painful. Work shouldn't be this frustrating. Churches shouldn't be this conflict-ridden. Life shouldn't be this lonely. So much of our life is marked by "This is not the way it should be," isn't it?

Fortunately, we have the Bible, which reveals to us what we were all made for as well as why things are not the way they should be. There is a relationship, a home, a purpose we were made for that Adam and Eve lost for us in that day they turned away from the goodness of God in the garden of Eden. It was their rebellion against God that ushered in the "This is not the way it should be" in this world. Fortunately, however, the Bible assures us that this is not the way it will be forever. Revelation 21 and 22 present us with a picture of the day when all who are in Christ will leave behind "This is not the way it should be" for good, to enter into the ultimate and eternal "I was made for this," because, in fact, we *were* made for this. Revelation 21 and 22 shows us the relationship we were made to share, the land we were made to inherit, the community we were made to be a part of, the glory we were made to bask in, and the satisfaction we were made to enjoy forever.

At the center of the passage is a declaration, which is actually the hope at the center of our existence, so we'll start there:

> He who was seated on the throne said, "Behold, I am making all things new." Also he said, "Write this down, for these words are trustworthy and true." (Rev. 21:5)

We're told lots of things by untrustworthy sources, by people who have an agenda. But here, we're presented with a truth that is solid enough to build a life on. The person speaking does have an agenda. His agenda is blessing, and his means of accomplishing this agenda is pervasive, permanent newness. This is the newness that we long for in a world in which everything breaks down, everything wears out, everything is impacted by the curse. The promise here is not that God is going to make all new things but rather that all of the things in his creation that have been impacted by the curse are going to be restored, renewed, and resurrected.

> He said to me, "It is done! I am the Alpha and the Omega, the beginning and the end." (Rev. 21:6)

The one who set things in motion in the beginning is the one who will bring all things to their intended end. We read about the beginning in Genesis 1 through 3, and now, we get to read about the end here in Revelation 21 and 22.

~ The Alpha and the Omega who, in the beginning, presented a bride to his son Adam will, in the end, present a bride to his Son, the second Adam. This is the happy marriage we were made to enjoy.

~ The Alpha and the Omega who, in the beginning, created a land for Adam and Eve and their offspring will, in the end, give that land—the whole world—as an inheritance to all who become his sons and daughters by faith (Rom. 4:13). This is the land we were meant to inherit.

~ The Alpha and the Omega who, in the beginning, instructed Adam and Eve to be fruitful and multiply and fill the earth, will, in the end, welcome a people from every tribe, tongue, and nation into a city that will fill the earth. This is the multicultural community we were made to be a part of.

~ The Alpha and the Omega, who, in the beginning, walked with his people in the sanctuary of Eden, will, in the end, dwell with his people in the most holy place, which will extend to every corner of the earth. This is the glory we were made to bask in.

~ The Alpha and the Omega, who, in the beginning, planted the tree of life in the center of the garden to nourish and sustain his people, will, in the end, welcome the nations into a new garden where all will find healing and wholeness, fullness of satisfaction and provision. This is the life, the healing, and the satisfaction we were made to enjoy forever.

Doesn't all of this sound good? This is the world, the life, we were made for. And it is exactly what John saw in his vision.

> Then I saw a new heaven and a new earth, for the first heaven and the first earth had passed away, and the sea was no more. (Rev. 21:1)

The "first earth," or the "old order" as some translations of Revelation 21:4 put it, the way things work in a world impacted by the curse, is no more. John saw what the creation will be like when "his blessings flow far as the curse is found,"[1] after the creation is purged of evil, when "the creation itself will be set free from its bondage to corruption and obtain the freedom of the glory of the children of God" (Rom. 8:21). The sea is portrayed as a place of chaos, evil, and danger throughout the Scriptures, and in Revelation the sea has been the abode of the beast. So when John says that the sea is no more, he's saying that nothing evil will ever arise in the new creation.

John then begins to use the imagery used throughout the Bible—the imagery of marriage, inheritance, the city, the temple, and the garden—to put the wonders of what the new creation will be like on display, beginning with the Bible's imagery of a marriage.

The Marriage You Were Meant to Share

In the beginning, God brought a bride to his son Adam. This was a marriage filled with so much promise. It was a marriage with a mission. They were supposed to fill the earth and subdue it, extending the boundaries of Eden so that the whole earth would become a garden paradise filled with God's image bearers. Two sinless people with nothing to hide and everything to share. But when sin entered the picture, the joy of being presented with a bride turned into finger-pointing at the bride, saying "The woman whom you gave to be with me, she gave me fruit of the tree, and I ate" (Gen. 3:12). The impact of the curse meant that their marriage became infected with power struggles and disappointment.

A more faithful bridegroom than Adam was needed, one who would obey rather than rebel, one who would faithfully lead his bride to eat from the tree of life together rather than cause them to be barred from it. And when Jesus showed up on the scene, that's how John identified him in his Gospel, as the faithful bridegroom. John records John the Baptist saying, "The one who has the bride is the bridegroom"

---

1   Isaac Watts, "Joy to the World," 1719.

(John 3:29). Paul presents Jesus in these terms as well, writing that ever since that first marriage in Eden, marriage has always been most profoundly about the greater eternal marriage of Christ and his bride (Eph. 5:32). In 5:31 he quotes Moses, who wrote, "Therefore a man shall leave his father and mother and hold fast to his wife, and the two shall become one flesh" (Gen. 2:24) and says, "This mystery is profound, and I am saying that it refers to Christ and the church" (5:32). Human marriage was always intended to tell us something about the relationship God desires to share with his people.

Of course, so far, as we await this eternal marriage to Christ, it has proved to be a very long engagement. And Revelation seems to recognize that it can be so very hard to stay faithful over a long-distance engagement. The book of Revelation has been a call for patient endurance, a call for the bride of Christ to patiently and expectantly watch for her bridegroom to come. And in Revelation 21, John sees a vision of the day when the waiting will finally be over:

> I saw the holy city, new Jerusalem, coming down out of heaven from God, prepared as a bride adorned for her husband. (Rev. 21:2)

It is the beautiful bride of Christ, ready for the wedding, ready for the consummation of an eternal marriage to her bridegroom. The separation will be over. Finally, bride and bridegroom will be at home together:

> And I heard a loud voice from the throne saying, "Behold, the dwelling place of God is with man. He will dwell with them, and they will be his people, and God himself will be with them as their God. He will wipe away every tear from their eyes, and death shall be no more, neither shall there be mourning, nor crying, nor pain anymore, for the former things have passed away." (Rev. 21:3–4)

This dwelling with man is what God has always wanted. And if you think about it, that's really quite amazing, isn't it, that God desires to dwell with us? He does. And clearly he wants to draw close, so close that he will be able to wipe away the tears from our eyes, all the tears we have shed over the suffering and losses of this life. Patient endurance in this life doesn't mean that what we experience as we wait doesn't hurt. There is so much to living in this world that brings pain. But we can be sure that our bridegroom has seen the hurts, the sacrifices, and the slights. He knows what it is like to live in this world because he entered into this world to live in it, and he experienced the worst of this world's hurts. One day he is going to come again for us. He will arrive as a warrior king on a white horse to do away with everything that has brought us pain and sorrow. And then he will come to us as a bridegroom so that our eternal marriage can begin. We'll finally have the intimacy with him we've always longed for but have never been able to achieve or maintain. We will love him who first loved us.

You may have been blessed in this life with a long and happy marriage. If so, you've had a foretaste of heaven. Or you may have spent a lot of years longing to be married or a lot of years disappointed in a marriage or have come to the place of giving up on marriage altogether. The truth is, as good as human marriage can be, no marriage can live up to the level of our desires for what only this eternal marriage to our divine bridegroom can and will provide.

One day God is going to present us as a bride to his Son, the one who loved us and gave himself up for us, that he might sanctify us, having cleansed us by the washing of water with the word, so that he might present us to himself in splendor, without spot or wrinkle or any such thing, that we might be holy and without blemish (see Eph. 5:25–27). His face will radiate with a joy that will be reflected in our faces. He will welcome us into his home so that the eternal marriage can begin.

The Land You Were Meant to Inherit

While the imagery of bride and bridegroom captures the intimacy we will share into eternity with Christ, the imagery of father and son captures the inheritance that will be ours in Christ:

The one who conquers will have this heritage, and I will be his God and he will be my son. But as for the cowardly, the faithless, the detestable, as for murderers, the sexually immoral, sorcerers, idolaters, and all liars, their portion will be in the lake that burns with fire and sulfur, which is the second death. (Rev. 21:7–8)

In the beginning, Adam and Eve were given dominion and told to be fruitful and multiply and fill the earth. Had they obeyed, the whole earth would have been theirs. But when Adam and Eve disobeyed, they were ejected from the garden and lost their access and claim to the land. So God began working in his people to give them an inheritance of land by calling Abraham to leave his family and his country to go to the land he was giving to him. Abraham's descendants went into exile in Egypt for four hundred years, but Moses led them out of Egypt, and Joshua led them back into the promised land giving each tribe, clan, and family an inheritance of land. To have land in the promised land was to have a share in all of God's promises to his people, all of his promised blessings.

Of course, Abraham always understood that the land God gave to him and his descendants was really pointing toward a far greater inheritance. The writer of Hebrews says, "By faith [Abraham] went to live in the land of promise, as in a foreign land, living in tents with Isaac and Jacob, heirs with him of the same promise. For he was looking forward to the city that has foundations, whose designer and builder is God" (Heb. 11:9–10). Abraham evidently saw through the promise of the land of Canaan into its deeper reality. Paul writes that "the promise to Abraham and his offspring [was] that he would be heir of the world" and that everyone who lives by faith is "his offspring" (Rom. 4:13, 16). That means that if you are in Christ, you, along with the rest of your brothers and sisters, stand to inherit . . . the world. One day, our greater Joshua is going to lead us into the land of which the promised land of Canaan was always a mere shadow. We will finally take full possession of our inheritance in the true land of milk and honey. This will be the land we've always longed for, the land that Canaan was always pointing toward, the land where we will finally be at home.

But to make this grand inheritance possible, Jesus had to be cut off from the land. Isaiah writes that "he was cut off out of the land of the living, stricken for the transgression of my people." (Isa. 53:8). Jesus was exiled from the land of blessing and descended into the realm of the dead so that you and I can anticipate living in the land of promise forever.

You may be blessed with a tremendous inheritance from your earthly family. Perhaps you stand to inherit a significant amount of wealth or some valuable property. Perhaps you've been given a name that commands respect and a great sense of belonging. Or perhaps you don't have any of these things. Perhaps you have been estranged from your family or have never really had a home or a place where you feel you belong. No matter what your earthly father and mother have or haven't provided for you or passed along to you, if you are in Christ, you can be sure that your heavenly Father intends to provide you with a vast inheritance. He has already given you his name. Your brother has gone ahead to prepare a place for you. A treasure is being stored up for you as you love and serve him. Arms are being opened for you. A table is being set for you. So you must refuse to make your home in this world, refuse to believe its false promises, refuse to indulge in its contaminating sins. Those who love this world will also have an inheritance, or as John describes it, a "portion" (Rev. 21:8), but it won't be in a cleansed creation, in a heavenly land. It will be in a lake of fire.

To be blessed is to live this life with no fear of receiving that portion, but instead to live this life anticipating that one day you are going to be welcomed into the new creation where you will receive an inheritance that will make up for every lack in your life. You'll be blessed by an undeserved, unfathomable, unlosable inheritance.

The Community You Were Made to Be a Part Of

Then came one of the seven angels who had the seven bowls full of the seven last plagues and spoke to me, saying, "Come, I will show you the Bride, the wife of the Lamb." And he carried me away in the Spirit to a great, high mountain, and showed me the holy city Jerusalem coming down out of heaven from God, having the glory of God, its radiance like a most rare jewel, like a jasper, clear as crystal. It had a great, high wall, with twelve gates, and at the gates twelve angels, and on the gates the names of the twelve tribes of the sons of Israel were inscribed—on the east three gates, on the north three gates, on the south three gates, and on the west three gates. And the wall of the city had twelve foundations, and on them were the twelve names of the twelve apostles of the Lamb. (Rev. 21:9–14)

In these verses John overlaps two metaphors to describe the same reality. The angel says he intends to show John the bride, the wife of the Lamb, and then shows him the holy city. So, the bride, all people who are joined to Christ, are a city, the holy city of Jerusalem. This city is said to come down out of heaven, because this city—these people—are the result of the transforming work of the Holy Spirit in the lives of ordinary sinners. There is no sign of that sin in their lives anymore. They radiate the beauty, the glory, and the holiness of God.

And when we read it, it should cause us to consider what cities have been like throughout the Bible. There was the first city built by Cain, named for his son Enoch, in Genesis 4, which was a city built with the express purpose of keeping God out. That has always been the way with cities built by men. That's the way it was for the next significant city we read about in the Bible—the city called Babel. This was a city built in defiance of God's command to spread throughout the earth. They were out to make a name for themselves. Instead of giving glory to God, they wanted to create their own glory. Of course, Babel came to an inglorious end. We read about the city of Sodom, which was inhabited by "wicked, great sinners" (Gen. 13:13) and the victims of their sexual violence and injustice. God destroyed Sodom and Gomorrah with sulfur and fire. The next significant city in the story of the Bible is Jerusalem. Jerusalem was meant to be a city in which the people of God would enjoy the presence of God in their midst. And she had her good days. But Jerusalem became thoroughly sullied by idolatry and other evils. The city God determined to use to judge and purge her evil was none other than Babylon, who took the inhabitants of Jerusalem to live in a refugee camp outside the city of Babylon. Eventually the people of God returned from exile to rebuild their city, but it was never as glorious as it once had been. This was the Jerusalem that Jesus came to and wept over. This was the Jerusalem that rejected and killed Jesus.

So in many ways, it is quite stunning that John describes the community of those who are joined to Christ as the "new Jerusalem." What does this reveal to us? This shows us that God is making out of the idol-loving, God-defying, Christ-rejecting city of man a holy city that he intends to live in with his people. This is at the heart of what it means to be made new. God is taking men and women like us who worship idols of pleasure and pride, men and women like us who love to hate God, men and women like us who continually reject the riches of Christ for the trinkets of the world, and he is remaking us into a city, a community, he wants to live in.[2]

There are twelve gates on four sides of the city: east, north, south, and west. In other words, people are going to come from every direction to live in this city. The gates have the names of the twelve tribes, and the wall has twelve foundations on which are written the names of the twelve apostles. What is John trying to tell us? Certainly one thing he's telling us is that there are not two communities—one for Israel and one for the church. God has one multinational, multicultural people. What defines them, no matter which corner of the earth they come from, is their embrace of the gospel of Jesus Christ proclaimed by the apostles. This is how a person enters into this city, by embracing this glorious gospel.

But there is more to what these gates are telling us. People are coming into this city from every direction. We live in a world of suspicion, elitism, racism, and nationalism that fills many with pride, rage, and resentment and creates deep divides between people groups. As we leave those things behind and embrace our brothers and sisters in Christ of

---

2   This paragraph is adapted from my earlier book *The Son of David: Seeing Jesus in the Historical Books* (Wheaton, IL: Crossway, 2013), 241.

different colors and cultures, we become a living preview of the beautiful community we're going to live in forever.

Just imagine it. No division. No discord. No distrust. We're going to live together with brothers and sisters in Christ from every tribe, tongue, and nation, sharing in the love of Christ forever.

This is a city with walls. Walls speak of security. You and I now live in a world that is insecure. We shut our gates and lock our doors. We are bombarded by scenes of bombings in the heart of major cities, refugees risking their lives to escape poverty and danger, news reports about deadly viruses, killer bees, natural disasters, polluted waters, nuclear weapons, cyber-attacks, and civil unrest. And we know we're vulnerable. But that vulnerability has an expiration date.

One day we're going to make our home in the new creation that will be completely secure. Perfectly peaceful. It will have unsurpassed beauty and abundant resources.

John has used the imagery of a bride, a son, and a city to help us to grasp the excellencies ahead for us in the new creation. And we've been seeing that each of these images overlaps to portray a particular aspect of what the world will be like and who we will be as a bride, a son, and a community in the new creation. Next, he uses the imagery that has been at the forefront of the Bible's story since the beginning, the imagery of the temple.

The Glory You Were Meant to Bask In

John is still speaking in terms of a city, but he lets us know that the city is also a temple, by the measurements he gives for the city:

> The one who spoke with me had a measuring rod of gold to measure the city and its gates and walls. The city lies foursquare, its length the same as its width. And he measured the city with his rod, 12,000 stadia. Its length and width and height are equal. (Rev. 21:15–16)

In the beginning, God made a sanctuary that was flooded with radiant light, embedded with beautiful jewels, filled with his permeating glory, and inhabited by his people. It was a holy place, and when Adam and Eve sinned, they could no longer dwell in this holy sanctuary with a holy God. So God began working out his plan to purify his people so they could enter into his presence once again. He had his people build him a sanctuary in the form of a tent and instituted sacrifices for cleansing. Inside the tent was the Most Holy Place, a room that was a perfect cube in which he came down to dwell among his people. The priests who entered after offering sacrifices for cleansing had beautiful jewels embedded in their garments. Later, when his people had a more permanent home in Israel, God came down to dwell among them in the Most Holy Place of the temple. But there was a problem. Only one person, one time a year, could ever enter into the presence of God. The high priest entered the Most Holy Place once a year, but everyone else had to keep their distance. The only way God's people could ever come into the presence of a holy God is if they were made perfectly holy. But how could that ever happen?

God is working out his plan to bring us into his presence through Jesus, who entered into this world that was sullied by sin and offered himself as a once for all sacrifice for sin. God "made him to be sin who knew no sin, so that in him we might become the righteousness of God" (2 Cor. 5:21). Even now God is at work in us making us holy so that we will be able to enter into his Most Holy Place that will no longer be confined to a 15 x 15 x 15–foot room in a temple in the Middle East. Instead, the whole of the earth will become the Most Holy Place of the temple. One day, when God's sanctifying work in us is complete, we will finally have the glory, holiness, and beauty that we were made for so that we will be able to enter into the presence of God to behold his beauty. It is this beauty that is pictured for us in the jewels embedded in this temple-city's foundations:

> He also measured its wall, 144 cubits by human measurement, which is also an angel's measurement. The wall was built of jasper, while the city was pure gold, like clear glass. The foundations of the wall of the city were adorned with every kind of jewel. The first

was jasper, the second sapphire, the third agate, the fourth emerald, the fifth onyx, the sixth carnelian, the seventh chrysolite, the eighth beryl, the ninth topaz, the tenth chrysoprase, the eleventh jacinth, the twelfth amethyst. And the twelve gates were twelve pearls, each of the gates made of a single pearl, and the street of the city was pure gold, like transparent glass. (Rev. 21:17–21)

C. S. Lewis writes in *The Weight of Glory*, "We do not want merely to see beauty, though, God knows, even that is bounty enough. We want something else which can hardly be put into words—to be united with the beauty we see, to pass into it, to receive it into ourselves, to bathe in it, to become part of it."[3] And one day we will. John's picture of this reality makes us long for it:

I saw no temple in the city, for its temple is the Lord God the Almighty and the Lamb. And the city has no need of sun or moon to shine on it, for the glory of God gives it light, and its lamp is the Lamb. By its light will the nations walk, and the kings of the earth will bring their glory into it, and its gates will never be shut by day—and there will be no night there. They will bring into it the glory and the honor of the nations. But nothing unclean will ever enter it, nor anyone who does what is detestable or false, but only those who are written in the Lamb's book of life. (Rev. 21:22–27)

There will be no temple in this city because the city will be a temple. And it will be filled with people—people who have been made clean by the blood of the Lamb, had their name written in his book, and made holy by the sanctifying work of the Spirit. We will all be in the immediate and abiding presence of the one who loved us and gave himself for us.

The holiness of heaven is a little intimidating to us now. There's a sense in which we know we just would not fit in in a place that is perfectly holy. We're afraid we'll leave muddy footprints of our moral

3   C. S. Lewis, *The Weight of Glory* (New York: HarperCollins, 2001), 43.

failures everywhere we step. But the blessing of the new creation is that he who began a good work in us will have been faithful to complete it. The one who said, "Be holy for I am holy," will have completed his sanctifying work in our lives so that we really will be holy as he is holy. Perfectly, pervasively, permanently holy. This is what we were made for.

The Satisfaction You Were Made to Enjoy

John has one more image to pile on to the images of marriage, inheritance, community, and temple: garden.

> Then the angel showed me the river of the water of life, bright as crystal, flowing from the throne of God and of the Lamb through the middle of the street of the city; also, on either side of the river, the tree of life with its twelve kinds of fruit, yielding its fruit each month. The leaves of the tree were for the healing of the nations. No longer will there be anything accursed, but the throne of God and of the Lamb will be in it, and his servants will worship him. (Rev. 22:1–3)

In the beginning, God planted a garden. The tree of life was in the midst of the garden. The tree of the knowledge of good and evil was there too, the tree at which Adam was meant to judge good as good and evil as evil according to what God had said. It was there that Adam should have crushed the head of the serpent when he tempted Eve to eat of this tree. But he didn't. Had Adam and Eve passed the test of obedience represented in the forbidden tree, they would have been able to feast on the tree of life in the garden and would have thereby been given a glorious, unending, fully satisfying life. But they didn't. The glory given to them became marred, life gave way to death, and satisfaction became elusive.

Because of their disobedience Adam and Eve were banished from the garden, and God placed the cherubim and a flaming sword that turned every way to guard the tree of life. So God sent his Son, a second Adam, who also faced temptation regarding a tree, the tree of

Calvary. To make it possible for his people to enter into the presence of God, Jesus came under the flaming sword. On the cross, Jesus was pierced by that flaming sword of judgment. Jesus entered into death so that we might one day be welcomed into this greater garden that John saw in his vision.

This garden will have a river of water. This is the water Jesus told the Samaritan woman about when he said, "Whoever drinks of the water that I will give him will never be thirsty again. The water that I will give him will become in him a spring of water welling up to eternal life" (John 4:14). And the tree of life will be in this garden. Except it will have expanded. No longer will it be one tree with one kind of fruit and one crop of fruit per season. It will be on each side of the river. It will produce twelve kinds of fruit, with a new crop every month. The number twelve here indicates that this tree is not going to simply provide for us; it is going to provide ultimate, complete, eternal satisfaction.

This will be a healing garden. All of the ways that sin has disfigured and diseased us will be healed. No longer will anything be accursed. Everything the curse has taken from us will be restored to us.

And then John gets to the best part of the new garden:

They will see his face, and his name will be on their foreheads. (Rev. 22:4)

This is what the psalmist gave us the words to pray for when he wrote, "One thing have I asked of the LORD, that will I seek after: that I may dwell in the house of the LORD all the days of my life, to gaze upon the beauty of the LORD and to inquire in his temple" (Ps. 27:4). It is what the Aaronic blessing promises to us when the words, "The LORD make his face to shine upon you and be gracious to you" are prayed over us (Num. 6:25). Face to face with his beauty. Marked and transformed by his beauty. Perfect acceptance and belonging. No more seeing in a mirror dimly, but then face to face. No more knowing in part; then we shall know fully, even as we have been fully known (1 Cor. 13:12).

And night will be no more. They will need no light of lamp or sun, for the Lord God will be their light, and they will reign forever and ever. (Rev. 22:5)

The story of the Bible began with man and woman being made in the image of God and told to exercise dominion over creation. But, of course, we know that they failed, allowing a creeping thing to exercise dominion over them. The writer of Hebrews describes the reality we have lived in ever since: "At present, we do not yet see everything in subjection to him" (Heb. 2:8). It seems like an understatement. We live in a world in rebellion against Christ. But that's only what we can see from our vantage point of the here and now. John was enabled to see what this world will be like on the day when all who are in Christ come into the dominion or reign that God always intended for his people. When that day comes, all the prayers we have prayed for his will to be done on earth as it is in heaven will have been answered. Our wills will perfectly coincide with his. Free from sin and self, we will live in this world in his radiant presence, wanting nothing other than what he wants, loving nothing other than what he loves. That's reigning forever and ever. That's his will done on earth as it is in heaven.

Hearing and Keeping Revelation 21:1–22:5

What are we to do with the wonder of the new creation that John presents to us in these verses? How do we hear and keep this incredible promise? First and foremost (and forgive me if I've become a broken record on this urgent implication of the book of Revelation, in fact the whole Bible), we must become joined to Christ. Paul writes, "Therefore, if anyone is in Christ, the new creation has come" (2 Cor. 5:17 NIV). In other words, the newness of this new creation—its intimacy with Jesus and belonging to Jesus, its beauty, security, community, satisfaction, illumination, holiness, healing, and happiness—is not solely reserved for the future. It is an increasing reality in the interior of our lives right now if we are in Christ.

- This picture of the new creation as a marriage sustains us as we await the coming of our bridegroom, Jesus. It causes us to direct our desires toward this eternal marriage.

- This picture of the new creation as an inheritance helps us to be content. We don't get so uptight about what we have or don't have here and now because we really do believe and anticipate that one day we, along with all of the other children of Abraham by faith, are going to inherit the world.

- This picture of the new creation as a multicultural community leads us to open the doors of our hearts, the tables in our homes, and the pews in our churches for people who may come through a different door, from a different culture, and have skin that's a different color. We love them and welcome them and invest in relationship with them now because we know we are going to be sharing eternity with them.

- This picture of the new creation as a holy temple causes us to increasingly hate what is evil and love what is good. Instead of holding on to our pet sins, we find that we have an increasing desire to be holy as he is holy.

- This picture of the new creation as a garden keeps us from expecting that this world is ever going to fully satisfy us. We're thirsty for the living water. We're hungry for the fruit of the tree of life. We long for the full and complete satisfaction that awaits us in the new and greater garden to come.

Revelation 21 and 22 provide us with new categories for defining what it means to be blessed. John has pulled back the veil so that we can see the blessing of the new creation, where we'll be:

blessed to be adorned as a bride for Jesus,
blessed to be at home with Jesus,
blessed to have our tears wiped away by Jesus,
blessed to drink the living water of Jesus,
blessed to share in the inheritance of Jesus,
blessed to gaze upon the radiance and beauty of Jesus,
blessed to live in the security provided by Jesus,

blessed to enter into the Most Holy Place because of Jesus,
blessed to be satisfied by Jesus,
blessed to be healed by Jesus,
blessed to worship Jesus,
blessed to see the face of Jesus,
blessed to belong forever to Jesus,
blessed to live in the radiant light of Jesus,
blessed to reign forever and ever with Jesus.

Truly blessed. Eternally blessed. Indeed this will be the life of blessing we were made for.

12

Blessed by Keeping the Words of Jesus

Revelation 22:6–21

A WHILE AGO, the editors of the *New York Times* asked their readers to write to them and tell them about a book that influenced how they think, act, or look at the world.[1] They received more than thirteen hundred responses that cited hundreds of books and published some of them in an article entitled "The Book That Changed My Life."

Beth Krugman wrote about how reading and working her way through cooking the foods in *Mastering the Art of French Cooking* by Simone Beck, Louisette Bertholle, and Julia Child opened her family's taste buds to new foods.[2] Rick de Yampert wrote that reading *Go, Dog. Go!* by P. D. Eastman as a child infused him with a love of reading as a way to have adventures.[3] G. Wayne Dowdy wrote that when he read the line, "All animals are equal, but some animals are more equal than others" in George Orwell's *Animal Farm* as an eighth grader, a chill went down his spine, and he never looked at politics or government the same way again.[4]

---

1   Susan Mermelstein and Thomas Feyer, "The Book That Changed My Life," *New York Times*, January 19, 2020, https://www.nytimes.com/.

2   Julia Child, Louisette Bertholle, Simone Beck, *Mastering the Art of French Cooking* (1961; repr., New York: Knopf, 2001).

3   P. D. Eastman, *Go, Dog. Go!* (New York: Random House, 1961).

4   George Orwell, *Animal Farm* (Orlando, FL: Harcourt, 1946).

We've come to the end of an amazing book—Revelation—a book that has far more to it than we've been able to bring out in these pages. And I can't help but wonder how what you've seen in Revelation will influence how you think, act, or look at the world going forward.

We've come to the final few verses of the book of Revelation, its epilogue. Ever since the prologue in Revelation 1:1–8, we've been reading John's recounting of the visions he was given that have allowed us to see this world and what is happening in it from the perspective of heaven. We've heard what Jesus has to say to the churches he loves. We've been invited into the throne room of heaven to catch a glimpse of the glory of God and the Lamb. We've seen how history is unfolding as the judgment of God is being poured out in partial and preliminary ways, and what that judgment will be like on the day it is poured out in a final and complete way. We've seen the temporary suffering and the ultimate security of the saints as well as the eternal suffering and ultimate insecurity of all who persist in refusing the grace and goodness of God. In these final few chapters, we've seen how the kingdom of this world will become the kingdom of our Lord and of his Christ. It will happen through a purifying work of judgment that will purge the whole of creation of evil so that a new creation will emerge, a new creation in which God and his people will enjoy face-to-face communion and eternal satisfaction.

There is no book, no story, that has a happier ending than this one. Of course, this ending isn't really the end. The ending is filled with anticipation and longing for a new beginning, the new marriage, inheritance, community, glory, and satisfaction that was described in the previous passage. The epilogue we're going to consider is filled with anticipation for the event that will usher in this new creation in all of its glorious fullness—the second coming of the Lord Jesus.

In these final fifteen verses we actually get to hear Jesus speak three times. Three times Jesus says to John, to his first readers in the seven churches in Asia, to every believer down through the centuries since then, and to you and me today, "I am coming soon." Three times he woos our attention away from all of our day-to-day concerns and all of our short-term ambitions and all of our short-sighted pursuits toward what he intends for us to orient our lives around and toward: his coming.

And can we be honest and admit that it can seem a little crazy in our modern world to really believe that one day the Jesus who lived on this earth for thirty-three years over two thousand years ago is going to come back to this earth, execute judgment on those who have rejected him, and establish a new city-temple-garden with all who have received him? Most people in the world today would think that is an absurd, archaic, and unsophisticated way to look at the world and the future.

But in the final words of Revelation Jesus repeatedly tells us to "behold" or fix our gaze in anticipation of this reality. A Christian life in which we simply orient our lives around the teachings and example of Jesus with no real expectation of his bodily return to this earth is not the Christian life at all. The orientation of a Christian is leaning forward in anticipation of the next big event on the calendar of redemptive history: the second coming of Jesus Christ.

Believing that Jesus is going to return to this earth may seem foolish to most people in the world. But it isn't foolish. Based on what we have read in the whole of the Bible, including what we've been shown in the book of Revelation, to live in expectation of the second coming of Jesus is the wisest way to live, because this truth is the most reliable truth in the universe. That's what the angel said to John after he wrote down the visions that make up the book of Revelation:

> He said to me, "These words are trustworthy and true. And the Lord, the God of the spirits of the prophets, has sent his angel to show his servants what must soon take place." (Rev. 22:6)

The day will never come that you will regret believing that what John has written about in this book is the way human history will progress and come to its culmination. Remember how this content came to John: it originated with God himself and was given to Jesus, who gave it to his angel, who gave it to John, who wrote it down for the church and for us. You can put your trust in the reliability of what you read in Revelation. And as you put your trust in it and live in light of it, you'll experience the promise inherent in it: the promise of blessing.

Blessed by Keeping Revelation's Message

All the way along in this book we've been tracing the promise of blessing in Revelation. And here in its final verses we find the same promise of blessing we read in the first chapter:

> Behold, I am coming soon. Blessed is the one who keeps the words of the prophecy of this book. (Rev. 22:7)

All the way along we've been asking what it is going to mean for us to keep the words of the prophecy of this book. And as the book comes to a close, the question before us is: Will we allow our lives to be changed by the images we've seen and the declarations we've heard? Will the reality of the coming of Jesus in judgment and salvation shape our priorities, our concerns, our finances, the way we use our time and energy, the way we speak about Christ to others, and the way we speak to ourselves about what is real and reliable?

As we think through all of the ground that we have covered in the twenty-two chapters of Revelation, we've seen that there is tangible and profound blessing to be experienced now and into eternity by those who:

- have their vision of Jesus Christ shaped by Revelation's vision of who Jesus is, what he has accomplished, and what he will accomplish in his second coming;

- are willing to evaluate their churches and themselves in light of the commendations and criticisms of the letters to the churches in Revelation 2 and 3;

- allow the heavenly worship of God portrayed in Revelation 4 and 5 to guide their own worship;

- persevere in their bold allegiance to Christ and witness for Christ even when it costs them;

- see through the false veneer into the true ugliness and evil of this world's systems, philosophies, and priorities;

- rest in God's providence, believing that God has the power to bring about everything pictured and promised in this book;

- expect that the wicked will experience judgment from God and that we will celebrate his justice and righteousness;

- orient their lives toward the new creation, refusing to expect that life lived under the current order will ever truly satisfy and sustain them;

- anticipate seeing their Savior face to face and enjoying communion with him into eternity.

Oh, how I hope this study of Revelation has been about so much more than nailing down how to interpret it. The goal is to live it, keep it, and obey it. The goal is patient endurance. The goal is to overcome this world's pull toward compromise and apathy and idolatry. The goal is to one day be clothed in the white robes of Christ's righteousness, to hear our names read from the Lamb's book of life, to be sealed and sanctified and saved. The goal, according to the next verse, in which John tells us about his own response to what he saw, is to worship the God who has provided this revelation of his plans and purposes to us:

I, John, am the one who heard and saw these things. And when I heard and saw them, I fell down to worship at the feet of the angel who showed them to me, but he said to me, "You must not do that! I am a fellow servant with you and your brothers the prophets, and with those who keep the words of this book. Worship God." (Rev. 22:8–9)

John's instinctual response to what he saw in the visions of Revelation was to fall down to worship at the feet of the angel who showed it all to him. But, of course, to worship a created being, no matter how glorious, would be to divert worship away from the one who is worthy of our worship. God, as we have seen him on the throne, pouring out righteous judgment, empowering his people for witness, and then making his forever home with his people—these are just a few of the things that make God worthy of our worship, according to Revelation.

If you have truly taken in what we've been reading in Revelation, your head and your heart have been filled with images that should keep you from being sluggish or detached in your worship. Revelation should fill your tank with energy to worship and a longing to worship.

> And he said to me, "Do not seal up the words of the prophecy of this book, for the time is near." (Rev. 22:10)

Over seven hundred years earlier, the prophet Daniel was given a similar vision. But the instructions he received in regard to his vision were quite different. Daniel was told to "shut up the words and seal the book, until the time of the end" (Dan. 12:4). John has been told *not* to seal up his written record of the visions shown to him. Why? Because he is living in the last days. The "time of the end" is at hand.

Once we realize that John is clearly writing verse 10 with Daniel 12 in mind, it helps us to make sense of what he writes in verse 11, which, on the surface, can seem fatalistic:

> Let the evildoer still do evil, and the filthy still be filthy, and the righteous still do right, and the holy still be holy. (Rev. 22:11)

When we compare what John writes here with Daniel 12:10, which reads, "Many shall purify themselves and make themselves white and be refined, but the wicked shall act wickedly. And none of the wicked shall understand, but those who are wise shall understand," we can see that John is signaling to us as readers that Daniel's prophecy is now being fulfilled, so we shouldn't be deterred by the resistance of those who persist in their evil; rather we should continue to pursue righteousness and holiness.

Over and over again in the Bible we see that when the word of God goes out, some are melted by it and respond to it in repentance and faith, while others are hardened by it and respond to it with resistance and rejection. What John is presenting here is the opposite of being blessed by hearing and keeping the words of this book; it's a picture of being cursed by hearing and becoming hardened to the message of this book.

Blessed by Experiencing Revelation's Grace

Once again Jesus identifies himself as the beginning and the end, as the one who is going to return to bring everything he set into motion to its intended end:

> Behold, I am coming soon, bringing my recompense with me, to repay each one for what he has done. I am the Alpha and the Omega, the first and the last, the beginning and the end. (Rev. 22:12–13)

When we read the words "recompense" and "repay," they sound familiar to us. We've read plenty in this book about Jesus giving people what they rightly deserve. Perhaps we're tired of hearing about it. But I have to imagine that the first readers of this book needed the repeated assurance that Jesus was going to come to repay those who had persecuted them and carted people they loved off to prison or to death. They would not have tired of hearing about it. They needed to be assured that they could trust that the one who is the Alpha and the Omega will be there in the end to dole out what those who have earned his wrath rightly deserve.

But Jesus is not only talking about what he will repay to those who deserve his wrath. His recompense will also include his reward. Remember that one of the purposes of Revelation has been to call believers to persevere in living out the newness of life we have experienced by being joined to Christ. Jesus wants us to know that we will not regret living for him; we will be rewarded for living for him.

It reminds us of the parable he told about the master who was going away and entrusted various resources to his servants before he left with an expectation that they would invest those resources while he was gone for a return for his kingdom. To the faithful stewards, the master said upon his return, "Well done, good and faithful servant. You have been faithful over a little; I will set you over much. Enter into the joy of your master" (Matt. 25:21). There's the reward, the recompense.

When Jesus declares he will repay each one according to what he has done, this is not salvation by works. Rather, this is reward for the works that demonstrate a person has been saved, works that flow out of the life of a person who has been saved by grace. We know this is what Jesus is talking about as his next words present a picture to us of this grace:

> Blessed are those who wash their robes, so that they may have the right to the tree of life and that they may enter the city by the gates. Outside are the dogs and sorcerers and the sexually immoral and murderers and idolaters, and everyone who loves and practices falsehood. (Rev. 22:14–15)

What dramatically different futures await those who respond to the offer of the grace of Jesus in humble repentance and those who reject the offer of grace in prideful resistance. One will experience the unmerited, all-encompassing blessing of an all-satisfying life in the presence of the Savior who has loved them and cleansed them. The other will experience the fully merited, all-encompassing curse of never-ending misery away from the presence of the Savior whom they rejected and dishonored.

Blessed by Anticipating Revelation's Promise

In the final verses of Revelation, we hear the voice of Jesus once again declaring himself to be the fulfillment of two Old Testament prophecies:

I, Jesus, have sent my angel to testify to you about these things for the churches. I am the root and the descendant of David, the bright morning star. (Rev. 22:16)

Isaiah wrote, "There shall come forth a shoot from the stump of Jesse, and a branch from his roots shall bear fruit" (Isa. 11:1). The "stump of Jesse" was a way of referring to the people of Israel who had been mowed down by the Babylonians so that they seemed like a dried-up stump. Jesus is saying that he is the green shoot that emerged from that seemingly dried-up stump. Isaiah went on to say that when this king that will descend from Jesse comes, "the Spirit of the LORD shall rest upon him" (11:2); "with the breath of his lips he shall kill the wicked" (11:4); "the wolf shall dwell with the lamb" (11:6); and "the earth shall be full of the knowledge of the LORD as the waters cover the sea" (11:9). In identifying himself as the root and descendant of David, Jesus is saying that he is this king, and when he comes he will bring everything Isaiah wrote about in Isaiah 11 into being.

"The bright morning star" is an allusion to Numbers 24:17, which records the prophecy of the mysterious pagan shaman named Balaam, who said, "A star shall come out of Jacob, and a scepter shall rise out of Israel." Balaam went on to speak of all the enemies who would be dispossessed when this star, this king, comes. So by calling himself "the bright morning star," Jesus is declaring that when he comes as king, it will be the dawning of a new day. He will shine like a bright morning star over a new creation. This will be God's eternal day that will never end. This is the day we long for. This is day we're waiting for with patient endurance. Envisioning and anticipating this day has the power to fill us with the courage we need to face whatever today brings.

Blessed by Responding to Revelation's Invitation

We've heard the angel speak, we've heard John speak, and we've heard Jesus himself speak. And now we hear the Spirit and the bride speak. In other words, this is the message the Holy Spirit breathes out into the world through the lips of those who are in love with Jesus:

The Spirit and the Bride say, "Come." And let the one who hears say, "Come." And let the one who is thirsty come; let the one who desires take the water of life without price. (Rev. 22:17)

As those who are engaged to be married to Christ forever, we say to the world around us: "Come." Until the day that he comes, we invite all who are thirsty for something more than this world has to offer to come to the only well that will never run dry, the only source that can quench our thirst for life and relationship and meaning. We say to those who are thirsty, "Stop expecting that you can fill yourself up in what this world has to offer. Do you have a desire for something more? That desire is all you need. This life and relationship are given freely to anyone and everyone who will bring nothing but their need to Christ."

Revelation ends with a final word from Jesus, a final response from John, and a final prayer John prays for us.

The final word from Jesus is what he hopes will be echoing in our ears and captivating our hearts:

He who testifies to these things says, "Surely I am coming soon." (Rev. 22:20a)

Think of how important a person's final words are. It's usually the most important thing they want to say. It's what they want those to whom they're speaking to hold on to and remember. Jesus wants you and me to hold on to his promise that he is coming.

John hears these final words of Jesus, and then John responds to what Jesus has said:

Amen. Come, Lord Jesus! (Rev. 22:20b)

John has taken it all in. He's written it all down. It has filled his heart with worship and wonder and a longing for the King to come, a longing for Jesus to put an end to evil for good, a longing for him to bring his people into the new creation, a longing for him to dwell with us and satisfy us forever. So he cries out in response to the promise of Jesus, affirming that he has heard it and that he is holding on to it. There's nothing he wants more than for Jesus to come.

John seems to know that there is going to be a time of waiting for Jesus's promised coming and that his people are going to need grace to be able to wait for that day and persevere until that day. And so he prays that we will experience that grace:

The grace of the Lord Jesus be with all. Amen. (Rev. 22:21)

That is also my prayer for you. I pray that your response to all you have read and thought through and prayed through in this book of Revelation will stir in you the same response as it did in John—that you will find yourself longing for Jesus to come. And I pray that he will give you the grace for patient endurance as you wait for his coming.

- May you be blessed with the spiritual strength you need to keep what is written in this book.
- May you be blessed with the grace of having your robe washed in Christ's cleansing blood so that you can live in the confidence that you will be welcomed into his presence in the cleansed creation.
- May you be blessed with the joy of calling thirsty people around you to come and drink from the water of life that can be found only in Christ.
- May you be blessed with a longing for your King to come and for the dawning of the eternal day.

Bibliography

Bauckham, Richard. *The Theology of the Book of Revelation*. Cambridge, UK: Cambridge University Press, 1993.

Beale, G. K., with David H. Campbell. *Revelation: A Shorter Commentary*. Grand Rapids, MI: Eerdmans, 2015.

Beale, Gregory K., and Donald A. Carson. *Commentary on the New Testament Use of the Old Testament*. Ada, MI: Baker, 2007.

ESV Study Bible. Edited by Wayne Grudem. Wheaton, IL: Crossway, 2018.

Ferguson, Sinclair. Sermon series on Revelation. "Resources," The Gospel Coalition. Accessed August 18, 2021. https://thegospelcoalition.org.

Goldsworthy, Graeme et al. *The Goldsworthy Trilogy*. Milton Keynes, UK: Paternoster, 2011.

Hamilton, James M. *Revelation: The Spirit Speaks to the Churches*. Wheaton, IL: Crossway, 2012.

Hendriksen, William. *More than Conquerors: An Interpretation of the Book of Revelation*. Ada, MI: Baker, 2015.

Hoekema, Anthony A. *The Bible and the Future*. Grand Rapids, MI: Eerdmans, 1994.

Johnson, Dennis E. *Triumph of the Lamb: A Commentary on Revelation*. Phillipsburg, NJ: P&R, 2001.

Kruger, Michael J. *Hebrews to Revelation*. Course 0NT5350, Reformed Theological Seminary. Accessed August 18, 2021. https://itunes.apple.com.

Leithart, Peter J. *Revelation 1–11*. Edinburgh: Bloomsbury, 2018.

Mackie, Tim. "Apocalyptic Literature." *Bible Project* podcast. Accessed August 18, 2021. https://bibleproject.com.

Morris, Leon. *Apocalyptic*. Grand Rapids, MI: Eerdmans, 1972.

Phillips, Richard D. *Revelation*. Reformed Expository Commentary. Phillipsburg, NJ: P&R, 2017.

Poythress, Vern S. *The Returning King: A Guide to the Book of Revelation*. Phillipsburg, NJ: P&R, 2000.

Riddlebarger, Kim. "Sermons on the Book of Revelation." The Riddleblog. Accessed August 18, 2021. http://kimriddlebarger.squarespace.com.

Ryken, Leland. *Words of Delight: A Literary Introduction to the Bible*. Ada, MI: Baker, 2003.

Sach, Andrew, and Andrew Latimer. "666: Armageddon and the End of the World: What Does the Bible Actually Say?" Sermon series. Grace Church Greenwich, January–May 2021. https://www.greenwich.church.

Schreiner, Thomas R. "Commentary on Revelation." *Expository Commentary Hebrews–Revelation*. Wheaton, IL: Crossway, 2018.

———. *The Joy of Hearing: A Theology of Revelation*. New Testament Theology. Wheaton, IL: Crossway, 2021.

Wilcock, Michael. *The Message of Revelation: I Saw Heaven Opened*. The Bible Speaks Today. Westmont, IL: InterVarsity Press, 1991.

General Index

Scripture Index

Also Available from Nancy Guthrie

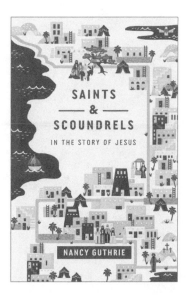

For more information, visit **crossway.org**.